a year in the garden

a year in the garden

a step-by-step guide to vital gardening projects through the year

Steven Bradley

photography by
Anne Hyde

RYLAND
PETERS
& SMALL
LONDON NEW YORK

For this edition:
Senior Designer Amy Trombat
Senior Editor Clare Double
Picture Research Emily Westlake
Production Sheila Smith, Simon Walsh
Publishing Director Alison Starling

Illustrators David Ashby, Leslie Craig,
Sarah Kensington, Amanda Patton,
Polly Raynes, Gill Tomblin, Ann Winterbotham

First published in the United Kingdom in 2000.
This new edition published in 2007 by Ryland Peters & Small
20–21 Jockey's Fields
London WC1R 4BW
www.rylandpeters.com

10 9 8 7 6 5 4 3 2 1

ISBN: 978-1-84597-356-8

A catalogue record for this book is available from
the British Library

Material contained in this book was originally published
in *Autumn in the Garden* (published in 1997), *Spring in the
Garden* and *Summer in the Garden* (both published in 1998).

contents

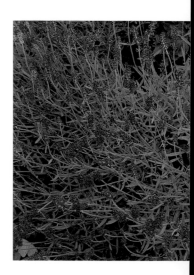

The gardening year begins in early spring and carries through until the first hard frosts of late autumn herald a period of dormancy for most plants. It is not possible to be precise about when specific tasks need to be undertaken, since so much depends not only on the prevailing climatic conditions for the part of the world you live in, but also on the microclimate that prevails in your garden. It is possible, however, to divide the gardening year up into three principal seasons of activity.

Spring can be a stressful period. Too much to do, too little time to do it and, of course, the plants can't wait to get started. Your timing is critical – how do you get the earliest possible start while beating those lingering spring frosts? Day temperatures can soar for hours at a time before plunging to freezing overnight. Strong winds thrash young foliage and heavy rain batters tender seedlings, yet still we are glad when spring finally arrives.

Spring provides a perfect opportunity to create something new – a short-term project, perhaps, such as planting a hanging basket for a summer display, or something more permanent, such as planting a climber to provide years of interest. Spring is also the time to renovate any shrubs that need pruning to stimulate new growth. The lawn, too, can look sad after the ravages of winter, and now is the time to undertake repairs, deal with any moss and begin feeding, weeding and mowing to encourage grass growth. Start the season by carrying out any repairs on machinery and equipment before they are needed for the coming year.

Summer is often the most colourful time of year in the garden. Growth is still rapid and, in order to sustain it, much of this season's work is aimed at keeping plants watered and fed. At times, it may feel as if the gardener has to run in order simply to stand still. The lawn grows overnight and needs constant mowing, hedges need clipping at every turn, blooms need dead-heading, young fruit trees need training and no sooner has one batch of

seeds been sown than another batch of seedlings needs thinning or staking. Regardless of all the hard labour, the summer is also a time when the garden can be enjoyed at close quarters. The warm weather and lingering daylight hours entice us out of doors for long periods; but even when they are apparently simply relaxing, experienced gardeners are using their time to note successful plants and planting schemes and record any failures or disappointments for moving or disposal. This helps to ensure that the same mistakes are not made next year, when the glorious technicolour experiment can be tried all over again.

Autumn signals a change of direction – as exciting as the other seasons, but in different ways. As the growing season draws to a close, the process of shutting down the garden for the winter begins, with annuals dying off and perennial plants storing food for the winter months to come. The shorter days also bring about some quite dramatic changes, with many deciduous plants, and a few evergreen ones, really making their presence felt in a glorious display of colour.

Autumn is a time for looking back on the year and noting successes and failures. Plans can now be made while the events are still fresh in the mind, because many of the operations carried out in autumn will determine the success of the coming year. Cleaning the garden is a good way to begin. Prune away unwanted branches and twigs and shred them into bags as a mulch for next year. Clear away all annuals that have died down and dig borders and plots to bury weeds and plant debris. This helps to eliminate pest and disease problems and provides vital organic matter. Rather than being thought of as the end of the present growing season, autumn should be regarded as the beginning of the new one.

Steven Bradley

new introductions

The prospect of adding new plants to the garden is irresistible. Either the acquisition of new plants or raising them from seed or cuttings for that little space in the garden will always be a source of excitement. There is a great sense of anticipation, too, as ideas for new planting schemes take shape, perhaps inspired by the vast range of plants on show at garden centres or in other people's gardens. The challenge may be to produce a display that changes with the seasons, providing interest and colour all year round. What often determines when new plants are introduced is their hardiness and growth patterns. In truth, there can be overlap in the gardening operations that are carried out in the different seasons, especially between autumn and spring.

planting bulbs

'Bulb' is the generic term that is often loosely used to describe bulbous plants such as bulbs, corms, rhizomes and tubers. Although most bulbs found in the average garden will have been propagated in Europe, they may have originated from as far afield as South Africa, South America, the Mediterranean or even the Middle East. The planting and maintenance of bulbs is relatively straightforward, but care when planting is important to ensure complete success. Most soil types are suitable, but try to avoid waterlogged soil during the winter. Consider location when you choose your bulbs; most prefer a sunny position, but some, such as snowdrops (*Galanthus*), prefer to grow in the dappled shade provided by trees.

tools and equipment

Trowel
This is the most popular planting tool for small plants and is probably the best one to use if only a few bulbs are to be planted, or if the bulbs being planted vary greatly in size.

Spade
A garden spade is the best tool to use for planting a large number of bulbs, or planting bulbs in groups.

Bulb planter
A hand-held bulb planter (almost a trowel with a circular blade) is useful where several bulbs are to be planted at the same time. This tool removes a core of soil, leaving a hole into which the bulb is placed. A larger version with a spade-like shaft and handle is useful where the soil is hard or heavy with clay. The main disadvantage of bulb planters is that all of the holes are the same size.

how deep to plant

Depth is particularly important when planning a display of bulbs, since inconsistent planting will lead to uneven flowering, and this can spoil the effect of mass groupings of bulbs. Depending on the bulbs being planted, the depth can vary from as shallow as 1 cm (½ in) to as deep as 25 cm (10 in). See below for the correct planting depths.

By planting bulbs fractionally deeper than the recommended depth, however, flowering can be delayed by up to ten days. A useful technique is to plant half of your bulbs at the correct depth and the other half of the bulbs slightly deeper; the flowering display of one particular cultivar can then be extended over a longer period.

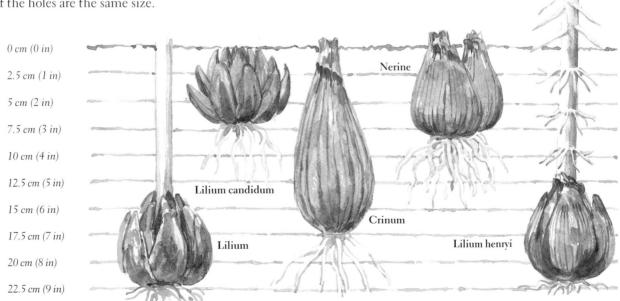

0 cm (0 in)
2.5 cm (1 in)
5 cm (2 in)
7.5 cm (3 in)
10 cm (4 in)
12.5 cm (5 in)
15 cm (6 in)
17.5 cm (7 in)
20 cm (8 in)
22.5 cm (9 in)

Nerine

Lilium candidum

Crinum

Lilium

Lilium henryi

planting a single bulb

Bulbs often look at their best when planted in groups, but some of the larger-flowering types, such as the giant onions (*Alliums*), make fine display plants when planted individually. The bulb planter below is ideal to use when introducing bulbs between established plants.

1   Push the bulb planter or trowel into the ground with a twisting motion to cut through the soil, rather than forcing it straight in.

2   After making the planting hole, break up the soil in the bottom with a trowel.

grouping

Make a shallow trench, positioning the bulbs in the bottom, then refill the trench and firm in gently.

3   Set the bulb in the hole in an upright position, then fill in around the bulb with soil until the surface is level. Firm in gently.

naturalizing bulbs

In order to achieve a randomized, natural look for a group of bulbs growing in grass, simply position them by throwing a handful of bulbs over the grass and planting them where they have landed.

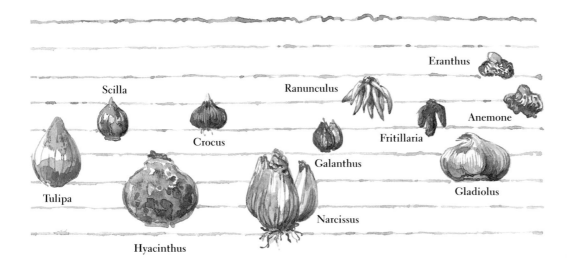

Scilla

Ranunculus

Eranthus

Anemone

Crocus

Fritillaria

Tulipa

Galanthus

Gladiolus

Narcissus

Hyacinthus

late-flowering bulbs

Bulbs that are intended to flower in the summer and autumn seasons must have a soil that retains plenty of moisture through the summer months while they are growing. However, the soil must also be free-draining during the winter in order to prevent the bulbs from rotting while they are dormant. Late-flowering bulbs are ideal for planting in mixed borders, where they can be used to extend the season of interest and give the border an 'early start'. Bulbs can be selected to develop and flower before many of the shrubs and herbaceous perennials have started to show colour. Another added attraction with some summer- and autumn-flowering bulbs is that the seed heads may be kept after the blooms are finished – for example, ornamental onions (*Alliums*) are particularly valuable for this purpose. The old seed heads can either be left in situ, where they will last well into the winter, or they can be cut down and hung to dry out before being used in dried-flower arrangements.

Gladiolus tristis 'Bowlby'

Alstroemeria

Lilium candidum

Lilium 'Enchantment'

Colchicum 'The Giant'

Amaryllis belladonna

Cyclamen hederifolium

Allium

preparing for planting

Bulbs that grow and flower later in the year frequently have to endure some of the driest growing conditions and will often root quite deeply into the soil in order to find moisture. Incorporating generous quantities of well-rotted organic matter before planting will aid moisture retention. Bulbs are normally sold and planted while they are dry, with no roots or leaves. However, snowdrops (*Galanthus*) will establish better if transplanted almost immediately after flowering – 'in the green' (see right) with the leaves still present, when new roots are produced very quickly.

Summer- and autumn-flowering bulbs
Arum lily (*Zantedeschia aethiopica*)
Crocosmia
Cyclamen hederifolium
Foxtail lily (*Eremurus*)
Giant lily (*Cardiocrinum*)
Gladiolus
Lily (*Lilium*)
Onion (*Allium*)
Peruvian lily (*Alstroemeria*)
Sorrel (*Oxalis*)

planting in baskets

Any type of bulb can be planted in a wire or plastic basket. This is a clever device to use if you wish to move your plants, for instance, once the foliage has died off in preparation for lifting, dividing and storing, or for tender bulbs that need to be put indoors over winter.

1 Line the bottom of the basket with enough soil so that the bulbs will be planted at their correct depth. Then position the bulbs you have chosen on top of the layer of soil, evenly spacing them out.

2 Fill the basket with soil and lower it into a hole, deep enough so that the top rim sits just below soil level. Cover the top of the basket with soil and mark its position.

3 After planting, cover the area with a mulch of sharp gravel – this will help to deter slugs and snails from eating the shoots as they emerge, since they do not like travelling across sharp surfaces. Applying such a barrier also reduces the need to use chemical baits.

lifting bulbs

1 Carefully lift 'old' spring bulbs and leave them in a cool, dry place for two or three days before brushing off any soil clinging to them. Trim away the old roots and any loose papery scales, and remove the dried stems level with the bulb 'neck'.

2 Gently pull away any 'bulblets' from around the mother bulb; these can be used to grow new plants. Discard soft or unusually light bulbs, since they may be infested with eelworms or bulb fly maggots, or be decaying due to damage caused by fungal rots.

3 Using clean, shallow trays or boxes lined with paper, arrange the bulbs in a single layer and place them in a cool, dry place until it is time for replanting in the autumn. Inspect the bulbs every two or three weeks and discard immediately the ones that show any signs of fungal rot or softness, otherwise the surrounding bulbs may become infected.

planting annuals and biennials

These plants provide an enormous variety of flower colour, form and foliage texture, making them ideal candidates for planting in containers and hanging baskets; in the garden soil, they can be used to great effect massed in a bed by themselves, or as 'fillers' in gaps between shrubs and other permanent plants. By choosing suitable species and cultivars, it is possible to have flowers for a large part of the year. Often, half-hardy annuals are used for summer colour, as they are very fast growing and provide an amazing display, which may last through until the first frosts of autumn or early winter.

planting for a summer display

Many summer bedding plants are half-hardy annuals whose seeds, if left to themselves, would not germinate until the early summer. Sowing seed in trays of compost in spring and keeping them under glass or on a warm windowsill means the plants will start growing early. Once the seedlings are large enough to handle without risk of damage, they can be transplanted from their seed trays into small pots. This will give them the space and food they need to keep them growing quickly. Gradually harden them off (see page 20), before planting them out into their flowering site.

Transplanting (pricking out) seedlings

1   Select several small pots and fill to the top with a suitable compost. Using your fingers or a dibber, gently firm down the surface of the compost to 1 cm (½ in) below the rim.

2   Using a label or a similar utensil, gently tease the seedlings out of the seed compost. Do this when the compost is slightly moist.

3   Make a hole with a dibber in the centre of each pot. Then lift the seedlings individually and place each one, root first, into a hole.

4   Water gently to settle the compost around the roots. Label the pots with the plant name and date, then place in a shaded spot.

5   For plants destined to go into troughs and tubs, grow in 8 cm (3 in) plastic pots and plunge them into the decorative container. The plant's roots will grow through the bottom of the pot and into the compost.

6   After flowering, the plant can easily be removed by twisting the pot from side to side to sever any roots that have pushed through the drainage holes. You can then drop a replacement plant neatly into the hole.

planting for a spring display

As well as annuals, many hardy biennials are grown through autumn and winter. They are usually sown in a seedbed during early summer, transplanted into a nursery bed six or eight weeks later, and planted out in mid-autumn in display beds.

Sowing seed outdoors

The seeds are sown in straight lines in 'drills' so that the seedlings are in rows about 20 cm (8 in) apart. A groove is cut in the soil (the depth depends on the seed involved) and the seed scattered along the bottom of the drill. Seeds should be sown as thinly as possible to reduce the need for thinning seedlings later. Sowing in drills is most commonly used for plants grown in nursery beds, which are later transplanted into permanent positions.

Lifting and transplanting

1   As soon as seedlings have grown to a manageable size, lift them with a hand fork to avoid injuring the roots and hold them by their leaves. For plants raised in pots, draw them gently from the container, or if they have been raised in biodegradable pots, plant them with the pot intact.

2   Start by digging a planting hole large enough to accommodate the root system. Hold the plant by its stem or leaves and place it into the hole, with the roots evenly spread out. For biodegradable pots, place the pots and plants directly into the hole.

3   Using a trowel, pull the soil back into the hole around the plant and gently firm. Tidy the soil around the base of the plant so that there is a slight depression around the stem to catch the water.

4   Check that the plant is firm by gently pulling a leaf in an upwards direction. The leaf may snap but the plant should stay firmly in the soil. Finally, carefully water around the base of the plant, filling up the depression.

seasonal interest

The spring season provides you with a perfect opportunity to create a short-term bedding display which will provide splashes of colour in spaces that will eventually be filled by more permanent plantings. Interest in the garden can also be provided by sowing patches of annual grasses into the border between other established plants. The gentle swaying movement and rustling of seed heads add an extra dimension. The easiest way to grow annuals and biennials is to sow them directly into the ground outside. This is done at the beginning of spring when the soil is starting to warm up again. For detailed instructions on planting annual seeds outdoors, see page 80.

Annuals and biennials for spring sowing	Season of interest	Height
Aster (*Callistephus*)	summer	38–60 cm (15–24 in)
Baby's breath (*Gypsophila paniculata*)	summer	1.2 m (4 ft)
Black-eyed Susan (*Rudbeckia hirta*)	summer	30–90 cm (1–3 ft)
Candytuft (*Iberis*)	late spring/summer	20–30 cm (8–12 in)
Canterbury bells (*Campanula medium*)	spring/summer	60–90 cm (2–3 ft)
Cornflower (*Centaurea*)	summer	90 cm (3 ft)
Cynoglossum	spring/summer	30–45 cm (12–18in)
Double daisy (*Bellis*)	spring/summer	10–15 cm (4–6 in)
Flax (*Linum*)	summer	38 cm (15 in)
Foxglove (*Digitalis*)	summer	90 cm–1.5 m (3–5 ft)
Gillyflower (*Matthiola incana*)	summer	80 cm (32 in)
Godetia grandiflora	summer	30–40 cm (12–16 in)
Hollyhock (*Alcea ficifolia*)	summer	2.5 m (8 ft)
Honesty (*Lunaria annua*)	spring/summer	75 cm (30 in)
Love-in-a-mist (*Nigella*)	summer	45–75 cm (18–30 in)
Mallow (*Lavatera trimestris*)	summer	1.2 m (4 ft)
Marigold (*Calendula officinalis*)	summer	30–70 cm (12–28 in)
Morning glory (*Ipomoea purpurea*)	summer/late autumn	3 m (10 ft)
Nasturtium (*Tropaeolum majus*)	summer	30–38 cm (12–15 in)
Pansy (*Viola*)	spring/autumn	15–20 cm (6–8 in)
Poppy (*Papaver*)	summer	20–45 cm (8–18 in)
Siberian wallflower (*Erysimum allionii*)	late spring/summer	30 cm (12 in)
Snapdragon (*Antirrhinum*)	summer	20–60 cm (8–24 in)
Sunflower (*Helianthus*)	late summer/autumn	60 cm–3 m (2–10 ft)
Sweet William (*Dianthus barbatus*)	summer	70 cm (28 in)
Tobacco plant (*Nicotiana*)	summer/autumn	30–60 cm (12–24 in)
Treasure flower (*Gazania hybrida*)	summer/late autumn	20–30 cm (8–12 in)

Dianthus barbatus

Lavatera trimestris

Lunaria annua

Annual and biennial grasses for spring sowing	Season of interest	Height
Fountain grass (*Pennisetum setaceum*)	summer	90 cm (3 ft)
Greater quaking grass (*Briza maxima*)	summer	50 cm (20 in)
Hare's tail (*Lagurus ovatus*)	summer	45 cm (18 in)
Job's tears (*Coix lacryma-jobi*)	autumn	45–90 cm (18–36 in)
Maize (*Zea mays*)	summer	90 cm–1.2 m (3–4 ft)
Squirrel tail grass (*Hordeum jubatum*)	summer	30 cm (1 ft)
Switch grass (*Panicum virgatum*)	autumn	90 cm (3 ft)

planting spring bedding

After what often seems like a long, bleak and colourless winter, there are few more heartening sights than flowers beginning to emerge from the soil to create bright patches of colour amid the otherwise drab surroundings and bare-limbed trees. So, one of the most rewarding, as well as one of the easiest and problem-free, groups of plants for the gardener to grow are those used for spring bedding. These plants are a mixture of bulbs, biennials and low-growing perennials, selected for their display qualities.

Crocus

Muscari and *Narcissus*

sowing seeds

Seed sown indoors		Seed sown outdoors
Aubrietia	Pansy (*Viola*)	Candytuft (*Iberis*)
Begonia	Primrose (*Primula*)	*Clarkia*
Crocus	Rock cress (*Arabis*)	Grape hyacinth (*Muscari*)
Daffodil (*Narcissus*)	Scarlet sage (*Salvia splendens*)	Marigold (*Calendula*)
Daisy (*Bellis*)	Siberian wallflower (*Erysimum allionii*)	Ornamental cabbage (*Brassica oleracea*)
Forget-me-not (*Myosotis*)	Wallflower (*Erysimum cheiri*)	Poppy (*Papaver*)
Iris reticulata		

Hardening off

Plants suitable for spring bedding that have been raised from seeds sown indoors, and young plants that have not reached maturity, have soft and sappy tissues that may easily be damaged if they are too suddenly exposed to low temperatures or cold, dry winds. To prevent this happening, these plants must first be hardened off, or acclimatized, for up to about two weeks before they can be successfully transplanted outdoors. Move them from the greenhouse or kitchen windowsill into a cold frame, or place them under cloches. Cloches covered in light-weight plastic must have their edges buried in the soil to prevent the covering from blowing off. Then, increase the amount of ventilation plants receive a little each day. Feed the plants with a suitable compound fertilizer – one that is low in nitrogen and high in potash – to promote harder growth and protect them from the cold.

Plants grown outdoors

Some spring bedding plants can be raised and grown in seedbeds in the open ground rather than as bedding plants in a greenhouse or cold frame. Treat these as annuals and hardy biennials (see page 18). Seeds are sown in early summer, replanted in nursery beds and then transferred to their permanent flowering sites in early autumn. Water the plants several hours before they are to be moved.

perennials

These plants can be introduced in spring or autumn. Planting them in autumn means that they can be put in soil that is still warm from the summer, which gives them a head start in spring when the weather improves. However, in very cold climates and for tender perennials it is more sensible to leave planting until spring. Tender perennials include: pincushion flower (*Scabiosa*), cardinal flower (*Lobelia cardinalis*) and pink (*Dianthus*). Bear in mind that what is an annual or biennial in one climate could be a perennial in another, so there may be some overlap between plant categories.

plant selection

Before you begin planting, plan the site, taking into account the size of the plot and the relationship of the various plants. Also consider the timing as well as the suitability of your soil. Look for plants with strong, healthy growth buds at the base of the plant.

Spring planting	Season of interest	Height
Alcanet (*Anchusa*)	summer	50 cm (20 in)
Aster amellus	summer	50 cm (20 in)
Blanket flower (*Gaillardia*)	summer	45–60 cm (18–24 in)
Blazing star (*Liatris*)	summer	1.2 m (4 ft)
Brunnera	spring	45 cm (18 in)
Campion (*Lychnis*)	summer	15–30 cm (6–12 in)
Catmint (*Nepeta*)	summer	40–80 cm (16–32 in)
Comfrey (*Symphytum*)	spring	25–50 cm (10–20 in)
Delphinium	summer	90 cm–1.8 m (3–6 ft)
Hedge nettle (*Stachys*)	spring/summer	15–45 cm (6–18 in)
Ligularia	summer	1.2 m (4 ft)
Lungwort (*Pulmonaria*)	spring	25 cm (10 in)
Nerine	autumn	60 cm (24 in)
Pearl everlasting (*Anaphalis*)	late summer	60 cm (24 in)
Phlox	summer	10–30 cm (4–12 in)
Pincushion flower (*Scabiosa*)	spring/summer	30–90 cm (1–3 ft)
Poppy (*Papaver*)	summer	20–45 cm (8–18 in)
Red hot poker (*Kniphofia*)	summer	90 cm–1.8 m (3–6 ft)
Spurge (*Euphorbia*)	summer	2–4 m (6½–13 ft)
Stonecrop (*Sedum*)	summer	5–20 cm (2–8 in)
Tanacetum syn. *Pyrethrum*	summer	30–75 cm (12–30 in)

Autumn planting	Season of interest	Height
African blue lily (*Agapanthus*)	mid- to late summer	1 m (39 in)
Baby's breath (*Gypsophila paniculata*)	mid-summer	90 cm (3 ft)
Bear's breeches (*Acanthus spinosus*)	mid- to late summer	1 m (39 in)
Bleeding heart (*Dicentra spectabilis*)	late spring	60 cm (24 in)
Elephant's ears (*Bergenia*)	early to mid-spring	30 cm (12 in)
Giant kale (*Crambe cordifolia*)	summer	2 m (6½ ft)
Ice plant (*Sedum spectabile*)	early autumn	60 cm (24 in)
Lenten rose (*Helleborus orientalis*)	spring	45 cm (18 in)
Michaelmas daisy (*Aster novi-belgii*)	late summer	45–75 cm (18–30 in)
Peony (*Paeonia lactiflora*)	early to mid-summer	60–90 cm (24–36 in)
Plantain lily (*Hosta*)	mid-summer	30–75 cm (12–30 in)
Regal lily (*Lilium regale*)	mid-summer	1 m (39 in)
Winter iris (*Iris unguicularis*)	winter	30 cm (12 in)

preparing the soil and planting perennials

Herbaceous perennials usually occupy the same site for three years, so soil must be well cultivated before planting. Test the pH and adjust it, if necessary, to a level of 6.5–7.0. Increase acidity (lowering pH) by adding peat, or raise the alkalinity by adding lime.

Planting depths

1   Plants with a fibrous root system should have the topmost root about 1 cm (½ in) below soil level.

2   Those with a thick, fleshy root, or a cluster or crown of buds, should be around 2.5 cm (1 in) below soil level.

3   In soils that are prone to waterlogging the base should be planted slightly proud of the soil level to avoid rotting.

Container-grown plants

1   Before planting, water the container thoroughly to moisten the plant's roots. Then dig a hole for the plant, large enough to accommodate the roots.

2   Take the plant by its stem or leaves, gently lift it from the container and remove the top 1 cm (½ in) of compost from the surface and discard it (this gets rid of any weed seeds or moss).

3   Hold the plant by its root ball and carefully place it in the bottom of the planting hole.

4   With a trowel, pull the soil back into the hole and firm it around the plant. Cover the compost with soil, leaving a depression around the stem.

5   Finally, water around the base, making sure you fill the depression.

Bare-root plants

The method for planting bare-root perennials is similar to that of transplanting spring bedding. Follow the steps here, and for illustrated reference see steps 2, 3 and 4 on page 18.

1 Dig a hole large enough for the plant's root system and place it into the hole.

2 Pull the soil back into the hole around the plant and firm in gently.

3 Leave a slight depression around the stem and check that the plant is secure.

4 Water around the base of the plant, filling the depression made earlier.

creating an instant display

It is important to buy perennials in the right season. The main advantage of buying them in the summer is that the plants can be seen in flower and close to their ultimate height and spread. This will be invaluable if you need to fill a gap in a group of plants, or want to hide another, perhaps early-flowering perennial that is no longer looking its best

It will be useful, too, if you are planning a border from scratch, as you should be able to get a clear impression of how the plants will look all together. There is no need to stick rigidly to the rule of putting the shortest plants at the front of the border, and the tallest ones at the back – a change in height often lends extra interest.

colour scheming

There are numerous ways of using colour in order to create a theme within a garden display. You can, for instance, give a border a rainbow theme, starting at one end with plants that have flower colours in shades of violet, merging into blues, and changing through greens and yellows to oranges and reds. This may be effective for a long border, giving it a feeling of harmony and drawing the eye easily from end to end. Another option could be to use colour groupings within a number of separate borders around the garden: blue, pink and white; pale yellow, cream and salmon shades; purple, magenta and brown-purple shades; or maroon, red, orange and deep yellows. Or you could adopt a temperature theme: borders in 'hot' colours, which include reds, yellows and oranges, can look spectacular in a warm, sunny position; for a 'cool' border in a semi-shaded site, use plants with flowers in shades of blue, green and white.

Plants for a cool border in semi-shade

Agapanthus Headbourne hybrids	*Euphorbia amygdaloides* var. *robbiae*	*Polemonium* 'Sapphire'
Alchemilla mollis	*Geranium* 'Johnson's Blue'	*Pulmonaria angustifolia* subsp. *azurea*
Anaphalis yedoensis	*Geum* 'Rubin'	*Scabiosa caucasica* 'Butterfly Blue'
Astrantia major	*Iris sibirica*	*Tradescantia* 'Osprey'
Centranthus ruber var. *coccineus*	*Liriope muscari*	*Yucca flaccida* 'Ivory'
Dicentra spectabilis 'Alba'	*Nepeta* 'Six Hills Giant'	

Geranium 'Johnson's Blue'

Plants for a hot border in a warm, sunny position

Achillea filipendulina 'Gold Plate'	*Hemerocallis* 'Stella d'Oro'	*Rudbeckia fulgida* var. *sullivanii* 'Goldsturm'
Bergenia 'Morgenrote'	*Incarvillea delavayi*	*Saponaria ocymoides*
Cosmos atrosanguineus	*Kniphofia caulescens*	*Schizostylis coccinea* 'Major'
Crocosmia masoniorum	*Ligularia* 'The Rocket'	*Sedum* 'Autumn Joy'
Dahlia 'Bishop of Llandaff'	*Oenothera missouriensis*	*Trollius* 'Orange Princess'
Dianthus 'Christopher'	*Penstemon* 'Garnet'	
	Potentilla 'Gibson's Scarlet'	

Rudbeckia fulgida

making a summer bed

The whole idea of summer bedding is to create a loud, bold display to reflect the brightest, warmest season of the gardening year. With the help of a good seed catalogue it is remarkably easy to create a flower bed that will provide colour and interest all summer long. No special growing facilities are required. The main display can be produced from hardy annuals sown directly into the border in mid- to late spring, or early summer in colder areas. More tender plants, such as half-hardy annuals, can be grown from seeds or cuttings raised on the kitchen windowsill.

MATERIALS & EQUIPMENT

garden rake and trowel

high-phosphate fertilizer

sand

plastic bottle

plant seeds (see page 26)

stakes and twine

Preparing the bed

1   The bed can be marked out into planned blocks before sowing any seeds.

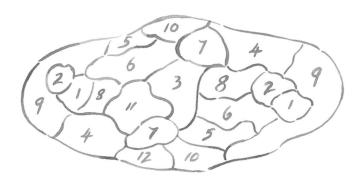

2   Prepare the ground thoroughly to give the seedlings a good start, and rake the soil down to a fairly fine tilth, adding a high-phosphate fertilizer at 30 g per sq m (1 oz per sq yd), to encourage rapid root development.

3   The easiest way to mark out the bed is to use dry sand. Slowly pour the sand out of a plastic bottle, forming narrow lines to indicate the intended margins of each group of plants. This will give a clear guide to where to sow or plant each group. If the sizes of the blocks are not quite right, you can rake the sand into the soil and mark out the border again.

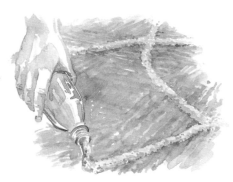

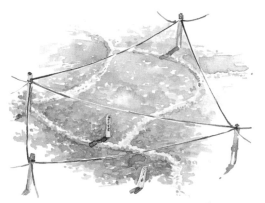

Sowing the hardy annuals

4   Sow the seeds into their respective segments, covering them lightly with soil to prevent them drying out. Label each group clearly. Provide protection from birds if necessary by stringing lengths of fine twine between short stakes.

5   At this stage, some segments should be left empty, with no seed sown in them. These accommodate the more tender half-hardy annuals when they are planted out.

6   When the seedlings emerge, gradually thin them out, to give them plenty of room to grow.

KEY TO PLANTING SCHEME	
1 *Solenostemon (Coleus) blumei** (red-leaved form)	7 *Gaillardia* x *grandiflora* 'Kobold'***
2 *Solenostemon (Coleus) blumei** (cream-leaved form)	8 *Verbena bonariensis****
	9 *Argyranthemum*** to ***
3 *Cosmos***	10 *Salvia viridis* 'Claryssa'***
4 *Coreopsis****	11 *Dahlia* (Collarette Series)**
5 *Gomphrena***	12 *Achillea ptarmatica****
6 *Zinnia elegans***	

Key: *=Tender   **=Half hardy   ***=Hardy

Transplanting the half-hardy annuals

7   You can now add the more tender plants that you have raised from seed indoors (or you can buy these as 'starter plants' from a garden centre). Start by digging a hole slightly larger than the plant's root system. Remove the young plant from its container and, holding it by its root ball, place it in the hole so that it sits firmly on the bottom.

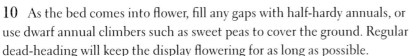

8   Using the trowel pull the soil back into the hole around the plant, and firm gently into place. Immediately after planting, water around the base of the plant.

9   Test that the plant is securely in place by tugging a leaf gently upwards. The leaf may tear, but the plant itself should not move.

10   As the bed comes into flower, fill any gaps with half-hardy annuals, or use dwarf annual climbers such as sweet peas to cover the ground. Regular dead-heading will keep the display flowering for as long as possible.

planting vegetables and fruit

The main purpose of growing fruit and vegetables is to provide a constant supply of fresh and tasty produce, and there are things to do at most times of the year. Spring is a time of intense activity in the vegetable garden, and this is when the bulk of the salad crops are planted, as well as alpine strawberries, ready for eating once the weather has warmed up. However, as with any other time of the year, we see both ends of the cropping cycle in spring, with seeds being sown and plants raised, as well as harvesting of some overwintered crops. Summer is essentially the season for planning and growing. Many of the vegetables planted in the spring will be ready to harvest in summer, while those that mature through the autumn, winter and spring of the following year will need to be propagated and the young plants raised. Also in summer, other rapidly growing crops will need to be sown at regular, frequent intervals to make sure the continuity of supply is not broken. Autumn is often seen as the quiet time in the vegetable garden, with harvesting being the main activity. However, some vegetables are tough enough to survive outdoors and need winter cold in order to produce a crop.

crop rotation

For larger gardens it is a good idea to follow a crop rotation plan in your vegetable garden: this is a system used to move vegetable crops from one plot to another on a regular basis over a number of years, reducing the effect of both pests and disease, and balancing the nutrients that are taken from the soil as the plants grow and develop. Simply divide the area to be planted into four separate plots, each one representing one of the rotational groups, then rotate the plots from year to year.

Root and salad crops	Brassicas	Legumes	Onions
Carrot	Cabbage	Broad bean	Bulb onion
Celery	Cauliflower	French bean	Garlic
Potato	Radish	Runner bean	Leek
Tomato	Swede		Salad onion
	Turnip		Shallot

bed systems

Where space is limited, a bed system can be used. This is a multi-row system where plants are grown close together and the distance between the rows is the same as the distance between the plants. The pathways between the beds are slightly wider than those on the row system, but because of the closer plant spacing more plants are accommodated. This arrangement makes the growth and shape of the vegetables more uniform. Weed control is made easier with the close spacing making the competition too fierce for the weeds to establish themselves, and the soil structure is kept in a better condition, since there is far less soil compaction.

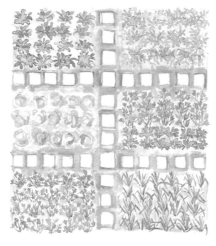

successional sowing

Quick-growing crops, especially the short-term salad vegetables such as lettuces and radishes, are the ones where gluts and shortages are the most likely to occur, but to a large extent this situation can be avoided by careful planning and sowing batches of seed on a regular basis.

Timing
This can be hard to gauge for inexperienced gardeners, since many plants mature more rapidly in warmer weather. Work out when to sow from the date you hope to harvest the crop, by counting back the number of weeks needed for the plants to grow. Sow the next batch of seed when the previous batch has germinated and emerged through the soil.

Vegetables for successional sowing	
French beans	Radishes
Runner beans	Spinach
Chinese cabbage	Spring onions
Lettuce	

sowing vegetable seeds

1   Firm and roughly level an area of seedbed using a large-toothed rake. Add a base dressing of fertilizer and rake it into the soil.

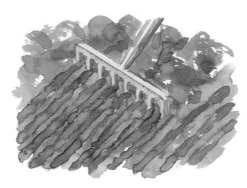

2   Insert a line and use a draw hoe to make a seed drill up to 2 cm (¾ in) deep. It needs to be the same depth all along its length.

3   Space the seeds evenly all along the bottom of the drill, then rake loose soil over the top. Check that the seeds are covered with a layer of earth, then gently press down the soil until it is firm. Write the name of the plant on a label and push it into the earth at one end of the row.

transplanting seedlings from beds or trays

After germination, seedlings are often too close together and they will need to be moved (transplanted) to a different site where they will have plenty of space to grow and mature. The seedlings are usually ready for transplanting when they are about 8 cm (3 in) high, and have four or five leaves each.

1 Dig a planting hole that is large enough to accommodate the root system of the seedling and, gently grasping the plant by its stem or leaves, place it in the hole, making sure that the roots are spread out evenly.

2 Using the trowel, pull the soil back into the hole around the seedling, leaving an indentation around the stem, and firm gently into place with your hands. Test the plant is secure by tugging a leaf upwards. Water immediately after planting by filling the indentation around the base of the plant.

Seedlings for transplanting	
Broccoli	Calabrese
sprouting	Cauliflower
Chinese	autumn
Brussels sprouts	winter
Cabbage	spring
Chinese	Kale
winter	Leeks
spring	Lettuce

transplanting pot-grown seedlings

1 More tender vegetables, sown in pots, need to be transplanted into a warm soil and grown through a sheet of black plastic, which will retain heat and moisture. Lay the plastic sheet over the soil and bury its edges.

2 Cut a cross in the plastic where the plant is to be inserted, fold back the flaps of plastic and dig a planting hole large enough to accommodate the plant's root system. Work carefully to avoid tearing the plastic.

3 Turn the plant upside down and remove the pot. Holding the plant by the root ball, place it in the hole.

4 Pull the soil back into the hole around the plant, and firm gently into place, leaving a slight depression at the base of the stem.

5 Immediately after planting, water around the base of the plant and fold the flaps back over the soil so they meet at the plant stem.

Pot-grown seedlings	
Aubergine	Peppers
Cucumber	Sweet corn
Marrow	Tomato

supporting vegetables

Tall-growing and climbing vegetables will need to be given some form of support as they develop in order to prevent the stems from becoming damaged or broken. The support will also help the plants bear the weight of the crop.

For French beans, use 2.5 m (8 ft) canes and erect them in two rows, at intervals of 60 cm (24 in). Join opposite canes together at the top and place a horizontal bar over them. Sow the seeds at the base of each cane.

Taller-growing broad beans are better with some support. Insert canes each end of the drills, on either side of them, and run string between them at a height of about 60 cm (24 in) from the ground to enclose the plants.

Once pea seedlings have emerged, plant pea sticks or twigs in the ground, either side of the drills. Then, as the peas grow, they will attach themselves with tendrils to the sticks and gradually climb up them.

pinching out

This is the process whereby the growing tip is removed by hand to encourage the formation of side shoots or flower buds – and thus fruit. Runner beans, broad beans and tomatoes all benefit from this treatment. Nip out the top buds once plants reach the required height or, for broad beans, once they are in full flower (this also deters aphids). If you want runner bean plants to form a bush, pinch them out when 25 cm (10 in) high.

protecting

Check your plants regularly for any early signs of pests and diseases (see pages 240–41 for more information). Remove any pests, such as slugs or caterpillars, and also remove any damaged growth as soon as it becomes apparent, treating where necessary. Another effective way to protect plants is to erect netting or other covers over plants to deter predators (see pages 238–39).

weeding

Weeds are particularly prevalent during the summer and you will need to check for them often, removing them as they occur to reduce competition for nutrients in the soil. Hand weeding is usually recommended for vegetable gardens, but other methods may also be appropriate. For more information on weed control see pages 229–31.

seeds sown outdoors

The vast majority of vegetables can be sown outdoors, directly into well-prepared beds, using either a broadcast (scattering) action or by sowing seeds in orderly drills, as shown on page 30. (For more detailed information on sowing seeds using both types of technique, see pages 80–81.) After sowing the seedlings will start to emerge above the soil level and it is at this point they must be thinned out to the appropriate spacing to encourage proper development – but only when the first true leaf has appeared (ignore the initial seed leaves). This information is often found on the back of the seed packets. At this time, they may also need to be transplanted to their permanent beds (see page 81 for more information). If you are sowing seeds outdoors in the autumn for harvesting in the spring of the new year, timing is critical. If you do this too early (in late summer, for example), the young plants may become too mature and 'bolt' in order to produce seed. If, however, you sow seed too late (say, in mid-autumn), then the young plants may not have sufficient time to mature enough to survive the cold winter months. Judging the time to sow is largely a matter of experience, since this can vary by a week or two earlier or later depending on the prevailing weather conditions in any given year.

seeds sown indoors

Some types of spring-sown seed need to be started off under protection, since the soil will be too cold for them to germinate successfully outdoors, and they also risk being damaged by any late frosts. Plant seeds in suitable seed trays or pots (see pages 86–87) and put them through a process of acclimatization, or hardening off (see page 34), once they have started to grow and before you begin any planting out.

Suitable seeds for outdoor sowing

Seeds sown	Row spacing	Plant spacing
Beetroot	30 cm (12 in)	10 cm (4 in)
Broad bean	30 cm (12 in)	23 cm (9 in)
Cabbage – summer/autumn	45 cm (18 in)	30 cm (12 in)
Cabbage – winter	45 cm (18 in)	45 cm (18 in)
Calabrese	35 cm (14 in)	30 cm (12 in)
Carrot	15 cm (6 in)	10 cm (4 in)
Cauliflower – early autumn	30 cm (12 in)	15 cm (6 in)
Cauliflower – autumn	30 cm (12 in)	15 cm (6 in)
Cauliflower – winter	30 cm (12 in)	15 cm (6 in)
Cauliflower – spring	30 cm (12 in)	15 cm (6 in)
French bean	30 cm (12 in)	7.5 cm (3 in)
Kale	60 cm (24 in)	45 cm (18 in)
Kidney bean	30 cm (12 in)	15 cm (6 in)
Kohlrabi	30 cm (12 in)	15 cm (6 in)
Leek	10 cm (4 in)	2.5 cm (1 in)
Lettuce	30 cm (12 in)	30 cm (12 in)
Onion – salad	10 cm (4 in)	5 cm (2 in)
Onion – seed	30 cm (12 in)	10 cm (4 in)
Parsnip	30 cm (12 in)	15 cm (6 in)
Pea	12.5 cm (5 in)	12.5 cm (5 in)
Radish	15 cm (6 in)	2.5 cm (1 in)
Swede	38 cm (15 in)	23 cm (9 in)
Turnip	30 cm (12 in)	15 cm (6 in)

Suitable seeds for indoor sowing

Seeds sown	Sowing density
Aubergine	1 seed per 7.5 cm (3 in) pot
Broccoli	40 seeds per tray
Brussels sprouts	40 seeds per tray
Cauliflower – summer	40 seeds per tray
Celeriac	40 seeds per tray
Celery	40 seeds per tray
Cucumber	1 seed per 7.5 cm (3 in) pot
Marrow	1 seed per 7.5 cm (3 in) pot
Pepper	1 seed per 7.5 cm (3 in) pot
Sweet corn	1 seed per 7.5 cm (3 in) pot
Tomato	1 seed per 7.5 cm (3 in) pot

hardening off

Plants raised under cover must go through a period of acclimatization for up to two weeks before transplanting. Move them from the house or greenhouse into a cold frame or under cloches and ventilate for a few hours each day, increasing the period until the frame is left open all day. Alternatively, bring them out from the greenhouse for a couple of hours each day, then for longer periods.

thinning and transplanting seedlings

Most seedlings need thinning out to some degree after they have germinated in order to provide room for the young plants to grow. If they need transplanting, do this when they are still young, since they are better able to recover. See page 81 for additional information.

Transplanting in spring		
Plant	Row spacing	Plant spacing
Cauliflower – early summer	45 cm (18 in)	60 cm (24 in)
Cauliflower – summer	45 cm (18 in)	60 cm (24 in)
Celery	45 cm (18 in)	45 cm (18 in)
Garlic	20 cm (8 in)	20 cm (8 in)
Onion – sets	20 cm (8 in)	15 cm (6 in)
Potato	50 cm (20 in)	30 cm (12 in)

harvesting vegetables

The summer is a particularly busy time for the vegetable gardener as many of the established plants will need constant attention to produce good crops. Routine, but very important, tasks include training, staking, protecting and weeding.

Salad crops

Salad crops – whether lettuce, radish, beans or tomato – can be harvested throughout the summer months. They should be picked as soon as they mature so that they do not deteriorate. This is especially true of lettuces, which tend to bolt if left in the ground for too long.

Autumn cauliflowers

Harvest autumn cauliflowers from late summer until mid-winter, when the covering leaves start to open and reveal the curd beneath. Remove the curd by cutting through the main stem with a sharp knife; leave a row of leaves around the curd to protect it from damage while it is being handled.

Onions

These are ready for harvesting when the leaves start turning yellow and the tops keel over. You can speed up this process by bending the tops over by hand. Lift the bulbs gently with a fork and allow them to dry on a wire or wooden tray. Onions store well if they are hung in a cool, dry, frost-free place.

Podded vegetables

Where both the pod and its contents are intended to be eaten, start harvesting the crop once it is well developed and the seeds are just visible as slight swellings along the length of the pod.

Where just the seeds are to be eaten, they must be allowed to develop and swell, but you should harvest them before the pods start to change colour and the seeds become hard and inedible.

harvesting spring vegetables

Some vegetables
that were sown in
the autumn will be
ready for harvesting
in spring. These
include the ones in
the table below. They
can all be dug up out
of the plot and either
used immediately
when they are fresh
or stored for later
use. Most brassicas

freeze well and cabbages can be stored on a bed of straw
under cover, either in a cold frame, or, if you do not have
one, a garden shed.

Spring harvesting vegetables	
Broccoli	Cauliflower – winter
Brussels sprouts	Kale
Cabbage – spring	Spinach

planting asparagus

Asparagus is a perennial and should not be planted with
your other rotational crops – set aside a separate bed.
Asparagus can be sown from seed in the spring, but it is
easier to buy 'crowns'. Dig 30 cm (12 in) wide trenches,
20 cm (8 in) deep and set the crowns 38 cm (15 in) apart.
Cover the roots with 2.5 cm (1 in) of soil at first, adding
more as the plants grow, until you reach the level of the
surrounding soil.

planting alpine strawberries

There are several different types of strawberry available and
they can be divided up into three different categories:
summer-fruiting, perpetual-fruiting and alpine. The first
two types should be planted in late summer to produce
crops the following summer. However, small, sweet-tasting
alpine strawberries should be started off in the spring.

Begin by sowing the
seeds indoors in early
spring into trays of moist
compost. Store the trays
in a darkened room to
aid germination (see
pages 86–87 for more
information on sowing
seeds indoors and
transplanting).

After the last spring frosts have passed, transplant the
seedlings into beds outside (see page 81). Top dress them
with compost. They should produce fruit in the autumn of
the first season or, failing that, the following spring.

Varieties
'Alpine Yellow'
'Baron Solemacher'
'Delicious'

planting potatoes

Seed potatoes are easy to grow and need to be planted in the spring, in a frost-free environment, once the temperature has increased. The sprouts on the seed potatoes should be at least 2 cm (¾ in) long for a high-yielding crop. Prepare your soil by digging in plenty of organic matter. Dig drills or holes about 7.5–15 cm (3–6 in) deep and plant the seed potatoes about 38 cm (15 in) apart. Cover them with 2.5 cm (1 in) of soil. In cooler climates, place a black plastic mulch over them, making holes in the cover for the emerging plants.

Varieties
'Ailsa'
'King Edward'
'Pink Fir Apple'
'Romano'
'Sante'

planting autumn-sown onions

Bulb onions are grown as annual plants, with the brown- or yellow-skinned cultivars being the most popular with gardeners. They are cool-temperature and even frost-tolerant plants, especially in the early stages of development, with low temperatures often promoting a better-quality crop. For this reason many are raised from seed sown in the early autumn, 2.5 cm (1 in) apart, in drills 1 cm (½ in) deep, with rows about 30 cm (12 in) apart. The time of sowing is critical: if sown too early, the seedlings become too mature and will begin producing seed; if sown too late, the seedlings may not be mature enough to survive the winter. Sow once the weather turns cooler but before the frosts begin.

Varieties
'Express Yellow'
'Imai Early Yellow'

planting garlic

This strong-flavoured hardy vegetable is surprisingly easy to grow. Garlic needs six weeks of temperatures between 0 and 10°C (32 and 50°F) to promote good growth. The bulbs are propagated by splitting them into individual segments or cloves, which are pushed base first into a light, deeply cultivated soil so that the pointed top of the clove is about 2.5 cm (1 in) below the soil surface, and spaced out at about 18 cm (7 in) intervals. As they develop, the bulbs work their way onto the soil surface.

planting early-summer cauliflowers

In early autumn, treat the soil with a low-level nitrogenous fertilizer. Then sow seed into trays, and when seedlings have developed their first true leaf, prick them out and place in pots 7.5 x 7.5 cm (3 x 3 in) of loam-based compost. Put them in a cold frame in autumn, ventilate on warm days and water sparingly.

planting broad beans

Broad beans are rich in protein and provide nourishment to the soil in the form of nitrogen. They can be sown both in the autumn and the spring and will need fertile soil and shelter over the winter months. The seeds can be sown outside in October to produce a May crop. Start by placing the seeds in double rows set 20 cm (9 in) apart, with 5 cm (2 in) deep drills, and 15 cm (6 in) spaces between each seed. As a protective measure, cover the plants with cloches or floating mulches.

Varieties
'Aquadulce Claudin'
'Express'
'Red Epicure'
'Witkiem Major'

planting blackberries

Blackberries come as bare-root plants and, because of their vigorous habit, they need to be supported on a fence or wall as they grow. Start by digging a shallow hole, large enough to spread out the roots of the plant. If using more than one plant, space them at least 3 m (10 ft) apart. Place the plant in the hole, fill with soil, firm in and water. Prune the plant back to about 22 cm (9 in) to encourage rapid growth.

Varieties
Summer-fruiting
'Bedford Giant'
'Himalaya Giant'
'Merton Early'

Autumn-fruiting
'Ashton Cross'
'John Innes'
'Oregon Thornless'
'Thornfree'
'Variegatus'

planting spring cabbage

Hardy cabbages are sown in a seedbed in late summer. Plant them out in cool autumn temperatures so that they can grow slowly over the winter period and be ready for harvesting in the following spring. The young plants are ready for transplanting when they have three true leaves. Firm the plants in to prevent them from drying out or being lifted by frozen soil.

Varieties
'Avoncrest'
'Durham Early'
'Spring Hero'

planting raspberries

Raspberries can be planted throughout the winter, provided the weather holds up. Choose a well-drained site and erect posts in the ground, about 4.5 m (15 ft) apart. Attach three wires to each post at 75 cm (30 in) intervals – if you are planting more than one row, set the rows 2 m (6 ft) apart. Dig trenches under the wires 15 cm (6 in) wide and 20 cm (8 in) deep. Plant the raspberries in the trenches 45 cm (18 in) apart, cover with soil, firm in and water.

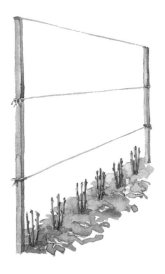

Varieties
Summer-fruiting
'Glen Clova'
'Malling Delight'
'Malling Jewel'

Autumn-fruiting
'American Fallgold'
'Autumn Bliss'
'September'

planting herbs

These aromatic plants, usually associated with culinary skills and food seasoning, also include a number of attractive ornamental garden plants that you can grow just for their looks. Almost all herbs prefer to grow in a sunny position with their roots in a fertile, free-draining compost. The site must be cultivated deeply and cleared of all perennial weeds before any planting can be considered.

a culinary herb border

Traditionally, herb beds are arranged in a formal design to define the individual herbs and prevent plants becoming too straggly. Shrubby herbs are used as a framework planting to provide focal points and boundaries, into which the annual and biennial herbs are used as groundwork or filling. A modern approach is to lay out the paths in a symmetrical pattern to create beds, but soften this effect with informal plantings within the beds, which will provide colour, aroma, leaf texture and variations in height and shape.

Use the plan (right) and the chart below as a guide to planting your herbs and see page 22 for planting techniques.

Common herbs		Season of interest	Height
A	Mint (*Mentha spicata*)	summer	30–90 cm (1–3 ft)
B	Borage (*Borago officinalis*)	summer	30–90 cm (1–3 ft)
C	Basil (*Ocimum basilicum*)	summer	15–45 cm (6–18 in)
D	Parsley (*Petroselinum crispum*)	summer	30–80 cm (12–32 in)
E	Fennel (*Foeniculum vulgare*)	summer	1.8 m (6 ft)
F	Coriander (*Coriandrum sativum*)	summer	50 cm (20 in)
G	Chives (*Allium schoenoprasum*)	summer	30–60 cm (1–2 ft)
H	Thyme (*Thymus vulgaris*)	summer	15–23 cm (6–9 in)
I	Lavender (*Lavandula angustifolia*)	summer	30–60 cm (1–2 ft)
J	Sage (*Salvia officinalis*)	summer	60–80 cm (24–32 in)
K	Bay (*Laurus nobilis*)	spring/summer	3–15 m (10–50 ft)
L	Rosemary (*Rosmarinus officinalis*)	spring	1.5 m (5 ft)
M	Dill (*Anethum graveolens*)	summer	60–90 cm (2–3 ft)
N	Horseradish (*Armoracia rusticana*)	summer	30–120 cm (1–4 ft)
O	Angelica (*Angelica archangelica*)	summer	1–2.5 m (3–8 ft)

Harvesting herbs

Harvest and dry your herbs to preserve their aromatic properties. Never wash them before drying, or they may start to rot. Tie short stems into bunches of eight to ten and hang them up in a warm, dry and well-aired room until the leaves become crisp. Once dry, store the leaves in an airtight container.

Spring-harvesting herbs	
Angelica	Lovage
Bay	Mint
Dill	Rosemary
Fennel	Sage
Horseradish	Thyme

making a hanging basket

Containers filled with plants are one of the most effective methods of linking the house and garden together. They brighten up a dull corner or provide interest on a plain, boring expanse of wall, adding colour for a large part of the year. This project features a classic planting plan with a large fuchsia in the centre, surrounded by smaller plants. However, you can use fewer varieties of plants in a looser formation, as seen in the arrangement of impatiens, petunias, verbenas and lobelias below, or a natural looking display of nasturtiums, lobelias and helichrysums.

MATERIALS & EQUIPMENT

40 cm (16 in) diameter wirework basket, rust-proofed and with a chain

wall bracket and screws

peat- or fibre-based lightweight compost

sphagnum moss

9 blue trailing lobelias (*L. erinus*)

1 large trailing fuchsia (*F.* 'Tom West')

3 swan river daisies (*Brachyscome iberidifolia*)

3 white impatiens (*I.* New Guinea Group)

3 begonias

Preparing the soil for watering

1   Perhaps the most difficult problem to overcome with plants in hanging baskets is providing enough water to keep them growing well. But there are solutions.

Mix 1 teaspoon of washing-up liquid into 9 litres (2 gallons) of water, and water the compost with this mixture before using it to fill the hanging basket. The detergent forms a film over the compost particles and acts as a wetting agent, attracting water.

Alternatively, fill a plastic bottle with water, leaving the cap slightly unscrewed, and bury it in the basket where the water will gradually seep out. Refill the bottle as necessary.

Securing the hanger

2   Choose the position for your basket carefully, taking into account both the display and ease of watering. Then attach a bracket to the wall, making sure it is secure and will take the weight of the finished basket.

3   Place the basket base down in a large pot that is half full of compost. This will make working much easier and stop the basket from rocking about.

Planting up

4   Start lining the basket by placing a 2.5 cm (1 in) layer of sphagnum moss in the bottom half of the basket, patting it firmly against the frame. Hold the moss in place with handfuls of moist compost.

5   Add more compost up to the level of the moss, and begin planting. Push the root balls of the small trailing lobelias through the mesh of the basket, from the outside, and bed the roots into the compost.

6 Continue lining the basket with a 2.5 cm (1 in) layer of sphagnum moss in the top half of the basket, patting it firmly against the frame of the basket. Add more compost up to the level of the moss, and continue to plant up the container.

7 Now plant the top section. Position the large fuchsia in the centre of the basket, pulling back the compost to bed in the plant and gently firming it into position. Place the small swan river daisies, begonias and impatiens around the fuchsia and firm them into the soil.

8 Once you have finished positioning the small plants around the central one, fill the basket with moist compost to within 2.5 cm (1 in) of the top of the basket (this will leave room to water the basket).

9 Soak the compost in the basket immediately after the planting has been completed. This will settle the compost around the roots and help the plants establish more quickly.

10 After the basket has drained, use the chains to lift the basket out of the pot and hang it in position.

planting hardy trees and shrubs

Trees and shrubs are easy to buy from nurseries and garden centres and come in three forms: container-grown, root-balled or bare-root. All types should be well balanced and with evenly spaced branches; this is particularly important for the main structural or framework branches. The plants should have no damaged or broken branches and stems, and should be free of all visible signs of pests and diseases. If possible, examine the root system of the plant and discard any plants with damaged roots, sucker growths, and containers where there are large populations of weeds in the growing medium.

plant forms

Container-grown

Root-balled

Bare-rooted

heeling in

If the intended transplanting area is not ready, plants can be placed in a site where they are 'heeled in' (a form of temporary planting), though this should only be for a few days. Dig a shallow trench in a sheltered part of the garden and place the roots in the trench with the stems laid at an angle of about 45°. Refill the trench with soil and firm in gently, making sure that all of the roots are covered with at least 20 cm (8 in) of soil. This will protect the roots from frost damage until the permanent site is ready.

container-grown trees and shrubs

Plants grown in containers can be purchased and planted at any time of the year, as long as the weather and soil conditions are acceptable. This makes them a very convenient way of adding plants to the garden.

Recommended plants

Beech	(*Fagus*)	Shrub althaea	(*Hibiscus syriacus*)
Firethorn	(*Pyracantha*)	Tagyosho pine	(*Pinus densiflora*
Horned holly	(*Ilex cornuta*)		'Umbraculifera')
Japanese maple	(*Acer japonicum*)	White cedar	(*Thuja occidentalis*)
Oak	(*Quercus*)		
Pfitzer juniper	(*Juniperus* x *media* 'Pfitzeriana')		

Acer japonicum

root-balled trees and shrubs

Plants bought as root-balled specimens are usually available in the autumn and spring when planting conditions are most suitable. When you buy your plant, check that the root system is well proportioned and tightly wrapped and has no exposed roots.

Recommended plants

Callery pear	(*Pyrus calleryana*)	Japanese red pine	(*Pinus densiflora*)
Catawba rhododendron	(*Rhododendron catawbiense*)	Kentucky coffee tree	(*Gymnocladus dioica*)
		Manchurian lilac	(*Syringa patula*)
Common hornbeam	(*Carpinus betulus*)	Red maple	(*Acer rubrum*)
Eastern hemlock	(*Tsuga canadensis*)	Serbian spruce	(*Picea omorika*)
Green ash	(*Fraxinus pennsylvanica*)		

Acer rubrum

bare-rooted trees and shrubs

These plants will normally have some packing, such as straw, around their roots to protect them from drying out or frost. They are only available when the plants are dormant and are best planted in the autumn.

Recommended plants

Aspen	(*Populus*)	Oak-leaved hydrangea	(*Hydrangea quercifolia*)
Bridal wreath	(*Spiraea* 'Arguta')	Ohio buckeye	(*Aesculus glabra*)
Crab apple	(*Malus prunifolia*)	Red-barked dogwood	(*Cornus alba* 'Sibirica')
Japanese barberry	(*Berberis thunbergii*)	River birch	(*Betula nigra*)
Manchurian cherry	(*Prunus maackii*)	Willow	(*Salix*)

Malus prunifolia

planting a container-grown shrub

1 Start by marking out the planting hole using two canes and a piece of string to scribe a circle about twice the diameter of the root ball.

2 Dig out the hole to at least twice the depth of the root ball, keeping the topsoil separate from the less-fertile subsoil.

3 Using a garden fork, break up the sides and bottom of the hole to allow the newly developed roots to penetrate into the surrounding soil.

4 For tall shrubs it may be necessary to use a stake. Position it in the side of the hole and knock it into place until it is firm – it should reach up to the head of the shrub.

5 Add a layer of soil back into the hole around the stake and firm in.

6 Take hold of the stem of the shrub and ease the plant out of its container, then tease out any enmeshed roots.

7 Place the shrub into the centre of the hole, and use a bamboo cane or broom handle to check that the tree is at the correct level. Container-grown shrubs should be planted with the compost level in the container 2.5 cm (1 in) below the level of the surrounding soil.

8 Start to back fill the hole with soil, spreading it evenly around the roots; hold the stem of the shrub steady while you do this. Fill the hole with layers of soil, finishing with the topsoil, and firm each layer with your boot heel until the hole has been filled up to its original level.

9 You will now need to fix the shrub to the stake, using a strap tie with a spacer; the point of the spacer is to keep the shrub and stake apart and prevent the stake from damaging the stem. The strap should be about 5 cm (2 in) below the top of the stake.

10 Apply a top dressing of fertilizer to the soil around the base and lightly mix this into the top 5 cm (2 in). This will gradually be washed down into the root zone in time for new growth to start in the spring.

planting a root-balled conifer

1 The method is very similar to that of planting a container-grown plant (see left), but when you mark out the planting hole make it at least 2 or 3 times the diameter of the root ball.

2 Dig the hole, break up the sides and add soil as for the container-grown shrub. Place the conifer into the centre of the hole and tilt the plant gently to help remove the wrapping. Check that the top of the root ball is 4 cm (1½ in) below soil level.

3 Back fill the hole with layers of soil, spreading it evenly around the root ball. Firm each layer with your boot heel, filling the hole to its original level.

4 Drive a support stake into the soil surrounding the planting hole at an angle of about 45°; this avoids breaking the root ball or damaging the root system. Point the top of the stake into the prevailing wind so that the stem is tugging against the stake, and as the wind blows it drives the stake further into the ground. Tie the plant to the stake about 30 cm (12 in) above ground level.

5 Apply a dressing of fertilizer around the base of the plant and mix this into the topsoil.

planting bare-rooted shrubs and trees

Some newly planted trees and large and standard shrubs require staking and supporting until the roots are sufficiently anchored. Position the stake in the hole on the windward side before planting to avoid damaging the roots. Anchor the plant close to the base with a tie 15 to 20 cm (6 to 8 in) above soil level to allow the roots to grow and establish, leaving the stem free to flex in the wind. This helps it to thicken and develop.

Planting a bare-rooted rose

Most roses are offered for sale as bare-root plants (with the soil removed from the roots). Exposing the roots means that they can become very dry. To overcome this, cover the roots in sacking and then soak them in a bucket of water for about half an hour before you begin planting. The best time to plant bare-rooted roses is in autumn and early winter, when the plant has just lost its leaves. With the soil still warm, they will establish very quickly. They prefer a rich soil in a sunny situation. Make sure the 'bud union', where the roots join the stem, is planted above soil level.

1 Dig out the hole to at least twice the width of the plant's root system and deep enough to accommodate all of the roots. Using a garden fork, break up the soil in the bottom of the hole to allow the new roots to spread into the soil surrounding the planting hole.

2 Trim the roots of the plant with secateurs to remove any broken or damaged pieces of root (damaged roots are often the sites where suckers develop).

3 Place the rose bush into the centre of the hole and use a bamboo cane to check that the plant is at the correct level.

4 Back fill the hole with soil, spreading it evenly around the roots, and shake the stem of the rose to settle the soil between the roots and to remove any air pockets. Fill the hole with layers of soil to the original level, firming each layer with the heel of your boot.

5 Prune the rose back to 7.5 to 10 cm (3 to 4 in) from the bud union. Do this after planting, since the long shoots provide something to hold during planting. Apply a top dressing of fertilizer around the plant, mixing it into the top 5 cm (2 in). This will be washed down into the root zone.

transplanting

In addition to introducing new plants into the garden, there are times when it may be desirable or even necessary to move existing plants within the garden to make way for other plants, to reduce competition between plants or to open up a particular vista. Careful planning and thorough preparation in advance of any move are essential.

Preparation

This process should begin in the early autumn, while the roots are growing and the soil is still warm. This means that any roots that are pruned at this time will quickly heal and regrow. The first stage is to mark

out the intended size of the root ball, the diameter of which should be about one-third of the plant's height. Dig a trench outside of this mark, 30 to 60 cm (12 to 24 in) deep and one spade's width, cutting through any thick roots. Refill the trench with a mixture of soil, compost and fertilizer to encourage plenty of new roots to form.

Lifting

In the following autumn, dig a trench outside the one made the previous year, about 30 to 60 cm (12 to 24 in) deep and the width of two spades. Cut under the root ball to sever any roots and separate it from the soil.

Rock the root ball to one side and place sacking underneath, then rock it to the other side so that the ball is sitting on the sacking.

Bring the four corners of the wrapping together and tie in position. The plant is now ready to be moved to its new site.

Re-planting

Position the root ball in a well-prepared planting hole and untie and remove the wrapping by rocking the root ball over on its side (hessian can be left to rot in the ground). The hole around the root ball then needs to be refilled with soil and firmed in.

Support taller plants with three angled stakes knocked into the soil, with guy-ropes fixed two-thirds of the way up the main stem; thread the rope through sections of rubber hose to stop it rubbing against the bark. Finally, water the plant and apply a mulch.

using trees and shrubs in containers

Growing trees and shrubs in containers is the ideal way for many gardeners to increase quickly the range of plants they grow, especially for those with only a little spare time, since there is no major soil preparation to be done. Autumn and spring are the usual times for planting, but if trees and shrubs are container-grown they will happily establish themselves in the summer, which is particularly useful for those wanting to create an instant display.

advantages of containers

There are many advantages to growing plants in containers, especially for those with only a small garden, or even no garden at all. It can offer solutions to problems of space, soil and climate, or provide a simple means of filling an unexpected gap in a border. We usually think first of bedding plants as the planting material, but trees or shrubs combined with perennials and annuals create a permanent feature and a continual source of pleasure.

Dealing with lack of space
Plants in containers can be used to add interest in a small garden since they can be moved from one site to another and so help to vary the seasonal display. The use of containers is also a very effective way of restricting the growth or spread of very vigorous plants.

Gardens with no soil
It is quite feasible to grow plants outdoors without having a garden. Plants can easily be grown in containers and positioned on a terrace or balcony. Bay trees and thyme make excellent pot-grown herbs.

Adapting to different climates
In more northerly districts or areas that are susceptible to late spring frosts, the growth rate of plants can be limited. By using containers, the plants can be moved to a more sheltered site or even taken indoors at certain times. This is particularly useful for pot-grown citrus fruits, such as lemons, which prefer to be overwintered under glass.

Different soil types

Some plants thrive only in certain soil conditions, but there are limits to how much you can modify the soil in your garden to suit. In some gardens, the soil may have a high lime content, which is difficult and expensive to adjust. This makes growing plants that need acid soil, such as rhododendrons and camellias, impossible. The easy answer to this problem is to grow the plants you want in a container, in a specially formulated compost.

choosing containers

Purpose-made containers are available in a wide variety of shapes, sizes and materials, including concrete, clay, plastic and wood. Alternatively, you can make your own, either from scratch or by giving a new lease of life to an object that started as something completely different (see project on page 244).

Size and shape

While the final selection of a container may be down to personal choice, there are some practical considerations to be taken into account. Tall plants and climbing plants may need some form of support if they are to keep growing well. In this situation the dimensions of the container are particularly important; a deep container is necessary so that a stake or cane can be driven into the compost. The shape of the container will also have a bearing on how rapidly the compost will dry out. One with a narrow base and wide top exposes a large surface area of compost to the atmosphere, and will, therefore, dry out more quickly than one with a narrow top.

Porous materials

Containers made from a porous material, such as terracotta or wood, often lose a good deal of water through their sides due to evaporation. To a large extent, this loss can be avoided by lining the inner walls of the container with plastic sheeting before potting begins. Do not line the base of the container as this may impede drainage and cause the compost to become waterlogged.

trees and shrubs suitable for growing in containers

Climbers and wall shrubs		
Actinidia kolomikta	*Euonymus fortunei* cultivars	*Wisteria sinensis* cultivars
Campsis x *tagliabuana*	*Jasminum nudiflorum*	(as a standard)
Ceanothus cultivars	*Lonicera* x *heckrottii*	
Clematis viticella cultivars	*Vitis*	

Pinus mugo 'Winter Gold'

Conifers		
Abies koreana	*Juniperus scopulorum* 'Skyrocket'	*Taxus baccata*
Cryptomeria japonica	*Picea abies* 'Nidiformis'	*Thuja occidentalis* cultivars
Cupressus macrocarpa cultivars	*Pinus mugo*	

Deciduous trees and shrubs		
Acer palmatum	*Eucalyptus gunnii*	*Spiraea japonica*
Berberis thunbergii cultivars	*Fuchsia magellanica*	*Viburnum carlesii*
Buddleja alternifolia	*Magnolia stellata*	
Davidia involucrata	*Philadelphus* 'Belle Etoile'	

Berberis

Evergreen trees and shrubs		
Brachyglottis (Senecio) 'Sunshine'	*Cordyline australis*	*Lavandula angustifolia*
	Escallonia 'Slieve Donard'	*Mahonia aquifolium*
Buxus sempervirens cultivars	*Eucalyptus*	*Yucca filamentosa*
Camellia	*Laurus nobilis*	

Buxus

planting a shrub in a container

Always try to match the size and growth habit of a plant to the size and type of container used, otherwise even quite a light wind could blow the whole arrangement over. For example, a tall-growing plant with a bushy head of foliage will require a heavier container than a shorter one with more sparse foliage. If planting a deciduous specimen during its dormant season, you will have to envisage how it will look when in full leaf.

1   Make sure the container has drainage holes and place a layer of pot shards over them to stop the compost being washed out. Add a layer of compost to cover them.

2   Make a small cross out of 3 x 3 cm (1½ x 1½ in) wood and wedge it horizontally into the pot, above the pot shards. Insert a stake and fasten it to the cross with strong wire.

3   Place the shrub in the container, spreading its roots out evenly over the compost. Then add compost around the roots and shake the stem of the shrub to settle the compost.

4   Fill the container with layers of compost and firm each layer until the compost reaches up to 10 cm (4 in) below the top rim.

5   Make another, larger, cross out of wood and wedge it horizontally into the sides of the container, level with the compost. Fasten the stake to this cross with strong wire and cover it with compost to hide it from view.

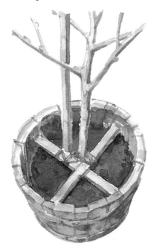

6   Fix the tree to the stake using a strap tie and spacer to prevent the stake damaging the stem. The strap tie should be about 15 cm (6 in) above the top of the container.

7   Using a saw, cut off any surplus stake about 5 cm (2 in) above the tie – use only a short stake, since this allows the roots to develop while allowing the stem to flex and bend in the wind and reduces the chance of the container blowing over in the wind.

8   Water the compost and apply a reflective mulch of light-coloured stones or wood chips to prevent the compost from drying out.

a shrub border for year-round interest

Summer offers the perfect opportunity to make plans for a border as you sit back and reflect on its present appearance and how you might like to change or improve it. Take inspiration from friends or neighbours and visit as many show gardens as you can so that you can design the border well in advance of the ideal planting time in the autumn. When choosing plants for a shrub border, there are different factors to consider: the size and shape of the shrub, which colours and forms complement one another, the suitability of a plant for a certain site, and whether or not it grows well in your type of soil.

planning the border

Perhaps one of the most interesting challenges for any gardener is to create a shrub border that will offer something of interest throughout the year. This is not simply a matter of selecting a range of shrubs that flower at different times; it also involves siting individual plants so that they draw the eye to various parts of the border.

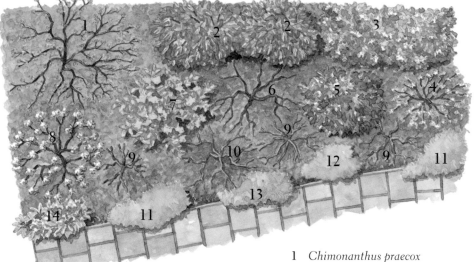

Creating seasonal interest

One of the best ways to draw attention deep into a border is to plant winter-flowering subjects at the rear, behind deciduous plants. The winter flowers can be seen through the deciduous shrubs, which will have no leaves on them at this time of year, but from mid-spring until mid-autumn, when winter-flowering shrubs tend to be relatively uninteresting, the foliage of the deciduous plants will hide them from view.

Using scented plants

Siting scented shrubs close to pathways allows anyone passing by to appreciate their fragrance, whether it comes from the flowers or from aromatic foliage. Even if the shrub does not have a strong shape or spectacular colour, its scent will add an extra delightful dimension to the border.

1   *Chimonanthus praecox*
2   *Camellia japonica*
3   *Lonicera fragrantissima*
4   *Abeliophyllum distichum*
5   *Choisya ternata*
6   *Hydrangea macrophylla*
7   *Mahonia aquifolium* 'Apollo'
8   *Viburnum x bodnantense* 'Dawn'
9   Shrub rose
10 *Paeonia officinalis*
11 *Lavandula* 'Hidcote'
12 *Rosmarinus officinalis*
13 *Santolina pinnata* subsp. *neapolitana*
14 *Salvia officinalis*

planting for year-round interest

Spring

The new season is heralded by many small blooms in shades of cream, pink, white and yellow. They are often highly visible due to the lack of foliage so early in the year, and many are also scented. Later on, more colour is provided by the newly opening leaves.

Plants with good flower colour	Plants with good foliage colour
Daphne tangutica Retusa Group	*Acer negundo* 'Flamingo'
Hamamelis mollis cultivars	*Berberis thunbergii* 'Atropurpurea Nana'
Kerria japonica 'Pleniflora'	*Elaeagnus* 'Gilt Edge'
Magnolia x *soulangeana*	*Mahonia fremontii*
Mahonia x *media* 'Charity'	*Pieris* 'Forest Flame'
Viburnum	

Magnolia x *soulangeana*

Summer

There is a huge choice of flowering shrubs for summer, and the plants can be combined to form a continuous display. Bear in mind that other colourful plants may offer stiff competition at this time, and interest can easily be diverted away from the shrub border.

Plants with good flower colour	Plants with good foliage colour
Buddleja fallowiana	*Berberis thunbergii* 'Rose Glow'
Calycanthus occidentalis	*Catalpa bignonioides* 'Aurea'
Cistus ladinifer	*Cornus alternifolia* 'Argentea'
Embothrium coccineum	*Luma apiculata* 'Glanleam Gold'
Rosa 'Blanc Double de Coubert'	*Pyracantha* 'Mohave Silver'

Catalpa bignonioides 'Aurea'

Autumn

Many of the shrubs grown for their spring or summer flowers provide a second season of interest in autumn. This is when many of the deciduous shrubs really come to the fore with their dramatic displays of changing leaf colours. Many others produce attractive fruits, which often remain on the branches through winter and into spring.

Plants with good flower colour	Plants with good foliage colour	Plants with good fruit colour
Ceanothus 'Burkwoodii'	*Acer palmatum*	*Cotoneaster* 'Rothschildianus'
Clerodendrum trichotomum	*Cercidiphyllum japonicum*	*Pyracantha* cultivars
Convolvulus cneorum	*Cercis canadensis*	*Rosa rugosa*
Hibiscus syriacus	*Hydrangea quercifolia*	*Symphoricarpos orbiculatus*

Winter

Conifers and broad-leaved evergreens take centre stage in winter, their attractive foliage often contrasting with orange, red and yellow berries. There are also flowers at this time of year, with yellow predominating, and deciduous shrubs with brightly coloured stems.

Plants with good flower colour	Plants with good stem colour
Chimonanthus praecox	*Cornus alba*
Garrya elliptica	*Cornus stolonifera*
Jasminum nudiflorum	*Kerria japonica*
Mahonia napaulensis	*Leycesteria formosa*
Rhododendron mucronulatum	*Rubus thibetanus*
Viburnum x *bodnantense*	*Salix sachalinensis* 'Sekka'

Cornus alba

making a tapestry hedge

A tapestry hedge is a selection of compatible plants with similar growth habits, used to create a hedge that provides a varied range of colours and textures. This type of hedge creates a feature in its own right, rather than being a backdrop for other ornamental plants, and the use of different plants often extends the season of interest. The most important aspect of a tapestry hedge is to choose plants (either deciduous or evergreen) that have very similar growth rates, otherwise the most vigorous species will dominate the hedge to the detriment of its partners.

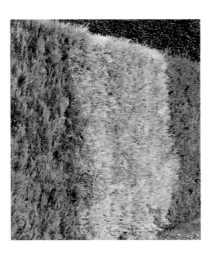

MATERIALS & EQUIPMENT

selection of suitable plants (see page 60)

organic matter, such as well-rotted manure

garden line

marker canes

garden spade and fork

root fertilizer

secateurs

1   Soil preparation

Hedges are usually permanent features in a garden, so it is essential to prepare the soil thoroughly. Start by marking off a hedge line about 1 m (3¼ ft) wide and double dig the site (see page 253). Add copious quantities of organic matter as you dig. This cultivation should be carried out at least a month before planting, together with an application of a systemic weed killer, such as glyphosate.

2   Plant selection

Choose three or four different plants from the examples below. Make sure they have a good root system, well-balanced stocky growth and branches starting at soil level – this avoids gaps during early growth.

Common green beech (*Fagus sylvatica*)
Copper beech (*Fagus sylvatica purpurea*)
Green holly (*Ilex aquifolium*)
Hornbeam (*Carpinus betulus*)
Purple barberry (*Berberis* x *ottawensis* 'Purpurea')
Quince (*Chaenomeles japonica*)
Yew (*Taxus baccata*)

3   Spacing

In most situations, a single row of plants is sufficient to establish a good hedge, but on exposed sites or where a dense barrier is needed quickly, a double row of plants can be used. For most species, for either a single or a double row, a spacing of 45 to 60 cm (18 to 24 in) between the plants is recommended. Where a double row is planted the rows are 30 cm (12 in) apart, with the plants staggered so that they will knit together more rapidly.

4   Planting a double row

Start by planning the positions for your plants. Mark out the first line of the hedge with garden line between two canes, then insert more canes along the length of the line at the correct spacings to indicate where the different plants are to be inserted.

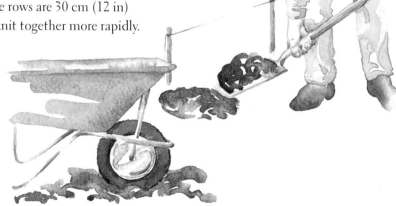

5   Dig a first hole by the first marker cane; the hole should be one spade wide and one spade deep in order to take the root system of the plant. As you dig, keep the soil from the first hole in a wheelbarrow (this will be used later to fill in the last hole).

6 In order to achieve a good tapestry effect, mix the plants together and stand them in a bucket of water to prevent the roots drying out. As planting progresses, the hedge plants are simply pulled out at random and planted to give a mixed population within the hedge. For the first plant, place the root system against the side of the hole and spread out the roots; do not fill in the hole with soil yet.

7 Dig another hole by the second marker cane and place the soil into the first hole, covering the roots of the plant already inserted. Firm the soil in gently with a boot heel. Repeat this procedure down the entire length of the first row.

8 Now mark out the second line of the hedge, as before, and insert canes where the plants will go.

9 Start planting the second row, working back along the hedge line in the opposite direction to the first row. At the end of the row, the last hole is filled with the soil that was placed in the wheelbarrow in step 5.

10 Apply a dressing of fertilizer to the soil surface around the young plants and mix this into the top 5 cm (2 in).

11 Add a layer of organic matter 10 cm (4 in) deep to act as a mulch over the surface and to retain moisture and suppress weeds.

12 Formative pruning

Pruning is essential to encourage even growth at the base and top of the hedge. Most hedges benefit from being cut back to two-thirds of their original height immediately after planting. At the same time, cut back any strong lateral branches by about half in order to encourage a dense bushy habit.

planting climbers

Apart from climbing roses, most climbers are purchased as container-grown plants. They can be planted at almost any time of the year, but planting in the spring offers a number of benefits. In spring, the soil is moist and starting to warm up as the days become longer and the sun warmer and this provides the longest possible growing period in the new site and allows plenty of time for the plant to establish successfully. In addition, the risk of frost is diminishing, which is particularly important for plants that may not be fully hardy.

Tropaeolum speciosum

Climbers for acid soil

Agapetes serpens

Asteranthera ovata

Chilean bellflower
(*Lapageria rosea*)

Coral plant
(*Berberidopsis corallina*)

Dusky coral pea
(*Kennedia rubicunda*)

Flame nasturtium
(*Tropaeolum speciosum*)

Herald's trumpet
(*Beaumontia grandiflora*)

Holboellia coriacea

Lardizabala biternata

Mitraria coccinea

Mutisia oligodon

Passiflora caerulea

Climbers for alkaline soil

Actinidia kolomikta

American bittersweet
(*Celastrus scandens*)

Blue passion flower
(*Passiflora caerulea*)

Campsis x *tagliabuana*
'Mme Galen'

Clematis heracleifolia

Chinese wisteria
(*Wisteria sinensis*)

Chocolate vine
(*Akebia quinata*)

Confederate jasmine
(*Trachelospermum jasminoides*)

Everlasting pea
(*Lathyrus grandiflorus*)

Humulus lupulus 'Aureus'

Climbers for clay soil

Boston ivy
(*Parthenocissus tricuspidata*)

Chinese wisteria
(*Wisteria sinensis*)

Clematis
(Large-flowered hybrids)

Common hop
(*Humulus lupulus* 'Aureus')

Common trumpet creeper
(*Campsis radicans*)

Dutchman's pipe
(*Aristolochia durior*)

Everlasting pea
(*Lathyrus latifolius* 'White Pearl')

Virginia creeper
(*Parthenocissus*)

Ipomoea

Climbers for sandy soil

Coral plant
(*Berberidopsis corallina*)

Dusky coral pea
(*Kennedia rubicunda*)

Flame nasturtium
(*Tropaeolum speciosum*)

Giant granadilla
(*Passiflora quadrangularis*)

Glory pea (*Clianthus puniceus*)

Holboellia coriacea

Ipomoea

Merremia tuberosa

Mutisia oligodon

Paradise flower
(*Solanum wendlandii*)

Vitis vinifera 'Purpurea'

planting a container-grown climber

1   Dig a planting hole large enough to accommodate the plant's root system, about 30 to 45 cm (12 to 18 in) away from the base of the support. Break up the soil in the base of the hole to encourage deep root penetration from the new plant.

2   Before planting, water the container thoroughly to moisten the plant's roots. Then, holding the plant by its stem, gently remove it from the container and scrape away the top 1 cm (½ in) of compost from the surface of the root ball and discard it (this layer will contain most weed seeds and moss, which may contaminate the planting site).

3   Tease out any roots that may be curling around the bottom of the root ball and place the plant in the hole, leaning the top of the plant against the support.

4   Mix a dressing of slow-release fertilizer into the soil that will be used to refill the planting hole. Using a spade, pull the soil back into the hole around the plant and firm it gently into place. Cover the surface of the compost with soil, leaving a slight depression around the base of the stem.

5   After planting, water around the base of the plant with at least 9 litres (2 gallons) of water, to settle the soil around the plant's roots and encourage the roots to grow into the surrounding soil.

6   Untie the shoots from the cane, spread them out against the support frame and retie them into position (even climbers with tendrils will need some initial help and guidance to start climbing in the right direction). Finally, cut out or reduce any surplus, weak or badly damaged shoots.

routine care

Climbers are usually planted close to a wall and may lose a lot of moisture to the wall's foundations. It is, therefore, essential to replace this loss, especially after planting. Mulching is a useful method of reducing surface evaporation from the soil, particularly with clematis, which prefers a cool, moist root system. Scatter the  mulch evenly around the root area at the base of the plant. It is especially important to ensure that newly planted climbers are well watered. To help keep them supplied with water, a useful tip is to install a section of plastic pipe close to the root system when the climber is planted. This pipe can be filled with water at regular intervals and the water from it will then seep out into the surrounding soil, encouraging deeper rooting.

making a rose arch

This rose arch provides the perfect opportunity to plant hardy roses in the autumn so that they bloom in the following summer. An arch creates a sense of mystery in the garden, inviting the viewer to walk through and discover another garden scene beyond. This rose arch, which is made from pre-treated timber, will become even more attractive as the wood slowly ages, while the red *Rosa* 'Excelsa' and *R.* 'Swan Lake' will bring colour and fragrance to the garden during the summer months and into the early autumn.

MATERIALS & EQUIPMENT

4 timber upright posts, 2.5 m x 10 cm (8 ft x 4 in)

6 timber cross rails, 1 m x 10 cm (3¼ ft x 4 in)

6 timber diagonal braces, 1.5 m x 5 cm (5 ft x 2 in)

2 timber main roof beams, 2 m x 5 cm (6½ ft x 2 in)

3 timber roof cross rails, 90 x 5 cm (36 x 2 in)

2 timber diagonal braces, 1.35 m x 5 cm (4½ ft x 2 in)

4 wooden marker pegs and garden line

4 metal support posts

spirit level and builder's square

screws, 10 cm (4 in) long

nails, 10 cm (4 in) long

sledge hammer

4 climbing or rambling roses

1   Rake the soil roughly level in the area intended for the structure. Mark out the positions of the upright posts using the wooden pegs and garden line, checking that the corners are at right angles with a builder's square. The overall area should be 1.5 m (5 ft) wide and 1 m (3¼ ft) deep.

2   Insert a piece of off-cut wood into the first metal post holder and drive it into the ground using a sledge hammer until approximately 2 to 3 cm (¾ to 1¼ in) of the holder is showing. The process should be repeated for the remaining post holders to support the upright posts.

Making the side panels

3   Make each side panel using three of the 1 m (3¼ ft) horizontal cross rails and two 2.5 m (8 ft) upright posts. Mark off the position of the cross rails on the upright posts. Cut bird-mouth joints in the two upright posts and cut both ends of each cross rail into a chamfered point (see Glossary, page 259). Take each upright post in turn and insert the tip of the cross rails into the bird-mouth joints and nail them together at an angle.

4   Take two 1.5 m (5 ft) diagonal braces and nail one onto each side panel. This provides further structural strength and additional support for the climbing or rambling roses.

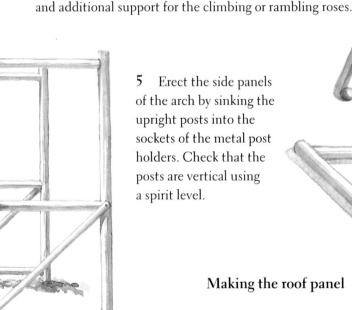

5   Erect the side panels of the arch by sinking the upright posts into the sockets of the metal post holders. Check that the posts are vertical using a spirit level.

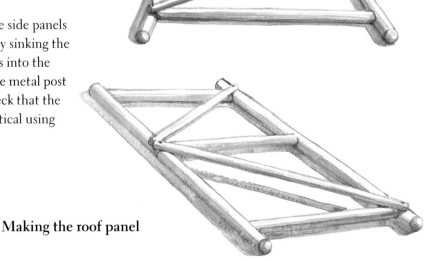

Making the roof panel

6   Make the roof panel in the same way as the side panels, using the two 2 m (6½ ft) main roof beams and three 90 cm (36 in) roof cross rails. Follow the instructions on making the side panels in step 3 in order to join the main roof beams to the cross rails. To provide further support, nail on two 1.35 m (4½ ft) diagonal braces, as in step 4.

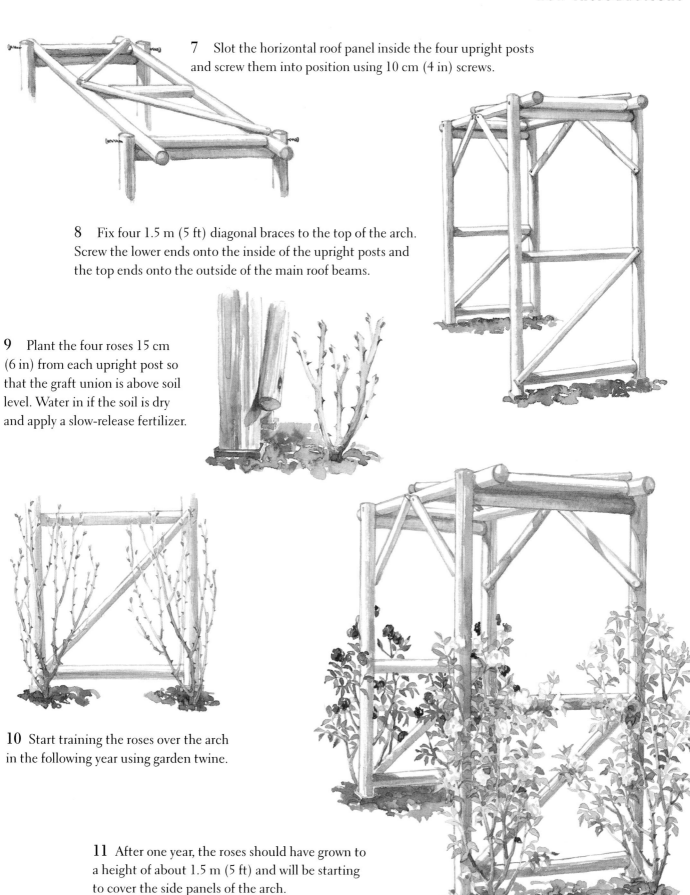

7 Slot the horizontal roof panel inside the four upright posts and screw them into position using 10 cm (4 in) screws.

8 Fix four 1.5 m (5 ft) diagonal braces to the top of the arch. Screw the lower ends onto the inside of the upright posts and the top ends onto the outside of the main roof beams.

9 Plant the four roses 15 cm (6 in) from each upright post so that the graft union is above soil level. Water in if the soil is dry and apply a slow-release fertilizer.

10 Start training the roses over the arch in the following year using garden twine.

11 After one year, the roses should have grown to a height of about 1.5 m (5 ft) and will be starting to cover the side panels of the arch.

caring for new plants

The most important task to consider when caring for new plants is careful planning to conserve water, which helps the new plants to grow well in dry conditions. Incorporating well-rotted organic matter into the soil increases the moisture-holding capacity of the soil, and mulching – covering the soil surface with a layer of material – is an ideal way of preventing surface evaporation of moisture. It is also vital that you keep an eye on the health of the plant, dealing with any pests or diseases at an early stage, before they can do any serious damage.

pests and diseases

Young plants and seedlings are particularly susceptible to pests and diseases and therefore need as much protection as possible in the early stages of growth. Healthy plants are better able to cope with invasion by pests and diseases, so the first stage in preventing lasting damage is to take the best possible care of your new plants. Always use clean containers and make sure that you choose a suitable planting site with sufficient spacing; the circulation of air helps growth and the health of the plant, as well as stopping the spread of pests and diseases from one plant to another. Also, water, prune and remove any suspect leaves or branches as soon as they appear, before problems can spread.

Diseases
The most common diseases are fungal, followed by bacterial. The commonest symptoms are discoloration and wilting or drying out of foliage and stems. Use either natural organic remedies or chemical controls for these problems (see page 240).

Pests
On new plants the best method of control is simply to pick off the offending pests, such as slugs, snails, beetles and caterpillars. Larger four-legged pests can be deterred by a chicken wire covering placed over your plants (see below).

watering seedlings

For seeds and seedlings, water must be in plentiful supply to enable germination and rapid development to take place. A moist seedbed is the best way to ensure that seeds will germinate quickly. If you water after sowing, the upper soil may dry out on a hot day, forming a thin crust that can prevent the seedlings emerging after germination. Young plants being transplanted often suffer from shock and stress due to the disturbance, and this is even worse in dry soil. When watering seedlings, use a light spray only; first check that your water flow is steady (see below) and then pass the watering can gently over the plants to settle the moist soil around the roots (see bottom).

competition

Any newly planted areas need all the help they can get to establish quickly; as well as feeding and watering these new plants you also need to make sure that they do not have to compete with weeds for supplies of food and water (see page 229). Some form of weed control will need to be planned and implemented, therefore, in order to reduce this competition. Chemicals that are usually sprayed onto the weeds can be used, but the best method is to tackle weeds by hand. For the most efficient weed elimination, use a hoe. The blade should penetrate no deeper than 1 cm (½ in) into the ground, to reduce the loss of moisture from the soil and minimize soil disturbance, which encourages more weed seeds to germinate.

When hoeing out weeds between plants, sever the weeds at just below soil level, leaving the plants intact.

mulching

A mulch is basically a covering over the soil. As well as retaining soil moisture, mulching also suppresses weeds. Problems can arise, however, depending on the material used. Straw tends to harbour insects, such as vine weevils and flea beetles, as well as potentially containing weed seeds. If you do use an organic mulch, make sure that it is at least 10 cm (4 in) deep in order to be effective. A good alternative is to use a black plastic film mulch, which not only warms the soil (essential at the beginning of spring) but also is easy to apply and remove. As the plants grow, you can cut a cross in the plastic and feed the new foliage through the opening.

shelter

Until they have established, many new plants benefit from shade and shelter to reduce water loss. To some extent these problems can be overcome by toughening the plants before they are planted out into the garden, but some form of protection for a few days can make a considerable difference to how quickly the plants start growing.

Polythene tunnels
These temporary structures are cheap, easily moved and very versatile crop covers. They can be laid over the crop (see below) and are ideal for vegetables that are grown in rows.

Fleece
For ornamental plants growing in beds, cut fleece into sheets or squares to make an effective frost protector and shade-giving cover. Fleece is more permeable to light and air than plastic film.

Plastic netting
This finely meshed material can be placed directly over seedlings or plants and anchored with pegs (see below). It is good for filtering the wind and providing overall protection.

constructing a rock garden

Rock gardens provide a unique growing environment for a wide range of interesting and beautiful plants, and they can be the ideal solution to an awkward area of the garden, such as a slope where mowing or other forms of cultivation are difficult. They are composed of rocks and free-draining soil arranged and built to imitate a rocky outcrop, with plants arranged and planted between the rocks.

MATERIALS & EQUIPMENT

sandstone, limestone, or granite rocks

spade, rake and trowel

coarse rubble and stones

protective gloves

crowbar or strong rope

rock cress (*Arabis*), trumpet gentian (*Gentiana acaulis*), pasque flower (*Pulsatilla vulgaris*), *Oxalis adenophylla*, moss phlox (*Phlox subulata*), meadow saxifrage (*Saxifraga granulata*), *Sedum spathulifolium* 'Cape Blanco', *Primula* 'Blossom', *Primula vulgaris*, *Lewisia tweedyi*, yarrow (*Achillea*)

coarse grit mulch

Planning and preparing the site

1   Choose the rock garden site carefully – alpines grow best in a sunny aspect, preferably on a sloping bank. Once you have found a location, it is a good idea to plan your garden on paper, since this largely avoids having to reposition the rocks as you go.

2   Remove the topsoil to a depth of 15 cm (6 in) over the site where the rock garden is to be built and stack this to one side for later use (if this soil is left at the base of the rock garden it will be covered over and wasted).

3   Fill the excavated hole with coarse rubble and stones to improve drainage. Rake soil and old compost over the rubble to form a slight mound.

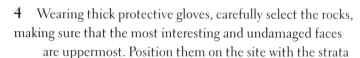

4   Wearing thick protective gloves, carefully select the rocks, making sure that the most interesting and undamaged faces are uppermost. Position them on the site with the strata running in the same direction and tilt them slightly to vary the overall height and allow any rain water to run off them. Move large rocks into position by dragging them on a sledge and lifting them onto the mound with a crowbar or strong ropes.

5 Build up the topsoil, put aside earlier, behind each of the rocks as the layers of the mound are formed. Bury the rocks by up to a third or until they are steady and secure in the soil.

Planting

6 Before planting, water each plant thoroughly and allow the pot to drain for a couple of hours.

7 Using a trowel, excavate a hole large enough to accommodate the plant's root ball. Gently remove the plant from its container and lower the root ball into the prepared hole.

8 Fill in with soil and firm gently around the plant. Level the soil surface so that it is just above the compost level of the root ball.

9 Finally, sprinkle a 2.5 cm (1 in) layer of coarse grit around the plant to form a mulch. Water the plant to settle the compost and grit.

Care and maintenance

• Keep the surface grit layer topped up so that the plants are always protected from pests and from being splashed with soil. This is usually done by top dressing in the spring, just after the plants have started to grow.

• Remove any dead leaves that accumulate on the rock garden, since once these have settled around the plants they tend to attract water and will eventually cause the plants to rot.

• Plants with hairy leaves are particularly susceptible to damage by wet conditions during the winter months or in early spring, and they may need to be protected by a sheet of plastic film.

propagation

One of the most satisfying aspects of gardening comes from the sheer satisfaction of producing your own plants, be it from cuttings, seeds or any other method of propagation. Many of the techniques used are quite easy, often very little equipment is required and the chances of success are high enough to make you want to keep trying. All methods of propagating plants other than from seed are known as vegetative propagation – this includes division and taking cuttings. The advantage of vegetative propagation is that you can be sure that any plant you reproduce vegetatively will be genetically identical to the parent plant. This is important in the propagation of especially fine forms of plants, or variegated plants.

seed

Using seed is the most common and, in most cases, possibly the easiest method of propagating quickly a large number of plants. Seeds can vary greatly in appearance, germination requirements, germination performance and growth rate. Some, such as birch (*Betula*), prefer cool, light conditions for germination, while others, such as *Verbena*, can take up to three weeks to germinate and prefer warm, dark conditions.

tools and equipment

In order to begin propagation by seed, there are a few items you will need to add to your gardening stocks, if you do not already have them. You will need a number of different sized pots – clay pots are the best kind, being both sturdy and deep. For seed trays, square or rectangular shapes will fit better on a shelf or window ledge. Use a multi-purpose free-draining compost as a growing medium, since garden soil is not sterile.

A selection of clay pots is invaluable when potting up seeds or seedlings.

Plastic seed trays can be bought with or without separate sections for your seeds. Use labels to avoid confusing seed types.

A rake and hoe can be used with pegs and string to keep your beds square and seed drills straight. Use a dibber (right) to make small planting holes.

Use a small can with a fine 'rose' head so that you do not wash away any compost and disturb the seeds.

A fine-mesh sieve is used to ensure that seed compost does not contain any lumps or debris.

collecting seeds and bulbs

Although it is very convenient to buy seeds or bulbs in packets or bags, it is a relatively simple task – and much more satisfying – to collect them yourself from your own plants, or from those of a friend or neighbour. In some cases, especially with certain modern cultivars, plants raised from seed will not be exactly the same as the parent – but this can be part of the fun.

collecting seeds

With many plants, the seeds can be collected as they ripen, but before they are dispersed from the fruit. It is much easier to pick the seed heads a day or two early and get all of the seed in one place; if you wait too long, you will find yourself having to pick up seeds from the ground, one by one. Observation is the key, because often the seed will mature before the fruit starts to split open. Once the pods begin to turn brown and you see the first signs of a split in the casing, the seed head and its contents can be collected.

Seed storage

1   Collect the seed heads complete with stalks, and remove any leaves or remaining petals. Place bunches of stalks, seed heads first, into paper bags, and tie the neck with string. Label the bags.

2   Hang the bags in a cool, dry place. Shake them occasionally to release the seeds. For smaller plants, lay the seed heads on trays lined with newspaper until the seed heads split open.

3   Carefully remove the seed heads and stalks from the paper bags or trays. Hold the seed heads over sheets of paper and shake them until the seeds fall out. Sift through with your fingers to clean out any bits of stalk or rubbish.

4   Place the cleaned seeds into dry envelopes or other paper packets (not plastic bags) and seal them up. Always take care to label the envelopes clearly with the plant name and variety, the flower colour (if appropriate), and the date.

5   Place the envelopes in a glass jar and seal the lid. Then put the jars in a cool, dry, dark place – this will make sure that the seed does not deteriorate. If they are properly dried and kept in the correct conditions, the seeds of most vegetables and flowering plants will survive from two to five years in storage.

Storage life of some seeds		
1 to 2 years	**3 to 5 years**	**5 to 10 years**
Callistephus chinensis	*Capsicum*	*Calendula*
Delphinium	*Centaurea candidissima*	*Cosmos*
Helichrysum monstrosus	*Phlox drummondii*	*Eschscholzia*
Iberis umbellata	Tomato	*Nigella*

pre-germination treatment

A seed is a complete plant in embryo, but it is dormant. Before germination it may require some preliminary treatment. Seeds that have extremely hard coats, or display cold-temperature dormancy, will take a very long time to germinate unless you prepare them first. Stratification is a simple method of treating your seeds prior to sowing.

Stratification

This chilling technique, used for many seeds encased in fleshy fruits, such as hips and berries, allows the fleshy fruits to rot away but prevents seeds from drying out. It is also used for seeds that germinate only in temperatures of 5°C (41°F) or lower. When you have treated your seeds (see below), label the pot and stand it in a cool, moist spot in the garden. Periodically turn the mixture. After this treatment the seeds can be sown in the normal way the following spring.

1   Collect the hips or berries before they are fully ripe and place them in a paper bag.

2   Place broken sections of clay pot over the drainage hole at the base of your pot.

3   Then place a 5 cm (2 in) layer of sand or seed compost in your pot with a 5 cm (2 in) layer of hips or berries over this.

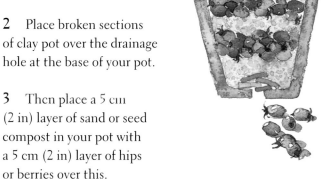

4   Repeat this process until the pot is almost full and finish off with a layer of sand.

> **Some seeds which require stratification**
>
> Aconite (*Aconitum*)   Maple (*Acer*)
> Barberry (*Berberis*)   Primrose (*Primula*)
> Birch (*Betula*)   *Sorbus*
> *Cotoneaster*   *Viburnum*
> Hornbeam (*Carpinus*)

collecting stem bulbils

Some species of lily produce embryo bulbs, known as bulbils, in the angle created where the leaf joins the flower stem (the 'leaf axil'). These immature bulbs can be collected after the flowers have died down and propagated to produce new plants that are identical to the parent. The bulbils are a dark green or blackish-purple colour, and they form through the spring and summer months on the flower stem as it develops.

1   The best time to collect stem bulbils is when they are ripe, about three weeks after the flowers have died down. Simply pick them from the stem by hand – they should come away quite easily.

2   Sow the bulbils (just like seeds) 2.5 cm (1 in) apart into trays of seed compost, so that they sit just below the surface. Now place the trays in a cold frame and leave them for a year. In the following autumn the young bulbs will be ready for planting out into a permanent site in the garden, although it will be a further two to three years before they produce any flowers.

> **Lilies that produce stem bulbils**
>
> *Lilium bulbiferum*
> *Lilium lancifolium*
> *Lilium sargentiae*
> *Lilium sulphureum*

sowing seeds outdoors

The growth rate and habit of your plant are important in determining the spacing of the seeds, for instance, low-growing plants with a spreading habit need more space than those with an erect habit. Also, sowing too thickly produces thin, weak seedlings, and sowing too thinly wastes space. Self-seeding plants need extra room, as the seed usually disperses over a wider area than the original plants.

sowing in drills

Sowing in drills is most commonly used for vegetables and plants that are to be grown in nursery rows and transplanted later into permanent positions. Drills are also used for

plants that are sown quite close together initially but are given extra space later by thinning out the seedlings when they are large enough to handle.

sowing broadcast

Most hardy annuals as well as some salad vegetables, such as radishes and salad onions, are broadcast-sown by scattering the seed evenly onto a well-prepared seedbed. This technique is most commonly used when the seedlings are intended to grow and mature in situ and is useful for creating a random planting effect.

1   Decide on the sowing rate per square metre (yard), according to the size and habit of the individual plant. Then on a prepared seedbed, rake the soil to establish a fine tilth.

2   Sow the seed by hand, and if the seeds are small, choose a calm day so that the wind does not blow them away. Work just above soil level so that the seeds do not bounce as they land.

3   Firm the seed gently into the seedbed with a flat board (make sure that the board is dry, since seeds will stick to a damp surface).

4   Next, cover the seeds with a layer of grit to a depth of 1 cm (½ in).

5   Using the back of a garden rake, level the grit over the seedbed. The large, coarse particles of grit allow light through to the seed, discourage slugs and suppress weed seed germination. It also absorbs the impact of rain droplets, preventing compaction and capping.

6   Finally, water the seedbed thoroughly to aid germination. It is a good idea to use a watering can fitted with a fine rose to avoid washing away the seeds.

Annuals that frequently self-seed		
Alyssum	Greater quaking grass	Nasturtium (*Tropaeolum majus*)
Candytuft (*Iberis*)	(*Briza maxima*)	Sunflower (*Helianthus*)
Clarkia	Marigold (*Calendula*)	Velvet bent (*Agrostis canina*)
Larkspur (*Consolida*)	Poppy (*Papaver*)	

seedling care

As the seedlings develop leaves they will benefit from a liquid feed of nitrogen and potash, every two weeks, to supplement the phosphates already in the seedbed. Use a liquid feed rather than a powder or granular formulated fertilizer, to reduce the risk of the seedlings being damaged by excessive nutrient levels.

Many seedlings are easily damaged by early spring frosts, especially in the first few weeks after germination. As an emergency measure, gently lay some sheets of newspaper over the seedlings whenever frost is forecast – although the paper may appear flimsy, its insulation properties can provide seedlings with as much as 2 to 3°C (4 to 5°F) of protection.

thinning seedlings

After germination the seedlings may be too close together and so will need to be spaced out. This involves removing some seedlings to provide growing room for those that are to remain and mature. Carefully prick out the weakest seedlings or any that are malformed or diseased, leaving an even, well-spaced row of healthy seedlings.

transplanting seedlings

1   With some plants, particularly vegetables, the seedlings are transplanted and grown in a new plot. Water the bed the night before to moisten the soil. Then, using a hand fork, lift the plants out, holding each seedling by its leaves to prevent the stem from becoming bruised or damaged.

2   In the new plot, make a hole in the soil using a dibber, deep enough to take the roots of the seedling. Place the seedling in the hole and fill in with soil around the base. Finally, gently firm in and water.

making a cold frame

Substantial structures, such as cold frames, are the best option for protection on exposed
sites, where other materials and structures may be damaged or blown away completely.
A cold frame will not keep out all frost but will reduce frost penetration to a minimum,
especially if it is also lined with an additional insulation material, such as fleece,
clear plastic film or bubble plastic. The best frames are those made with
good insulating materials – use wood for the sides and a single or double glazed
glass lid, either with or without a wooden frame.

MATERIALS & EQUIPMENT

softwood timber cladding as follows:

14.5 m x 10 x 2 cm (48 ft x 4 x ¾ in) for body

3 m x 5 x 5 cm (10 ft x 2 x 2 in) for posts, two side supports and central spar

1.2 m x 7.5 x 1.2 cm (4 ft x 3 x ½ in) for front of frame

7.5 x 2.5 x 1.2 cm (3 x 1 x ½ in) for fixing glass

1.2 m x 5 x 2.5 cm (4 ft x 2 x 1 in) for back rail

grooved timber 3.6 m x 5 x 2.5 cm (12 ft x 2 x 1 in) with 1 cm (⅜ in) wide
and 1.2 cm (½ in) deep groove for frame sides and back

brass screws, 2.5 cm (1 in) long

4 butt hinges

1 litre (1 quart) clear wood preservative

2 sheets horticultural glass 52 x 60 cm x 6 mm (21 x 24 x ¼ in)

Preparing the wood

1 Start by cutting the cladding into appropriate lengths for the body. For the front and back you need eight 1.2 m (4 ft) long boards: cut one of these in two along its length (use the other half for the sides). For the sides you need eight 60 cm (24 in) long boards, plus the spare length from the front and back, cut in two across its width.

Constructing the main body

3 Pre-drill three boards for the front at the short ends and screw them to two posts, with the excess at the top. Repeat this for the back panels using four and a half boards; place the narrow board at the top.

5 To create the sloping edge on the side panels you need to saw a 15 cm (6 in) diagonal 'fall', from the back to the front of the main body of the box. Discard the excess wood.

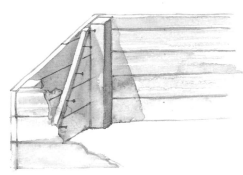

7 Cut the central spar to 60 cm (24 in) and bevel the ends so that it fits exactly inside the box, positioned in the centre and level with the top edge at both the front and the back. Pre-drill and screw it in place from the outside to form a supporting and strengthening bar.

2 Next, cut out the wood for the four corner posts: the front two posts measure 32.5 cm (13 in) and the back two posts measure 45 cm (18 in).

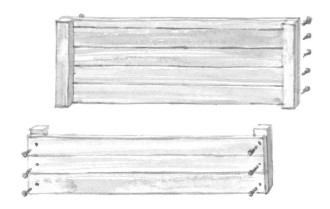

4 Now construct the sides using four and a half boards for each side, placing the narrow boards at the top. Pre-drill and screw them to the front and back, covering the end grain of the front and back boards.

6 Now cut the two side supports, each measuring 40 cm (16 in) and nail them to the inside of both sides, positioning them at an angle so that they join and secure the side boards together (this stops the sloping sections flapping around).

Constructing the frames

8   Cut the grooved wood into four 60 cm (24 in) lengths for the sides and two 60 cm (24 in) lengths for the back. Cut halving joints at the ends of all these pieces. Next, cut the front frame wood into two 60 cm (24 in) sections.

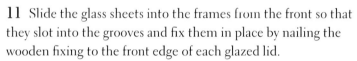

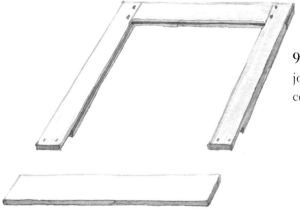

9   Assemble the frame back and sides by slotting the halving joints in place, then attach the front section. Secure all the corners with brass screws.

10   Now treat the frame and the main body (including the back rail, to be fixed later) with clear wood preservative, inside and out, and allow it to dry before joining the frame and body.

11   Slide the glass sheets into the frames from the front so that they slot into the grooves and fix them in place by nailing the wooden fixing to the front edge of each glazed lid.

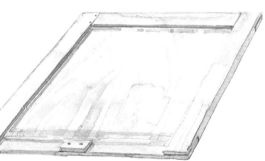

Assembling the box

12   Nail the back rail flush to the back edge of the body. Then place the glazed lids next to one another on top of the main body, butting the inside edge of the back rail. Screw two hinges to the top of each frame.

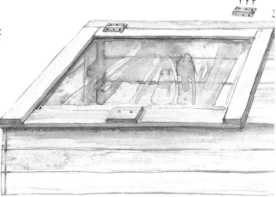

Using the frame

13   The completed frame is now ready for use. It can be used with the lid either fully closed or fully open. Also, sometimes it may be useful to have it half open in order to improve ventilation; to do this hold the lid open by wedging a brick or similar object between the frame and the main body, along the front edge.

sowing seeds indoors

Many summer bedding plants are half-hardy annuals and their seeds would not germinate in garden soil until early summer, since they need extra warmth. Other shrubs, trees and vegetables are perfectly hardy once established, but are frost-tender during their seedling stage and benefit from protection or extra warmth early on. Some seeds also need light to germinate, whereas others must be kept in a dark room with no windows or where the windows have been blacked out.

seed sowing

1   Select a seed tray or pot and fill it to the rim with a suitable compost. Firm gently until the compost is 1 cm (½ in) below the rim of the seed tray, and for very fine seeds, such as begonia, sieve an additional thin layer of fine compost over the surface.

2   For fine- and medium-sized seeds, sow broadcast, half in one direction and the remainder in the opposite direction, to ensure even distribution over the tray.

3   For large seeds, create a regular pattern of holes in the compost (you can use a pencil or dibber for this task) and sow the seeds into the prepared holes.

4   Sieve a thin layer of fine compost over the seeds and gently firm. For very fine seeds, simply press them into the surface rather than covering them with more compost.

5   Label and date the seeds. Insert the seed tray into another shallow tray of water and allow the compost to take up water by capillary action; let the surplus water drain away.

Seeds that require light to germinate	Seeds that require darkness to germinate
Begonia	*Amaranthus*
Floss flower (*Ageratum*)	Love-in-a-mist (*Nigella*)
Impatiens	*Nemesia*
Lettuce (*Lactuca sativa*)	Onion (*Allium*)
Lobelia	Pansy (*Viola*)
Musk (*Mimulus*)	*Phlox*
Snapdragon (*Antirrhinum*)	Scorpion weed (*Phacelia*)
Tobacco plant (*Nicotiana*)	Sowbread (*Cyclamen*)

Allium

transplanting seedlings

As with seeds sown outdoors, the seedlings will need pricking out and transplanting. This is to remove weak seedlings and to give the remainder more growing space.

1   Select a tray or pot of an appropriate size and fill it to the rim with a suitable compost. Firm gently until the compost is 1 cm (½ in) below the rim of the container.

2   Using a label or similar utensil, gently tease the seedlings out of the seed compost, making sure you do not damage the roots. Hold each seedling up by pinching a leaf between your finger and thumb.

3   Make carefully positioned holes in the transplanting pot or tray with a dibber and lift the seedlings, placing them root first into the holes. Tap a small quantity of compost into each hole to cover the roots of the seedling.

4   When the pot or tray is completed, water each seedling to encourage growth. Use a watering can with a fine rose to settle the compost around the roots without damaging the delicate leaves.

5   Write the name of the plant and the date on a label (this will help you to predict the speed of germination in future years) and insert it in the side of the pot or tray, which should then be placed in a warm, shaded area to aid growth.

creating a suitable environment

As plants start to grow, they are at their most vulnerable and often need 'intensive care', which means controlling temperature and moisture levels in an enclosed environment. However, warm humid conditions are an ideal breeding ground for fungal diseases, so make sure you remove any damaged or rotting plants to protect the others.

Protecting seedlings

In many situations a polythene bag or sheet of clingfilm over a plant pot or tray will provide the type of growth environment that is suitable for many plants, but it is worth remembering that on hot, sunny days some form of shading will also be required to prevent sun-scorch.

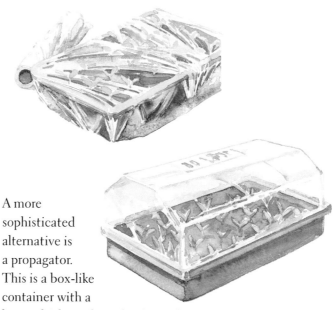

A more sophisticated alternative is a propagator. This is a box-like container with a base, which can be either heated or unheated, and a transparent cover. Where a heated propagator is used, always try to select one with a thermostatically controlled heater so that you can accurately monitor the temperature.

taking hardwood cuttings

This is an important method used by gardeners for the vegetative propagation of woody plants. The techniques used are not difficult to master and little equipment is required. The formation of new root growth can be aided by the use of rooting hormones; these are available as powders (the base of the cutting is dipped into the powder and the excess gently tapped off) or liquids. Rooting hormones are available in a variety of different strengths – use the strongest for hardwood cuttings.

techniques

This technique is suitable for propagating a wide range of easy-to-grow deciduous trees and shrubs, and is probably the easiest and cheapest method of propagating plants from cuttings, since no special facilities or equipment are required. The cuttings are taken immediately after leaf-fall, in the autumn, when the soil is still warm from the summer. During winter they will form a callus over the wound on the base and start to root. As they develop in the spring they will start to produce leaves and shoots.

1   Select healthy shoots of the current season's growth, which may be 22 to 60 cm (9 to 24 in) long, and remove them from the parent plant with secateurs (discard any thin or damaged shoots or those with obvious signs of pests or disease).

2   Using secateurs, prepare the cuttings by trimming them into lengths of approximately 25 cm (10 in). Make a cut straight across the stem at the bottom of the cutting with sharp pruning secateurs. Make the second cut at the top of the cutting an angled cut (or straight if the buds are opposite); the length of each cutting is dictated by the position of the buds on the shoot.

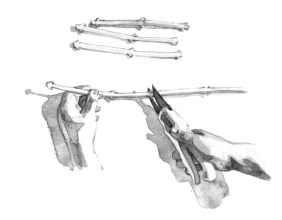

3   Prepare the ground by forking it over and roughly levelling it (there is no need for a fine seedbed-like tilth).

4   Cover the soil with a sheet of black polythene and bury the edges in the soil (this reduces the need for irrigation, checks weeds and encourages rooting just below the surface).

5   Insert the tines of a garden fork vertically through the plastic into the soil below to a depth of about 15 cm (6 in) – the holes are just the right diameter for most cuttings.

6 Gently push the cuttings, base first, through the holes in the plastic and into the soil, to the right depth (see table, right). Shrub cuttings are inserted with the bottom two-thirds in the soil, for a multi-stemmed plant. Tree cuttings are inserted until only the top bud shows, for a single-stemmed plant.

Multi-stemmed shrub or climber   *Single-stemmed tree*

7 Finish by pouring water into each hole containing a cutting (this firms in each cutting and builds up a reservoir of moisture beneath the plastic). After a hard frost it may be necessary to firm the cuttings into position with the heel of your boot, since the frost may loosen the cuttings in the soil. Over winter, the cuttings will start to root.

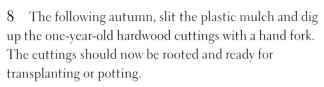

8 The following autumn, slit the plastic mulch and dig up the one-year-old hardwood cuttings with a hand fork. The cuttings should now be rooted and ready for transplanting or potting.

> **Some plants that can be increased by taking hardwood cuttings**
>
> **Single-stemmed trees**
> (Plant with the top bud above soil level)
>
> Black mulberry (*Morus nigra*)
> Common laburnum (*Laburnum anagyroides*)
> *Cordyline*
> Dawn redwood (*Metasequoia glyptostroboides*)
> Fig (*Ficus*)
> London plane (*Platanus* x *hispanica*)
> Mulberry (*Morus*)
> White poplar (*Populus alba* 'Richardii')
> Willow (*Salix*)
>
> **Multi-stemmed shrubs and climbers**
> (Plant the lower two-thirds below soil level)
>
> *Actinidia kolomikta*
> *Bougainvillea*
> Butterfly bush (*Buddleja davidii*)
> Common box (*Buxus*)
> *Clematis montana*
> Currants (*Ribes*)
> Elder (*Sambucus*)
> *Forsythia*
> Grape vine (*Vitis vinifera*)
> Honeysuckle (*Lonicera*)
> Mock orange (*Philadelphus*)
> Red-barked dogwood (*Cornus alba*)
> Russian vine (*Fallopia baldschuanica*)
> *Weigela*

using a cold frame

As well as rooting hardwood cuttings directly into a prepared bed outside, you can also use a cold frame. Cuttings raised in this way, because of the protected environment, will usually root more quickly – typically by the following spring. Harden the rooted cuttings off (see page 20) before transplanting them into their final positions.

taking softwood cuttings

As the temperature rises and the days lengthen many plants surge into growth and it becomes too late for propagating by hardwood cuttings, as the plants are no longer dormant. For many broad-leaved evergreens, and some conifers, it is too early to take semi-ripe cuttings, as the growth is not sufficiently mature. However, many plants can be propagated by softwood cuttings when they are in active growth, and for a number of plants the most opportune time is in the spring.

techniques

Select only strong, vigorous shoots that are free from obvious signs of pests and disease, and avoid thin or weak shoots that originate from the centre of the plant, since these tend to be too soft and sappy with long internodes (space between the leaf joints).

1   Remove the shoots from the parent plant with a sharp knife or secateurs.

2   If the stem of the cutting is more than 10 cm (4 in) long, reduce it to a length of 7.5 to 10 cm (3 to 4 in) by making a cut at right angles to the stem with a sharp knife, cutting 3 mm (⅛ in) below a node.

3   To keep the cuttings fresh and moist, place them in a polythene bag with a few drops of water inside. Keep the bag closed but do not seal it, since excess moisture may cause the cutting to wilt.

4   Remove all the leaves from the bottom third of the cuttings, since they will be of no use and would rot if left attached to the stem.

5   Dip the base of the cuttings into a hormone rooting preparation – this consists of chemicals that are replicas of substances that occur naturally in the plants to promote rooting. Treat only the cut surface at the base, since contact with the rooting preparation may cause the soft, juvenile bark on the cutting to rot. Tap off any surplus.

6   Select an appropriately sized tray or pot and fill it with a suitable compost. Remove a little compost from the top so that it sits 2.5 cm (1 in) from the top, but do not firm.

7   Push the cuttings, base first, vertically into the free-draining compost, with the bottom third in the compost.

8   When all the cuttings have been inserted, water them gently to settle the compost around the base of the cuttings, without damaging them. The cuttings may appear very loose and floppy for a few days but they should soon recover and look quite healthy, provided that they are not allowed to dry out. Write the name of the plant and the date of propagation on a label and insert it at the end of the tray or pot.

9   Place the completed tray or group of pots in a shaded, damp environment to encourage the cuttings to root. With the more difficult subjects, a heated propagator can be used to help promote rapid callus development (healing) and root formation. Place the tray or pots under the cover and control the temperature to create the most suitable environment.

Some plants that can be increased by taking softwood cuttings

Alpines

Alpine pink
(*Dianthus alpinus*)

Androsace lanuginosa

Horned violet
(*Viola cornuta*)

Hypericum olympicum

Italian bellflower
(*Campanula isophylla*)

Shrubs

Abelia schumannii

Caryopteris x *clandonensis*

Ceanothus gloriosus

Forsythia x *intermedia*

Hydrangea paniculata

Mock orange
(*Philadelphus coronarius*)

Trees

Caucasian maple
(*Acer cappadocicum*)

Erman's birch (*Betula ermanii*)

Eucryphia lucida

Golden-rain tree
(*Koelreuteria paniculata*)

Indian bean tree
(*Catalpa bignonioides*)

Smooth-leaved elm
(*Ulmus minor*)

Perennials

Argyranthemum gracile
'Chelsea girl'

Beardlip penstemon
(*Penstemon barbatus*)

Bergamot
(*Monarda didyma*)

Clover (*Trifolium*)

Delphinium bellamosum

Mallow (*Lavatera*)

Osteospermum jucundum

Ozark sundrops
(*Oenothera macrocarpa*)

Verbena bonariensis

Climbers

Allamanda

Boston ivy (*Parthenocissus
tricuspidata*)

Cape ivy (*Senecio macroglossus*)

Clematis montana

Climbing hydrangea
(*Hydrangea petiolaris*)

Japanese wisteria
(*Wisteria floribunda*)

Morning glory (*Ipomoea*)

Solanum

Thunbergia

Woodbine (*Lonicera
periclymenum*)

Clematis montana

Betula ermanii

Monarda didyma
'Cambridge Scarlet'

91

taking semi-ripe cuttings

With higher temperatures and long hours of daylight in summer, many plants have a surge of growth and can be propagated by softwood cuttings well into the season. As this growth starts to harden and gradually matures it becomes semi-ripe; this stage of development is ideal for taking cuttings of such plants as broad-leaved evergreens and some conifers. It is important to use only the best plants for propagation: the cuttings will be put under stress until they have rooted, and poor cuttings from poor plants will only deteriorate, never improve.

techniques

When collecting semi-ripe cuttings, choose only strong, vigorous shoots of the current season's growth. Do not select any thin or weak shoots, since these tend to be soft and sappy and usually rot. Discard any shoots showing signs of pests and disease.

1   Remove the shoots with secateurs and place in a polythene bag with a little water to slow down wilting. Keep the bag closed but not sealed. Leave in a shady place if the cuttings are not to be potted up immediately.

2   There are two types of semi-ripe cutting: nodal and heel. The latter is more effective when propagating evergreens.

Nodal cuttings

If the shoot is more than 20 cm (8 in) long, reduce it to 10 to 12 cm (4 to 5 in) by making a cut straight across the stem with a sharp knife, 3 mm (⅛ in) below a node or leaf joint. The positioning of the cut is important – the bark at the base of a cutting should be a light brown colour, indicating that the semi-ripe wood is forming.

Heel cuttings

Pull a side shoot away from the main shoot, tearing it off with a strip of the older wood (a heel) attached. The large wound stimulates root formation at the base of the cutting.

3   Strip away all leaves from the bottom third of the cutting. If you leave them in place, they will rot in the compost and encourage the cutting itself to rot.

4   Dip the cuttings into a hormone rooting powder to speed root formation. Treat only the exposed woody surface at the base of the cutting; if the hormone powder comes into contact with soft juvenile bark, it may cause the cutting to rot. Tap off any excess powder.

5 Insert the cuttings in a tray or pot of free-draining compost, or root them in a cold frame, planting the bottom third of the stem.

6 Water the cuttings gently to settle the compost. They may appear loose and floppy for a few days but they should soon recover.

7 Write the name of the plant and the date of propagation on a label and insert it in the container or cold frame. Place pots or trays in a shaded, damp environment and keep the top of the cold frame shaded in very sunny weather. Check the compost regularly to ensure it does not dry out. Covering the cuttings with clear plastic will speed up callus development and root formation.

Some plants that can be increased by taking semi-ripe cuttings

Climbers	Conifers	Shrubs
Akebia quinata	*Chamaecyparis*	*Berberis* (deciduous)
Fremontodendron	x *cupressocyparis*	*Callicarpa bodinieri*
Hedera	*Cupressus*	*Ceanothus* (evergreen)
Humulus lupulus 'Aureus'	*Juniperus*	*Choisya ternata*
Jasminum nudiflorum	*Taxus*	*Escallonia* 'Iveyi'
Passiflora	*Thuja*	*Hydrangea*
Trachelospermum	*Thujopsis*	*Photinia* 'Birmingham'
Wisteria	*Tsuga*	*Viburnum carlesii*

Passiflora caerulea

Thuja orientalis

Hydrangea 'Blue Wave'

division

This is one of the simplest and easiest propagation methods. As a basic technique, division involves separating one large plant into lots of smaller ones, or a number of small clumps, which are exact replicas of the parent plant. Although most plants are divided when they are dormant, there are some exceptions. Flag iris (*Iris germanica*) and some primulas establish better if divided and transplanted soon after flowering, in early summer.

simple division

1   There are various different methods of division, according to the type and size of your rootstock. 'Simple' is the most basic technique and works well for young perennials. Start by carefully lifting the plant to be divided with a fork, making sure you do not damage the roots.

2   Shake the plant to remove as much loose soil as possible, and take off any debris, such as dead leaves and stalks. Then wash the plant thoroughly so that all the buds are clearly visible; this will reduce the amount of wear and damage on any knives and secateurs used to divide the clump.

Geranium x *magnificum*

Bergenia 'Beethoven'

Hosta

Some plants propagated by division		
Aster	Daylily (*Hemerocallis*)	*Phormium*
Astilbe	Plantain lily (*Hosta*)	*Phyllostachys*
Bergenia	*Imperata*	Rhubarb (*Rheum*)
Gentian (*Gentiana*)	*Iris*	*Schizostylis*
Geranium	Campion (*Lychnis*)	*Stachys*

simple division of fibrous-rooted plants

These plants often form a dense, overcrowded clump, which may become thick and matted with age. The performance of the clump will gradually deteriorate as those plants in the centre become old and unproductive, often harbouring disease. With this type of plant, and particularly members of the primula family, the problem is often one of getting some leverage on the plant without causing it too much damage. The leaves may be relatively soft and fleshy, and any attempt to pull the plant apart with your bare hands often results in two handfuls of leaves and the clump remaining intact.

1   Once the plant has been lifted and the soil washed off, force the prongs of two garden forks into the centre of the clump so that they meet back to back. Apply pressure by levering the fork handles apart then pulling them together again until the clump starts to tease apart and splits in two.

2   This process can be repeated again and again, until the clumps are of the desired size. Each time, aim to inflict as little damage on the plant as you can. Before replanting, cut away old, dead or diseased areas.

Gentiana sino-ornata

Alchemilla mollis

Pulsatilla vulgaris

Rock plants that can be increased by division

Achillea ageratifolia	*Artemesia schmidtiana* 'Nana'	*Gentiana sino-ornata*	*Pulsatilla*
Alchemilla mollis	*Chiastophyllum oppositifolium*	Golden creeping Jenny	*Saxifraga apiculata*
Allium sikkimense	Fairies' thimble (*Campanula*	(*Lysimachia nummularia*)	*Sedum kamtschaticum*
Antennaria dioica	*cochlearifolia*)	*Oxalis adenophylla*	
Arenaria montana	Garden violet (*Viola odorata*)	Primula (*Primula*)	

Persicaria bistorta 'Superba'

Pulmonaria 'Blue Ensign'

Epimedium x *rubrum*

simple division of rhizomatous plants

Plants such as the flag iris (*Iris germanica*), which have a thick, fleshy, modified stem, or 'rhizome', spreading horizontally across the ground, can be propagated by cutting the rhizome into sections and then replanting.

1   Using a garden fork, dig up the plant, easing it out of the ground with as much root as possible. Wash the soil off the clump so that you can identify growth buds.

2   Cut the thick fleshy stem, or rhizome, into pieces with a sharp knife, making sure that each section has a growth bud.

3   Check the rhizome pieces and discard any that are showing signs of decay or disease. Strip away any withered foliage, leaving four or five healthy leaves on each section. Trim these back to about 15 to 20 cm (6 to 8 in).

4   Dig a shallow planting hole large enough to accommodate the rhizome's root system. Then, holding the rhizome by its leaves, lay it flat on the floor of the hole and gently spread out its roots.

5   Pull the soil back into the hole around the plant and firm it gently into place. Then water around the base of the plant to settle the soil and encourage the roots to grow.

planting

1   Divisions should be replanted at the same depth as the original plant, but any cultivars which are prone to the crowns rotting should be planted slightly proud of the soil level.

2   When replanting, ensure that the roots are well spread out in the planting hole and the plant is firmed in. Water newly planted divisions thoroughly with a fungicidal solution, to prevent rotting.

simple division of suckering shrubs

1 Dig carefully around the shrub with a fork and ease a section of root, with suckers on it, out of the ground.

2 Cut this section from the main plant with secateurs or a sharp knife, making sure it has plenty of fibrous roots attached.

3 To prepare the root for planting, remove some of the leaves from the top section of the cutting.

4 Dig a planting hole for the shrub's root system, breaking up the soil in the base of the hole to encourage deep root penetration from the new plant.

5 Replant the sucker, firm in around the base and water thoroughly.

division of snowdrops

1 After the flowers have died off, lift clumps up with a hand fork, making sure you do not damage the bulbs with the tines of the fork.

2 Shake all the loose soil from the roots and then carefully divide the clump, removing the individual bulbs.

3 Gently pull any bulblets away from the parent bulb – these can be replanted as well if they are in a good condition. These bulblets will simply take longer to develop than the main sections of the bulb, but they will eventually flower.

4 Replant the bulbs in the same depth of soil as they were originally planted. (See pages 12–13 for planting techniques.)

Suckering shrubs that can be increased by division

Amelanchier lamarkii	Creeping dogwood (*Cornus canadensis*)	*Mahonia repens*
Berberis buxifolia		*Polygala chamaebuxus*
Bush honeysuckle (*Diervilla lonicera*)	*Euonymus fortunei*	Red chokeberry (*Aronia arbutifolia*)
	Gaultheria mucronata	*Sarcococca humilis*
Butcher's broom (*Ruscus aculeatus*)	Glory flower (*Clerodendrum bungei*)	*Spiraea japonica*
Cassiope lycopodioides	*Kerria japonica*	Sweetspire (*Itea virginica*)

bulb scaling

This technique is possibly the easiest method of propagation and is suitable for both lilies and fritillaria, the bulbs of which consist of clusters of scales attached to a basal plate. Very simply, the process involves encouraging the development of bulblets around the base of the scales; the bulblets can then be removed and potted up to form new plants.

simple scaling

1   In late summer after flowering, as the stem begins to turn brown and dry, lift the bulbs from the ground and lay them in a seed tray to dry for two or three days. Then gently brush the soil from the outer scales of each bulb and remove the dead flower stem.

2   Detach the outer scales from the bulb by breaking them off at the point where they join the basal plate. Up to 80 per cent of the outer scales can be removed from the parent bulb, which will still grow if it is replanted.

3   Put the scales into a polythene bag and add fine grade, moist sphagnum moss peat, so that the bag contains equal proportions of peat and scales. Then add a small amount of fungicide, close the top, and turn the bag over several times to mix the contents evenly. Label the bag with the name and date and put it in a warm, dark place, such as an airing cupboard, for two to three months.

4   After this time, each scale should have produced at least one small embryo bulb (there may be three or four). The bulblets will be about 6 mm (¼ in) long, with tiny white fibrous roots growing from the base.

5   Plant each scale, complete with bulblets, in a small 8 cm (3 in) pot of compost, with just the tip of the old scale showing. Top dress with sand and place outdoors.

6   As the weather becomes warmer in the spring, new grass-like leaves will appear through the compost, growing from the bulblets. In the autumn these young bulbs can be planted in the garden soil and may flower the following year.

twin scaling

Twin scaling is a modification of scaling often used on daffodils and narcissi. Its advantage is that it produces many more plants from a single bulb, although the bulb is destroyed in the process and it does take longer for the new bulbs to reach flowering size.

1 Lift the dormant bulbs in mid-summer, and lay them in a seed tray to dry for two or three days, before brushing the soil from them and removing the dead, dried roots.

2 Trim the top of the bulbs and peel away the outer brown scales from each one.

3 Using a clean, sharp knife, cut the bulb into eight equal segments. Cut each bulb from top to bottom, and make sure that each segment has a piece of the bulb's basal plate attached to it.

4 Divide each segment into pairs of scales by peeling apart the layers and cutting them off, again making sure they have a piece of basal plate attached. Each segment should provide three or four twin scale sections.

5 Soak the twin scales in a fungicide solution for 10 minutes, then leave them to drain on a wire rack for a further 10 minutes.

6 Place the twin scales in a polythene bag containing moist vermiculite (equal parts vermiculite and bulb scales) and mix them together. Blow air into the bag then seal it, and tie on a label with the plant's name and the date of propagation. Put the bag in a warm, dark place for 12 to 14 weeks, turning it occasionally to keep the air moving.

7 By now, each twin scale should have formed at least one bulblet. Plant them into 5 cm (2 in) pots of compost and then place them in a heated frame or greenhouse.

8 In spring, the bulblets will produce grass-like leaves. As these die down, remove the bulblets from the scales. Repot in 5 cm (2 in) pots and place in a cold frame. After another year the young bulbs can be planted in the garden; they may flower three years later.

layering

This is ideal for plants that are difficult to root or would need specialist knowledge and facilities to make rooting cuttings a realistic proposition. The method involves the formation of new shoots on the new plant before it is separated from the parent plant.

the principles of layering

A whole range of plants can be propagated by layering, provided the correct method is used, as some plants have slightly different requirements. There are three basic treatments: the first includes simple, serpentine and tip layering and involves planting a section of the stem in the soil; the second is stooling, which involves mounding soil over the stem; the third method, used for stiff or high branches, is referred to as air layering.

Simple layering

1   In spring, select a strong, healthy shoot of the previous season's growth and bend it down into a horizontal position. Two-thirds of the way along the shoot make a mark in the soil.

2   Where the soil has been marked, dig an oval-shaped hole about 15 cm (6 in) deep, using a trowel.

3   With a sharp knife, scrape away a 2.5 cm (1 in) long section of bark to cause a wound on the section of stem to be buried. Bring down the shoot into a horizontal position and gently bend it into the prepared hole.

4   Pin the stem into the bottom of the hole with a 20 cm (8 in) long 'staple', made from heavy gauge wire, to prevent the stem from springing back out of the ground.

5   Fill the hole with soil and firm gently. Water the soil if it becomes dry to keep the stem moist and encourage roots to form.

6   In late winter, remove the soil and expose the roots that have formed at the base of each shoot. Cut off these new plants with as much root as possible and a small section of stem; they can now be replanted. (See 'New Introductions' chapter for planting.)

Serpentine layering

This is a variation on simple layering, used for vigorous plants with long flexible stems, such as clematis, climbing roses and lonicera. This technique has the advantage that one stem can yield as many as five or six plants, rather than just the single plant per stem that is obtained by simple layering. Follow the method used for 'Simple layering', opposite, but make several wounds on one long trailing shoot, in between buds, and peg down each wounded section leaving the section of stem in between exposed. Once they have rooted, cut each rooted section into an individual plant, ready for replanting.

Tip layering

Some plants naturally layer themselves; they have long arching stems that curve down to the ground, and where the tip of the stem comes into contact with the soil, adventitious roots form and grow into the soil. This can be encouraged by using a trowel to bury these tips about 15 cm (6 in) deep in the soil, so that a better root system is formed. In the late autumn, sever the rooted layer from the parent plant, lift the new plants and transplant them.

Stooling

Stooling, or mound layering, is often used to produce large numbers of plants, or to rejuvenate an old plant that has become tall and straggly or bare and open in the centre.

1   In the early spring, cut down the plant to a height of about 5 cm (2 in) and remove and discard all of the top growth.

2   The plant responds to this by producing lots of new shoots. When these reach 10 to 15 cm (4 to 6 in) high, rake up soil to form a mound about 5 to 7.5 cm (2 to 3 in) high around the base of each shoot.

3   Repeat this process in the summer when the shoots are 30 cm (12 in) high, and again when they are 45 cm (18 in) high. Each time the bottom half of the shoots are covered until the mound is about 20 cm (8 in) high.

4   In late autumn or early winter, carefully remove the mound of soil and expose the roots, which will by now have formed at the base of each shoot.

5   Once all of the soil has been removed, cut off these new plants with as much root as possible, but always leave a short stub of growth on the parent plant, since this is where the next layers will emerge. These plants can now be potted up or planted out in the garden.

Air layering

This method of propagation is used for plants with high branches or stiff shoots, which cannot be lowered to soil level without them breaking.

1 Choose a section of branch consisting of the current season's growth and clear any leaves or side shoots along a 15 cm (6 in) stretch, starting about 30 cm (12 in) down from the shoot tip.

2 Make a diagonal cut on the underside of this bare section, about 5 cm (2 in) long. Then bend the stem slightly to open the cut and wedge a small stone or twig into the cut to prevent the wound from healing.

3 Cut the bottom out of a polythene bag, pull it over the stem and tie the bottom end about 5 cm (2 in) below the cut.

4 Fill the polythene sleeve with moist, open compost, making sure that there is plenty of compost around the cut. Fasten the top of the sleeve about 10 cm (4 in) above the cut and leave the plant for about 12 weeks.

5 Finally, untie and carefully remove the polythene sleeve, without damaging the new roots. Cut off the shoot just below the newly formed root ball and replant it in a pot of compost (see the chapter 'New Introductions' for planting techniques). Keep the new plant well watered to encourage the roots to establish.

Plants suitable for simple, serpentine and tip layering	Plants suitable for stooling	Plants suitable for air layering
Blackberry (*Rubus*)	Apple (*Malus*)	Bay laurel (*Laurus nobilis*)
Clematis	Flowering currant (*Ribes*)	Calico bush (*Kalmia latifolia*)
Corylopsis	Heath (*Erica*)	Chinese witch hazel (*Hamamelis mollis*)
Hazel (*Corylus*)	Lavender (*Lavandula angustifolia*)	Common holly (*Ilex aquifolium*)
Honeysuckle (*Lonicera*)	Smoke bush (*Cotinus*)	Dove tree (*Davidia involucrata*)
Hops (*Humulus*)	Willow (*Salix*)	
Ivy (*Hedera*)	Wormwood (*Artemisia absinthium*)	
Winter jasmine (*Jasminum nudiflorum*)		
Wisteria		

grafting

This method of propagation involves a process of joining separate plants together; the upper part, or 'scion', is a section of stem taken from the plant that is to be increased in numbers, and the lower part, or 'rootstock', needs to be as closely related to the scion as possible. Grafting is ideal for plants that are slow to root or will not produce roots of their own.

Whip and tongue grafting

It is possible to propagate most plants successfully with whip and tongue grafting, which is the most frequently used and simplest method of permanently interlocking two plants. All you need to begin is a good-quality, sharp knife and a little practice.

1   To get the scion, select a healthy shoot of the current season's growth and remove it from the parent plant using a pair of secateurs. Trim the scion into a 10 to 15 cm (4 to 6 in) length; the top cut is made just above a bud and the bottom cut is made just below one.

2   Having chosen your rootstock, prepare it by making a flat cut across its top, 15 to 20 cm (6 to 8 in) above soil level.

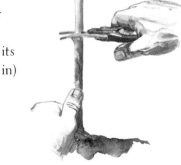

3   On the upper section of the rootstock, make a shallow upward-slanting cut, approximately 7.5 cm (3 in) long on one side.

4   Starting 2.5 cm (1 in) down this exposed side, make a shallow downwards cut, about 1 cm (½ in) deep, into the rootstock; this acts as a groove into which the scion is inserted.

5   Now prepare the scion in the same way by making a slanting cut approximately 7.5 cm (3 in) long on the bottom section.

6   Then 2.5 cm (1 in) from the bottom of this cut surface, make another cut upwards, 1 cm (½ in) deep (try to avoid handling the cut surface), to match the groove in the rootstock.

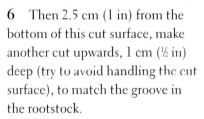

7   Place the scion and rootstock together so that the cut surfaces match and the grooves interlock.

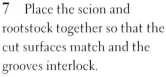

8   Bind the graft with waterproof plastic tape. After 3 or 4 weeks, when the stems start to heal together, slit the tape and allow it to split open.

seasonal pruning

It is easy to dismiss pruning as a winter task, and for some plants winter is the main season for pruning, but for many others summer is the most appropriate time. Pruning includes the shaping and training of young plants, particularly those that must be clipped or trimmed into a particular shape or pattern, such as for topiary or formal hedges. Techniques used to control the growth habit of plants, such as training fruit trees into fans or espaliers, make it possible to grow them in a relatively confined space. Other forms of pruning include removing old flowers, pinching out the tip of a plant to form a large single bloom or a multi-stemmed plant with clusters of small flowers and renovation pruning for old or neglected specimens.

selecting and using your tools

It is important to select the right tools for particular pruning jobs and to ensure that they remain in good working order. Keeping your pruning equipment clean and sharp and using the correct tool make the task in hand much easier. Wipe the blades with an old rag soaked in oil and invest in a proper sharpening device if you do not already have one.

secateurs

There are many types available. The anvil type has a single, straight-edged cutting blade that closes down onto an anvil, which is a bar of softer metal. The ratchet type is a usefully modified version, which enables the user to cut through a branch in stages. It is very good for reducing fatigue and ideal for gardeners with a small hand span; the cutting action is slower but easier than that of other models. The parrot-bill type has two curved blades that bypass one another very closely and cut in a scissor-like fashion.

Anvil type   *Parrot-bill type*

long-handled pruners

Long-handled pruners, or lopping shears, are basically strong secateurs with long handles that give extra leverage when cutting thick stems or branches. They are extremely useful for cutting out the old stumps that gradually build up at the base of bush roses.

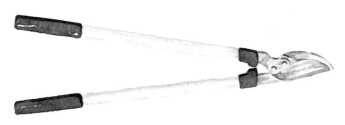

pole pruners

Pole pruners are used for pruning tree branches that would normally be out of reach and are capable of cutting through branches up to 3 cm (1¼ in) thick. They consist of a pole 2 to 3 m (6½ to 10 ft) in length with a hooked anvil and a curved blade at the tip, which is operated by a lever at the opposite end. Some models are available with a small pruning saw attached to the end, which is useful for removing both small and medium-sized branches.

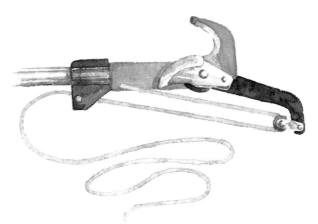

hand shears

These are available in several designs, but most have straight blades with a deep notch at the base of the blade for cutting thicker stems. There are models available with a wavy edged blade, which prevents the plant growth being squeezed back out of the mouth of the shears. Choose shears that are well balanced, strong, light and comfortable to use, with a sharp cutting edge.

pruning saws

Pruning saws are needed for cutting larger branches. Several designs are available, some of which are especially suitable for small spaces and in the narrow angles between branches. One type has a set of teeth at the bottom and the top of the blade; however, care has to be taken not to damage nearby branches with the set of teeth not in use.

General-purpose saw
The small size of the blade on this saw means that it will fit into most spaces and can tackle those awkward-to-reach branches.

Grecian saw
This saw has a curved blade tapered to a sharp point and sloping teeth designed to cut on the return stroke. It is useful in confined spaces.

Bow saw
For extra thick branches you are better off using this specially designed bow saw, which can cut quickly and easily through tough wood. The disadvantage of this saw is that it cannot be used in confined spaces.

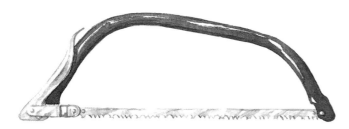

pruning knives

Pruning knives can easily be identified by their weight and the bulky appearance of the handle, and more often than not they are designed with a concave blade. A general-purpose knife is effective for most jobs; however, the slightly larger curved blade on specialist pruning knives is better for cutting through thicker branches.

General-purpose knife   *Pruning knife*

principles of pruning

There are three main categories of pruning. Formative pruning is carried out on young plants and is used to develop a strong, balanced structural framework of stems and branches. The amount of pruning required depends on the type of plant and the effect you want. Routine pruning, carried out when the plant is well grown, is used to keep the plant within its allotted space, to maintain its vitality or to induce flowering or fruiting. The third main type is known as renovation pruning, which is a drastic treatment necessary to restore old or neglected trees or shrubs. The first stage in any form of pruning is to remove diseased, damaged, dying or dead wood. Next you should prune out any thin, weak stems. It is then possible to decide which shoots should be cut back or removed.

Pruning wounds
Whenever a plant is pruned there is a risk of rot developing in the wound. It was usual to cover cuts with a wound paint, but new research indicates that this is not effective. In fact, paints may even encourage disease by sealing the spores of infectious organisms into new wounds. The surest way to prevent wound damage is to prune at the right time, when the plant is at its healthiest and therefore best able to recover quickly.

annuals

There are various techniques you can use to extend the growing period of the annuals in your garden, and so ensure a long and colourful display throughout the seasons. These tasks involve removing dead growth and any overgrown or overcrowded stems, as well as supporting and training tall or slender stems that may bend if left to their own devices.

shoot thinning

This technique allows more air to flow through the plant, which in turn reduces the chances of mildew occurring. For well-established plants, thin out some of the shoots by removing them completely, cutting them off at the base, before pinching out the tips of the strongest shoots. Select the thinnest and weakest shoots for removal; or, if the shoots are of equal size but are overcrowded, remove about one-third of them.

supporting stems

In addition to shoot thinning and pinching out shoot tips, many plants will also benefit from being provided with some form of support. Twigs or stakes should be positioned before the top growth is 15 cm (6 in) high, since this encourages the plant to grow up or through the support, disguising it in the process. If left unsupported for too long, the plant may fall over and there is a danger of the stems becoming bent and kinked.

Supporting sweet peas
To get plenty of really large blooms, sweet peas need to be grown up sticks or canes as cordons, with the plants being tied to the supports at 20 cm (8 in) intervals. Although climbing sweet peas normally support themselves by means of leaf tendrils, which curl around the canes, this self-clinging uses up a lot of energy. To encourage the plant to channel its resources into the production of flowers, it is better to remove the tendrils as soon as they appear, and to tie the stems to the support with soft garden string.

pinching out

To check the growth of plants that tend to become too tall and fall over, such as chrysanthemums and dahlias, create multi-branched stems by pinching out the growing point of each shoot. Do this when the shoots are about one-third of their ultimate height, and at least a month before they are due to flower. In mid-summer, remove the top 10 cm (4 in) of the most dominant shoots. This may delay flowering by a couple of weeks, but it will not affect the length of the flowering period and will encourage more flowers to develop. It may, however, reduce the ultimate height of the plants by a quarter.

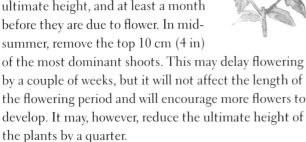

dead-heading

Both hardy and half-hardy annuals will need to be regularly dead-headed throughout their flowering season in order to get a good show of blooms over the longest possible period and to remove unsightly spent flowers. Cutting off the dying flower heads before the seed has developed will stimulate the plant to throw up more flowers in a determined attempt to produce the seed that will ensure the plant's survival the following year.

Flowers for dead-heading	
Achillea	Peony (Paeonia)
Anthemis	Scabious (Scabiosa)
Dahlia	Sidalcea
Gaillardia	Sweet pea (Lathyrus
Oenothera	odoratus)

Paeonia lactiflora

Sweet pea

disbudding

If blooms with long, clean stems are required, some of the stems can be disbudded. Keep the top 'primary' bud and remove the two smaller 'secondary' buds. This technique will produce fewer, larger blooms, which are ideal as cut flowers. Alternatively, to increase the number of flowers, leave the two smaller 'secondary' buds on the stem and remove the top 'primary' bud. The flowers will be smaller as a result, but they will create an excellent garden display throughout the season.

cutting back

As soon as the blooms on your earlier-flowering plants, such as columbine (*Aquilegia*), foxglove (*Digitalis*), *Erigeron* and mulleins (*Verbascum*), have faded and gone over, cut down the flowering stems to leave about 8 cm (3 in) above soil level. Although this is unlikely to result in a further display of flowers, it should encourage the plant to produce a new flush of leaves, which will provide good ground cover and help to suppress weeds for the rest of the year.

shrubs

There are some shrubs, although not many, that will hardly ever need pruning; they are usually the broad-leaved evergreens, such as *Cotoneaster conspicuus*, *Ruscus aculeatus* and *Sarcococca humilis*. However, by far the greater number of shrubs, if left to grow naturally, will eventually become overgrown and look unattractive, and will deteriorate over a period of time as the overall growth suffers and the health of the shrub declines. Careful, accurate pruning cuts will reduce the risk of damage to an absolute minimum. Cuts must be clean, with no crushing of the tissue or ragged edges. Always position the stem to be cut close to the base of the blade, where it can be firmly held; if the cut is made with the tip, the blades are liable to be strained or forced apart.

pruning techniques

Any cut you make should be in relation to a growth bud. This is important because rapid healing is greatly influenced by the close proximity of growth buds. Haphazard pruning is likely to result in the introduction of disease, die-back and a bush with an unbalanced and unattractive appearance. Thin or twiggy branches can be safely pruned back using secateurs.

As with any type of pruning, at any time of year, the position of the cut is important in promoting healthy growth. Even quite sturdy branches can be pruned with the right type of secateurs (see page 106); however,  some people prefer to use a pruning knife. Choose a knife with a weight that suits you and a handle that comfortably fits into your hand. Handle pruning knives with care – they must be kept very sharp to do a proper job so treat them with respect to avoid accidents.

positioning of pruning cuts

Select an appropriately placed bud facing the direction in which you want the new shoot to develop and cut the stems no more than 5 mm (¼ in) immediately above a healthy bud or pair of buds. The direction of the cut varies depending on the arrangement of the buds (see below). As the shoot grows, it can be tied in to form part of a branch framework or be used to replace an old shoot. To encourage a plant to develop an open centre, cut back to an outward-facing bud or shoot.

formative pruning

Shrubs transplanted as root-balled plants and container-grown plants usually require no root pruning. However, bare-rooted shrubs may need to be pruned lightly to remove any damaged or broken roots.

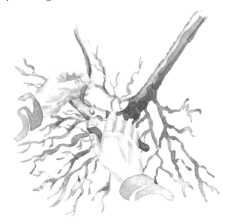

Generally speaking, deciduous shrubs need more formative pruning than evergreens. The shoots and stems may need some pruning to remove damaged or broken shoots, and in exposed locations it is a good idea to thin the shoots to reduce wind resistance.

routine pruning of flowering shrubs

Most types of flowering shrub are best pruned soon after they have finished flowering, although some shrubs are grown more for their berries, which develop after flowering has finished. Many deciduous shrubs that flower in spring or early summer carry their flowers on wood that has been produced during the previous year and these will benefit from being tidied up in the summer.

Shrubs with a naturally twiggy habit

Shrubs such as *Chaenomeles* and forsythias, which have a naturally twiggy habit with numerous crossing branches, will need little pruning. They will, however, respond well to 'spur' pruning. This will encourage heavier flowering and prevent the shrub becoming too straggly; this is particularly important when they are grown as wall shrubs. 'Spur' pruning involves removing the tips of the main shoots – about 15 cm (6 in) or so – to encourage side shoots (laterals) to develop. These side shoots can be trimmed back to three to five leaves later in the summer.

Dense, bushy shrubs

Shrubs that produce shorter side shoots, such as *Deutzia*, *Philadelphus* and *Weigela*, will become a dense thicket of matted and untidy growth if they are left unpruned, often becoming top heavy with crowded twiggy growth that will gradually, over a period of years, produce fewer and fewer flowers. The best way to prevent this happening is to prune the shrub in mid-summer, immediately after the flowers have faded. You should aim to cut the old flower-bearing shoots back to within about 5 to 8 cm (2 to 3 in) of ground level. This pruning treatment will encourage the shrub to produce new flower-bearing shoots for the following year.

Shrubs pruned in summer after flowering	
Deutzia	*Philadelphus*
Escallonia	*Rubus cockburnianus*
Euphorbia	*Spiraea* 'Arguta'
Fremontodendron	*Stephanandra*
Kerria	*Weigela florida* cultivars
Kolkwitzia	
Lonicera x *purpusii*	

Evergreen shrubs

For winter- or spring-flowering shrubs, such as *Berberis darwinii* and *Viburnum tinus*, prune immediately after flowering. Others, such as *Olearia macrodonta* and *Osmanthus heterophyllus*, which flower from mid-summer onwards, are pruned in mid-spring.

Remove all dead, diseased and damaged wood and any thin, straggly shoots. Cut back flower stems to a healthy bud and reduce the length of any strong vigorous shoots affecting the shape and balance of the plant.

renovation pruning

Old, neglected or badly shaped shrubs often respond to severe pruning, which can be used to encourage young growth from the base. Early spring is the best time to carry this out on evergreens – deciduous shrubs are best renovated during autumn and winter. Not all shrubs take kindly to this. For instance, broom (*Cytisus*) will die rather than produce new growths when pruned in this way. For these types of plants, cut out only a portion of the main stems, and remove the remaining old growths after flowering in summer or the following winter. But for a badly diseased plant, replacement may be the only option.

First year
Cut back the main stems to within 30 cm (12 in) of the ground in order to promote new growth from the base of the plant.

Second year
Cut back the new shoots to their point of origin, leaving only 2 or 3 of the strongest and best-placed shoots to create a balanced framework.

Subsequent years
In the third and subsequent years, prune according to the technique appropriate to your shrub as part of a normal growing cycle.

Magnolia

Lavandula angustifolia

Camellia reticulata

Drastic renovation

For the more drastic pruning in one season, cut away any weak shoots back to the stub and prune stronger growth to within 30 cm (12 in) of the soil level. If there are any suckers, cut them off at the base. Plants that have been grafted require special care; if cuts are made below the graft union, the ornamental part of the plant may be cut away leaving only sucker growths coming from the rootstock, particularly with some hybrid lilacs.

Pruning cuts should always be clean and go straight across the stem or branch.

Suitable shrubs
Berberis thunbergii
Common lilac (*Syringa vulgaris*)
Hazel (*Corylus*)
Cotinus coggygria
Spiraea japonica

Two-stage pruning

A two-stage operation is best if you want your plant to maintain its original shape and size. In the first year, remove all dead, diseased and damaged wood and cut back half of the old stems to within 5 to 8 cm (2 to 3 in)

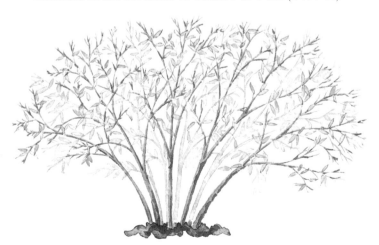

of ground level. Always select the oldest growths for cutting back in the first year, since these are the ones most likely to harbour pests and diseases. When removing branches lift them upwards out of the shrub – this does far less damage to the remaining stems. The most efficient method is to cut through the largest (usually the oldest) stems with a small pruning saw and lift these clear of the plant. Cut large or tall stems into two or three sections to ease their removal. In the following year, cut back the remaining old stems and trim any over-vigorous new growths.

pruning to create a barrier

If properly pruned, shrubs make attractive barriers in gardens. Barriers can be used to define a garden's boundaries, to divide the area up into a variety of 'rooms', to direct the eye in specific directions, or to screen an unattractive feature, such as a storage area or compost heap. Aim to create, perhaps over a period of two years or more, thick growth right from the base of the shrub to ensure you have a complete barrier.

Suitable shrubs
Beauty bush (*Kolkwitzia*)
Deutzia
Firethorn (*Pyracantha*)
Flowering maple (*Abutilon*)
Japonica (*Chaenomeles*)
Mock orange (*Philadelphus*)
Wintersweet (*Chimonanthus*)

115

berries and fruits

The general rule with shrubs is that those which flower during the summer months are pruned immediately after the flowers have faded. However, there are exceptions to this, especially with those that provide additional seasonal interest in the form of attractive autumn fruits and berries. These plants are often pruned in the late winter or early spring (once the danger of frosts has passed), by cutting back the previous season's growth. This encourages the formation of flowering spurs for the new season.

Shrubs left unpruned for display

Aronia

Berberis

Colutea

Cotoneaster

Hippophae

Ilex

Pyracantha

Rosa rugosa

Symphoricarpos

Pyracantha

Ilex

Rosa rugosa

Prunus

sap bleeding

Although, generally speaking, shrubs should ideally be pruned either after they have finished flowering or when they are dormant during the winter, some species will bleed large amounts of sap if they are pruned in the late winter or early spring, when the sap is rising. Examples include such common plants as some of the maples (*Acer*), some *Magnolia* species and *Prunus*. To prevent this happening, these shrubs should be left longer and pruned only when they are in full leaf. If you prune them in summer instead, when they are growing rapidly and the leaves have expanded, the leaves will search for any available moisture and will, as a result, draw the sap from the pruning wounds. This leaves them relatively dry and so less susceptible to bleeding.

Shrubs that bleed and thus need summer pruning

Acer japonica

Acer palmatum

Aesculus parviflora

Magnolia stellata

Prunus

Sophora

---

pinching out

This is a useful technique often used for shaping a plant or getting it to produce lots of side shoots or branches. It is a technique best employed when a shrub has almost reached the maximum height required. Pinching out involves removing the tip or growing point of each shoot. If this is done when the growth is soft and sappy, no pruning equipment is required, since the shoot tips can be pinched out between your finger and thumb. The trick is to pinch while the shrub is growing rapidly, since then the wound will quickly heal and so minimize the danger of disease entering the plant.

116

making a topiary design

Topiary is the clipping and training of plants into formal shapes. It involves early training followed by repeated restrictive pruning, the frequency of which depends on the intricacy of the design. The real secret to topiary is to prune little and often, constantly checking the plants and trimming them as necessary to form a dense, compact growth habit. Plants grown in pots are particularly convenient subjects for topiary, since they can be brought into the house and used for indoor display, although they will deteriorate rapidly if kept in for more than a few days.

MATERIALS & EQUIPMENT

pruning shears and secateurs

for a cone: 3 bamboo canes, several metres of wire and garden twine

for a spiral: thick wire

for a ball: bamboo cane and garden twine

suitable plants (see page 120)

Choosing a shape

Most topiary designs are easy to form if a template or framework is used. This will help to avoid accidents, such as uneven trimming or, even worse, the removal of the wrong branch. For simple shapes, such as a cone or pyramid, canes can be used for the template; for more complex shapes, you may need a framework of wrought iron or chicken wire or a cane and wire structure. Other shapes, such as balls – single or multiple – can be clipped freehand. Bear in mind that the more elaborate the design, the greater the maintenance required.

Selecting suitable plants

The plants that make good subjects for topiary must have certain characteristics if the growing and training is to be successful. Those that respond well include plants with easily trained pliable growth, dense and compact leaves, and attractive foliage.

Plants suitable for topiary

Barberry (*Berberis darwinii*)

Bay (*Laurus nobilis*)

Box (*Buxus sempervirens*)

Cotton lavender (*Santolina chamaecyparissus*)

Daisy bush (*Olearia nummulariifolia*)

English yew (*Taxus baccata*)

False holly (*Osmanthus heterophyllus*)

Holly (*Ilex aquifolium*)

Italian cypress (*Cupressus sempervirens*)

Jasmine box (*Phillyrea latifolia*)

Poor man's box (*Lonicera nitida*)

Privet (*Ligustrum ovalifolium*)

Sagebrush (*Artemisia abrotanum*)

Making a topiary cone

1   In the first summer, cut back any long vigorous shoots that are spoiling the overall shape. The aim is to encourage the plant to grow as evenly as possible. Apply fertilizer if necessary to ensure the plant is growing strongly before clipping begins.

2   The following summer, make a framework of bamboo canes and wire. Place the canes over the plant, tie them together at the top and wrap a few lengths of wire around them, spacing these evenly up to the top of the plant.

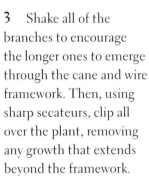

3   Shake all of the branches to encourage the longer ones to emerge through the cane and wire framework. Then, using sharp secateurs, clip all over the plant, removing any growth that extends beyond the framework.

4   When the clipping is finished, remove the framework. Next, cut back or pinch out the growing point by one-third to encourage the plant to produce side shoots and so become more bushy. This clipping and pinching will need to be repeated at least two or three times each year, depending on the plants used and their rate of growth.

Making a topiary spiral

1 A spiral can be achieved in two stages, but it will take several years to complete. First trim the plant as for a cone. Once it has reached the required height, wind a thick wire evenly around the cone to act as a guide.

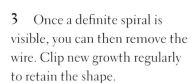

2 Clipping from the bottom, remove some of the growth around the wire until a spiral channel is formed.

3 Once a definite spiral is visible, you can then remove the wire. Clip new growth regularly to retain the shape.

Making a topiary ball

1 This shape can be achieved without the use of a template. In the first season, tie the main stem to a cane for support, then trim away the lower shoots.

2 Cut back the growing tip by one-third once the plant reaches the required height. Trim the horizontal branches where necessary to encourage a dense, bushy habit.

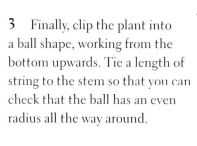

3 Finally, clip the plant into a ball shape, working from the bottom upwards. Tie a length of string to the stem so that you can check that the ball has an even radius all the way around.

Care and maintenance

• Do not clip topiary after late summer since soft young shoots are particularly vulnerable to frost damage in the late autumn and winter.
• If any stems or branches become damaged or broken, they can be removed with secateurs.
• In order to conceal any holes quickly, branches can be drawn together and tied with thin plastic-coated wire. The manipulated shoots will soon produce new shoots to fill the gaps, and these can be trimmed as necessary as they develop.

climbing and wall plants

Pruning is essential to the successful cultivation of almost all established climbers. Without control the plants eventually produce only a sparse display of flowers. More importantly, some of the most vigorous climbers may engulf neighbouring plants or damage property. Climbers and wall shrubs are usually pruned with the remaining strong, healthy stems being trained and tied to supports while they are still supple, to achieve the desired structure and appearance.

types of climber

Some climbers produce masses of long, slender shoots that need to be tied in. Vigorous climbers can be left to grow freely, and *Wisteria* produces its best flower buds on horizontally trained branches. This demonstrates the importance of growth habits and basic cultivation in influencing the training and pruning of climbers and wall plants.

Scramblers and ramblers
These have rapidly growing stems, which clamber through other plants on hooked thorns, as on firethorn (*Pyracantha*), or by rapidly extending lax shoots. They will need a support structure on which to climb.

Twiners
Climbers, such as honeysuckle (*Lonicera*), *Clematis* and *Wisteria*, climb on rapidly growing stems, supported by curling or twining tendrils, leaf-stalks or stems. They may require additional support.

Climbing shrubs
Shrubs that are tender enough to require some form of protection may be grown next to a wall or fence, or be supported by it, depending on the plant grown. They will need to be tied in with garden twine.

Natural clingers
The natural clingers, such as ivy (*Hedera*) and Virginia creeper (*Parthenocissus*), support themselves by aerial roots or sucker pads. For these types of climber, an additional support structure is not usually necessary.

positioning of pruning cuts

The position of the cut and the technique employed are essential to improving the appearance of your plant and extending its life. Secateurs will be strong enough, since most climbers have relatively thin stems. The best place to make the cut is just above a healthy bud, say 2 to 3 mm (¹⁄₁₆ to ⅛ in). If the cut is too close to the bud, you may damage it, and one placed too far from the bud will leave an exposed stem that will die back and encourage disease.

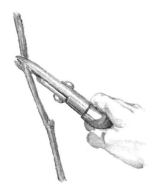 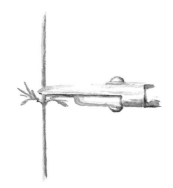

Decide on the direction you wish the climber to grow in and cut at an angle in that same direction.

If the buds are opposite one another, then make the cut so that it goes straight across the stem.

supporting climbers

Check 'self-supporting' climbers regularly and coax them into growing in the desired direction; twiners and scramblers may need fixing in place with ties until their tendrils or twining stems have attached themselves. Tying in also helps to control the growing direction. Stems to be kept for a number of years should be retied annually, when the plant is pruned, to prevent the ties strangling the stem.

A twiner in a wire frame support.

A scrambler tied to trellis.

formative pruning and training

Soon after planting, tie in the strongest stems to the support system to achieve a well-balanced framework of shoots. This is essential with newly planted climbers, since the woody stems, which develop as the shoot becomes mature, cannot be bent into position without damaging them. As the plant grows, prune weak or damaged shoots, stems growing in the wrong direction and crossing branches.

routine pruning

Climbing plants and wall shrubs are often used as decorative coverings for walls and fences, as garden dividers, or to give privacy or protection from winds around a patio or other seating area, so it is important to maintain their shape and health in order to promote vigorous new growths and attractive flowers. When you are dealing with established plants, the easiest approach is to prune them twice each year. The first pruning is carried out in the summer, when the new, long lateral growths are cut back to just above a growth bud. Framework shoots are then tied into position and left to twine around the supports provided for them (if they are self-supporting). The second pruning is carried out in late winter. At this time of year, all of the summer-pruned shoots should be cut back to form the spurs that will carry next year's flowers. Any secondary growths you find, which were formed as a result of the summer pruning, should also be reduced at this time, except with some evergreens, which require a different approach (see opposite). At any time of year, however, it is appropriate to remove damaged or diseased parts of the plant to maintain its health and vigour, or any stems that are growing in the wrong direction or are causing an obstruction.

The lateral branches, which are primarily responsible for carrying the next season's flowers, should be shortened to just above a bud in the late winter to encourage new flowering shoots.

Always keep a check on, and prune, any tangled and crossing branches. This can be done at any time of year in order to maintain the plant's overall appearance and good health.

The dormant winter season is usually the best time of year to reposition ties. Make sure that they are secure, but they should not be so tight that they rub against the stems or branches.

Pruning evergreens

Those evergreens that flower on the current season's growth are usually best pruned in the early spring – not in the summer, as is the more common practice with climbers. Remove all weak growth and damaged or congested stems, and retie the shoots securely, making sure that they are not restricting or rubbing the branches.

Wall shrubs

Wall shrubs grown for their ornamental fruits, such as pyracantha, produce most of their new growth in mid-summer, after flowering. If left unpruned, these shoots will obscure the berries. In late summer, prune the new growths back to within 10 cm (4 in) of the main stem. These short shoots then form spurs that will bear next year's flowers.

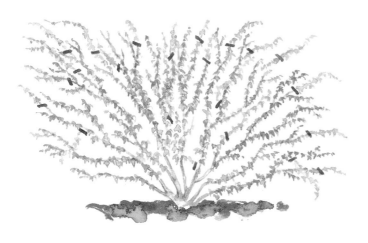

Climbers suitable for winter pruning

Clematis texensis	Trumpet creeper (Campsis)
Grape vine (Vitis)	Virginia creeper (Parthenocissus)
Oriental bittersweet (Celastrus orbiculatus)	Winter jasmine (Jasminum nudiflorum)
Pineapple broom (Cytisus battandieri)	Wisteria sinensis

Wisteria

Climbers suitable for spring pruning

Birthwort (Aristolochia)	Clematis 'Henryi'
Cissus	Clematis 'Nelly Moser'
Clematis 'Barbara Jackman'	Distictis
Clematis 'Carnaby'	Ivy (Hedera)
Clematis 'Duchess of Edinburgh'	Passion flower (Passiflora)
	Trachelospermum

Escallonia

Climbers suitable for summer pruning

Aristolochia	Cotoneaster
Billardiera	Escallonia
Campsis	Hydrangea
Ceanothus	Parthenocissus
Chaenomeles	Pyracantha
Clematis armandii	Thunbergia
Clematis montana	Wisteria
Clerodendrum	

Clematis

renovation pruning

Neglected climbers soon become a tangled mass of woody stems that produce very few flowers. When this happens you have to decide whether or not your plant is worth saving. However, they can usually be renovated; either vigorously in one year or, for climbers that are in particularly bad shape, over several years. A very badly diseased or infested plant may not be worth saving, and replacement is the only option.

Drastic renovation

If the plant is relatively healthy and vigorous, prune it very hard to rejuvenate it. Most deciduous climbers will tolerate being cut back close to the base or main framework of stems – the exception is evergreens, which are less suited to such drastic treatment. Cut the plant down to 30 cm (12 in) with clean angled cuts, and as the new growth develops, train it over the support system. Less healthy plants will not survive this type of drastic pruning treatment and so will need to be renovated in stages.

Staged renovation

For staged renovation, remove the oldest stems (usually the darkest coloured bark) each year, over a two- or three-year period. To avoid the new growth becoming tangled up in the old growth, in the first year cut down one half of the plant and train the new shoots into the open spaces. In the second year, the remainder of the old stems are cut away and replacements trained into the remaining space. However, be prepared to wait for two or more years before the new growth is mature enough to produce flowers.

First year

Train and tie in the new shoots as they develop in response to renovation.

Second year

Untie new stems, cut out weak or damaged growth and then retie the stems.

Climbers that tolerate renovation pruning

Clematis	Honeysuckle (*Lonicera*)
Confederate vine (*Antigonon leptopus*)	Passion flower (*Passiflora*)
Glory bower (*Clerodendrum thomsoniae*)	Russian vine (*Fallopia baldschuanica*)
Golden trumpet (*Allamanda cathartica*)	Trumpet creeper (*Campsis*)

wisteria

The vigorous habit of wisteria puts many gardeners off growing it, since they are unsure how to tackle the prolific growth in order to contain the stems and produce plenty of flowers. Provided pruning is carried out regularly, however, the task is fairly simple.

Pruning methods
In order to give an overview of the life-cycle of wisteria, the illustrations below follow the pruning process from planting to maturity.

On planting
Fix support wires to a fence or wall. Tie the main stem to a cane then cut it back to 75 to 90 cm (30 to 36 in). Remove any side shoots.

First year – summer
Train long, twining shoots into position to form a framework of branches. Cut back other shoots to 15 to 20 cm (6 to 8 in) to encourage flower-bearing spurs to form.

First year – winter
In winter, cut back the leading shoot and the lateral or side shoots until just three buds remain on each one. This will help in the formation of strong, new branches.

Second year – summer
Pinch out the tip of the leading shoot to the required height and cut back thin, spindly side shoots to encourage a bushy habit.

Second year – winter
To encourage the formation of spurs, which will eventually produce flowers, cut back the new lateral growth to two or three buds.

Third and subsequent years – summer
By now, only routine maintenance pruning will be needed. Keep the main framework branches in check by cutting back any over-long growths. Cut back the lateral growth to 15 cm (6 in) to encourage flowering spurs.

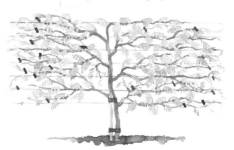

Third and subsequent years – winter
Cut back the flowering spurs to just two or three buds. This will stimulate growth and ensure the climber flowers well the following season. Check the ties on the main stem each year and replace if necessary.

installing a trellis

Adding a trellis panel to a wall is a good way of creating a new dimension
in a garden by providing a support frame for climbers and wall shrubs, and making an
expanse of plain wall interesting by covering all or part of it with attractive plants. The
basic trellis offers many design possibilities and provides an almost limitless
variety of garden options for the imaginative gardener. By attaching the trellis
to hinges, the whole structure can be lowered down away from the wall,
either to change the plant or paint the surface behind.

MATERIALS & EQUIPMENT

1.2 m x 5 x 2.5 cm (4 ft x 2 x 1 in) sawn timber batten

1.2 x 2 m (4 x 6½ ft) hardwood trellis, with 10 cm (4 in) square grids

plastic rawl plugs, to fit 8 cm (3 in) screws

2 rustproof butt hinges

rustproof screws, 8 cm (3 in) long

5 blocks of wood, 2.5 cm (1 in) square to act as spacers

screwdriver and hammer

electric drill, and wood and masonry bits

chalk and measuring tape

hardy climber, such as *Campsis* or *Wisteria*

organic matter, mulch and garden ties

1 Making the trellis

Prepare the timber batten by drilling five holes through it, spaced evenly from end to end.

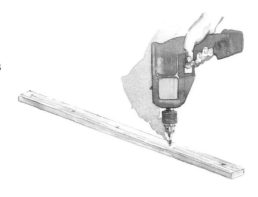

2 Hold the timber batten horizontally against the wall, about 30 cm (12 in) above ground level, and mark the wall with chalk to indicate the position of the holes.

3 Drill five holes into the wall as indicated by the marks, using a masonry bit, and insert a plastic rawl plug into each one, tapping it with a hammer so that the top of the plug is flush with the surface of the wall.

4 Place the batten against the wall, lining up the holes with the rawl plugs. Insert a screw through each hole in the batten, going into a plastic rawl plug behind. Screw the batten securely to the wall using an electric or a manual screwdriver.

5 Take the hardwood trellis and lay it on the ground, then position the hinges along the bottom edge about 15 cm (6 in) from the corners. Screw them into place.

6 Leaving the top of the trellis on the ground, lift the base until it is level with the wall-mounted batten. Then position the hinges against the front edge of the batten and screw them into place.

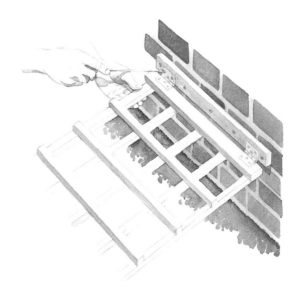

7 Swing the trellis up on its hinges and mark the wall and trellis with chalk to indicate where holes will go in the corners and centre of the top horizontal strip. Also mark where holes will go in the middle of the side sections.

8 Drill the five marked holes, going right through the trellis frame. Then drill five corresponding holes into the wall using a masonry bit. Insert a plastic rawl plug into each hole and tap it in, flush with the wall.

9 Spacers are now inserted so that the stems can be trained between the trellis and the wall. Drill a hole through each wooden block and position them between the wall and trellis. Insert a screw through the hole in the trellis, going though the block and into the plastic rawl plug. Screw securely in place.

10 Planting and training

Choose a hardy climber, such as *Campsis* or *Wisteria*. Remove the weeds from the soil and incorporate bulky organic matter. Dig a hole 45 cm (18 in) away from the wall, large enough to allow the roots to spread out.

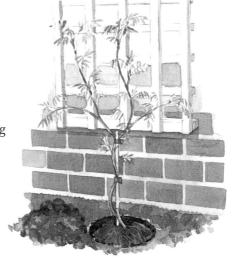

11 Insert a stake and place the root ball in the hole, level with the surrounding soil. Fill the hole with soil, firm in and tie the stem to the stake. Finally, water around the base and lay a mulch to deter weeds and keep the soil moist.

12 Using plastic ties or garden twine, tie the main stems to the trellis support system, spreading them out evenly so that as they grow they will cover the main framework.

roses

In nature, the habit of most roses is to produce strong new stems from close to the base of the plant each year. As the new stems develop they take priority for water and nutrients at the expense of the older existing stems, and these, in turn, gradually become weaker and eventually die of starvation. These old stems remain as dead wood before slowly rotting and falling to the ground. This is the closest plants come to being pruned in nature but illustrates that, in effect, the plant does prune itself.

rose types

The technique for pruning roses is relatively simple and only becomes complicated due to the different rose types and their varied growth rates and habits. Roses range from the low-growing patio and ground-cover types, which are often no more than 30 cm (12 in) tall, to the very vigorous climbers, ramblers and species roses, which can reach up to 10 to 15 m (30 to 45 ft) tall. When and how you prune your rose can significantly affect the health of the plant, so it is important to follow the correct method. Some roses do not respond well to the recommended treatment for their particular classification, in which case you need to adapt your methods to suit their habit.

You may not know to which group the roses in your garden belong, particularly if you moved house when the plants were dormant. If you are unsure, confine your pruning to the points listed under 'Principles of pruning' on page 134. Next summer you will see from their flowering which group they belong to and can plan your pruning accordingly. Pruning techniques may vary slightly in different conditions, but with experience you will quickly learn how to deal with them to suit your own local soil and microclimate.

Modern bush – roses that grow in a cup-like shape and require more pruning than most species.

Shrub – a varied group, they tend to be mound forming but can also spread their branches quite widely.

Climbing – with long, strong shoots, these roses need to be trained and kept tidy to create the best display.

general tasks

In order to keep all your roses growing and flowering well, or to improve their performance and the quality of the blooms, there are a number of tasks that should be tackled throughout the season, depending on the individual habit of your rose.

Disbudding

This is a technique that can be used to make fewer but larger blooms on a rose bush. With most hybrid roses, as the new flower-bearing stem develops, the cluster of blooms will consist of one central bud and a number of small lateral buds. Snap off these lateral buds while they are still soft and sappy so that all of the plant's energies will be directed into the one remaining bloom, creating a much larger individual flower.

Dead-heading

After flowering, dead rose blooms may remain on the plant for several months and in this situation the plant will divert a good deal of energy into producing seed. Once this process starts, the plant gradually stops producing flowers altogether. A common mistake is to remove the flower with a length of stem bearing four or five leaves; removing the leaves is unnecessary and only a small section of stem, about 10 cm (4 in) long, should be cut off with the dead bloom.

Sucker removal

A very important pruning task in the summer is removing suckers from roses. You can usually identify a sucker by its leaves. With most rose cultivars the leaf consists of 5 to 7 leaflets, but suckers have leaves with 7 to 11 leaflets, each ending with a sharp point, and they are usually a much paler green than those on the rest of the plant.

1   Using a trowel, carefully dig the soil from around the base of the sucker, to the point where it is attached to the parent plant.

2   Wearing a thick leather glove to protect your hand from the thorns, grip the sucker firmly, just above the point where it is growing from the root of the parent.

3   Tear the sucker free from the parent plant and trim any loose bark on the parent with a sharp knife. Discard the sucker and replace the soil around the base of the plant.

Standard roses often produce suckers above ground, on the stem, in addition to those originating from the roots, and these may compete with the top growth and eventually take over. Wearing thick leather gloves, snap off the sucker growths where they are attached to the main stem, or 'leg', of the plant. Do this while the suckers are still soft and sappy.

principles of pruning

For all types of rose, keep the centre of the plant open, well-spaced and clear of crossing branches. This allows air to flow freely through the plant and avoids the still-air conditions that encourage fungal diseases, such as black spot and mildew. Good spacing prevents rubbing, which can open up wounds where fungal problems, such as coral spot, can enter. Burn or shred all fallen leaves and prunings to avoid pests and diseases overwintering and returning to attack the following year. Finally, always use sharp secateurs and knives, since ragged cuts leave damaged tissue, which is prone to attack.

Cut at an angle, 5 mm (¼ in) above an outward-facing bud, with the bud near the top of the cut. This promotes rapid healing and an open-centre habit; prune to inward-pointing eyes for more upright growth.

Make sure you always cut back into healthy wood. If the middle of the stem is brown or discoloured, it is not healthy and you will need to cut the shoot back further until healthy white wood is reached.

Remove any dead, damaged and diseased stems, and any weak or spindly growth. This sometimes means pruning stems to ground level, or with side shoots, cutting back to where they join up with a healthy stem.

topping

One thing to watch out for is strong winter winds, since they can loosen roses and weaken or damage their roots, which makes them vulnerable to injury from frost and often leads to sucker growths developing from the injured roots. To prevent this happening, cut the plants down to half their height in the autumn; this lowers their wind resistance and reduces the likelihood of wind-rock.

renovation pruning

This is best carried out in autumn for all types of roses. It is possible to take drastic action and cut back your rose close to ground level; this can be very effective for a particularly neglected plant. Alternatively follow a gradual programme of renewal over two years by shortening and reducing the plant in two stages. This helps maintain the shape and form as the plant recovers. Start by cutting out any dead, diseased or damaged wood and reduce half the stems to about 15 cm (6 in) above ground level. In the following year, cut back the remaining old growth and then prune the laterals on the new growths.

spring pruning

Not all roses need a spring pruning, but for those that do, this is best done just before the plants come out of dormancy – earlier pruning can cause too much early growth, which is often damaged by the weather, and later pruning often wastes the plant's energy by cutting off new growth. If you are unsure when to prune, the best advice is to prune when the growth buds halfway up the most vigorous stems are just beginning to swell.

Frost damage

This can occur with fluctuating spring weather, where warm spells are followed by frosty periods. If the new shoots are damaged by frost, cut them back to healthy dormant buds further back on the main stems, making sure you remove all the dead wood. If there is a chance that frosts may return, particularly at the beginning of spring, then leave the damaged stem in place until the danger has passed.

modern bush roses

Modern bush roses, particularly those grown in colder climates, will have been pruned in autumn to reduce wind-rock. Once the danger of frost has passed in the following spring, they can be pruned normally. Most modern roses flower on the current season's wood, which means many of them need to be pruned severely in the spring or they tend to become tall and 'leggy', with flowers forming high on the plant. Slow-growing miniature roses will flower for many years with little or no formal pruning: simply cut out dead, diseased or damaged stems. The only planned pruning is to prevent them spreading too far.

Modern bush roses
Rosa 'Alexander'
Rosa 'Baby Masquerade'
Rosa 'Chinatown'
Rosa 'Clarissa'
Rosa 'Fragrant Dream'

Rosa 'Madame Knorr'

Rosa 'Roseraie de l'Haÿ'

Rosa 'Iceberg'

Rosa 'Amber Queen'

shrub roses

This category includes modern shrubs, old garden and species roses. These flower on old wood and need only be pruned when they become untidy or to remove dead, diseased or damaged wood; the best time to prune is after flowering. The main task is to remove the oldest stems just after the leaves have started to fall, usually in early autumn. Due to its dense growth, this is one of the few times when you can see into the centre of the plant, which provides an opportunity to get rid of diseased or damaged wood that may have an adverse effect on growth the following season. The drawback is that plants grown for their ornamental hips may have their overall display spoiled as a result.

rambling roses

These will flower quite satisfactorily for a number of years without any regular pruning, but they will eventually become a tangled mass of overcrowded, unmanageable shoots prone to attack by pests and diseases if they are completely neglected. The best time to prune ramblers is in the late summer, after their single flush of flowers is over.

Pruning cuts

As with all types of rose, you need to use clean, sharp secateurs or a pruning knife in order to prevent ragged edges on the plant that may then become susceptible to invasion by pests and diseases. Make each cut at an angle, 5 mm (¼ in) from an outward-facing bud. This helps to keep the centre of the plant open. Make sure to cut back into healthy white wood.

Routine pruning

Start by removing any dead, damaged or diseased shoots, before cutting out about a quarter to a third of the oldest shoots; the aim is to leave only young, vigorous stems that are no more than two years old. Any side shoots should be cut back to two or three buds, from which many of the next year's flowers will originate.

Rosa 'Constance Spry'

Shrub roses	
Rosa 'Autumn Sunset'	
Rosa 'Canary Bird'	
Rosa 'Canterbury'	
Rosa 'Fountain'	

Rambling roses	
Rosa 'Albéric Barbier'	*Rosa* 'Rambling Rector'
Rosa 'Albertine'	*Rosa* 'Sanders' White'
Rosa 'Complicata'	*Rosa* 'Silver Moon'
Rosa 'Emily Gray'	*Rosa* 'Veilchenblau'
Rosa 'Goldfinch'	*Rosa* 'Wedding Day'

climbing roses

Climbing roses flower on the current season's growth and are repeat flowering. Do not prune climbing roses in the first and second years after planting, except to remove any dead, diseased, damaged or weak growth. Then prune only if necessary. Never prune climbing sports of bush roses in the first two years, since they may revert to bush form.

Begin training as soon as the new shoots are long enough to reach their supports. Training them sideways along horizontal supports will encourage flowering

(see below). Many of these will produce flowers from the base of the plant without special training. The strong main shoots can be left unpruned unless they are getting too long, in which case shorten them as appropriate. Otherwise, simply shorten the side shoots.

Climbling roses

Rosa 'Aloha'	*Rosa* 'New Dawn'
Rosa 'Altissimo'	*Rosa* 'Rosy Mantle'
Rosa 'Dublin Bay'	*Rosa* 'Royal Gold'
Rosa 'Elegance'	*Rosa* 'Summer Wine'
Rosa 'Handel'	*Rosa* 'Warm Welcome'
Rosa 'Meg'	

Renewal pruning

Occasional renewal pruning may be necessary if the base of the rose becomes bare. To do this, simply cut out several of the older, main shoots to within 15 cm (6 in) or so of ground level; this will encourage strong new shoots to develop and replace the older growths. This process should be repeated in subsequent years, if and when required.

Rosa 'Pink Perpetue'   *Rosa* 'Madame Caroline Testout'

137

trees

Trees have the effect of imparting a sense of permanence and maturity to a landscape and they are often responsible for the overall structure and theme within a garden. In nature, trees are left to develop their natural form and no pruning is required or provided. Since a garden is an artificial environment, regular pruning and training can be used to manipulate a tree's growth, shape and size, and even to extend its life. For pruning larger trees it is sometimes better to consult a qualified tree surgeon.

types of tree

The main types of tree are deciduous, which shed their leaves in the winter, and evergreen, which retain their leaves throughout the year. Evergreens can be sub-divided into broad-leaved and conifers. The vast majority of deciduous trees should be pruned when they are dormant, in late autumn or winter, but they can also be pruned at other times, depending on the reasons for pruning (see below). Most evergreen trees require little or no pruning other than the removal of any dead, damaged, or diseased branches.

reasons for pruning trees

There are many different reasons for pruning trees. These include routine operations, such as removing crossing branches to avoid rubbing and breakage, and thinning the crown to lessen wind resistance and allow more light and air in through the crown to counteract root damage or structural faults. Tree pruning can also be carried out in order to change the overall size of your specimen. This may simply be to improve the balance or shape of semi-mature and mature trees or actually to make a tree smaller – an essential operation where a tree has outgrown its allotted space. Finally, dead and dangerous branches will need to be removed after storm damage, or to clear pedestrian or vehicle access.

Deciduous	**Broad-leaved evergreens**	**Conifers**
Ash (*Fraxinus*)	Common box (*Buxus sempervirens*)	White cedar (*Thuja occidentalis*)
Beech (*Fagus*)	Gum tree (*Eucalyptus*)	Cedar (*Cedrus*)
Birch (*Betula*)	Holly (*Ilex*)	Juniper (*Juniperus*)
Hornbeam (*Carpinus*)	Holm or evergreen oak (*Quercus ilex*)	Lawson cypress (*Chamaecyaris lawsoniana*)
Horse chestnut (*Aesculus*)	Laurel (*Laurus nobilis*)	Pine (*Pinus*)
Maple (*Acer*)	Strawberry tree (*Arbutus unedo*)	Spruce (*Picea*)
Sweet gum (*Liquidambar styraciflua*)		Yew (*Taxus*)
Walnut (*Juglans*)		

Acer leaf on *Berberis*

Ilex

Chamaecyaris

positioning of pruning cuts

Careful, accurate pruning cuts will reduce the risk of damage to an absolute minimum. Stems should be cut at an angle, 2 to 3 mm (1/16 to 1/8 in) above a healthy bud and facing the direction in which you want the new shoot to develop. All cuts must be clean, with no crushing of the tissue or ragged edges. To encourage a plant to develop an open centre, cut back to an outward facing bud or shoot. As the shoot grows, tie it in to form part of a branch framework or to replace an old shoot.

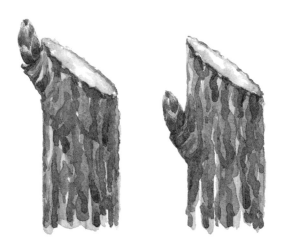

A cut too close to the bud (left) may damage it, and one too far away (right) will leave a stub that may die back and allow pests and diseases to enter.

Position the stem that you are cutting close to the base of the blade for a firm hold – using the tip is less likely to make a clean cut and can damage secateurs.

branch removal

To remove extra-large branches it is best to employ a qualified tree surgeon. For more manageable jobs, the method used depends on its size and position above the ground. Small branches can be hand-held and removed with a single cut close to the main stem or trunk. Larger branches are removed in sections. If some of the weight is not removed first, the branch may tear down into the trunk and cause a large gaping wound, which is a potential site for fungal invasion. If the flush cut is made from the bottom, the weight will cause the saw to jam, so remove the main part of the branch first.

1 Adopt a safe pruning procedure that reduces the weight of the branch first, before the final cut is made. Using an appropriate pruning saw, make the first cut on the underside of the branch at a convenient distance from the trunk and about a quarter of the branch's diameter in depth

2 Make the second cut on the top of the branch, further out along the branch from the first cut but parallel to it. The distance between these two cuts is normally 5 to 7.5 cm (2 to 3 in).When the second cut reaches the point where it overlaps the first, the branch should snap along the grain and fall.

3 The final cut to remove the branch stump is then made parallel to the trunk. Start by making an undercut near to the trunk and then cut along the collar of the branch in line with this undercut. Make sure your final cut is completely smooth, trimming with a pruning knife if necessary.

formative and routine pruning

Some trees are sold as one-year-old whips. These are young plants (often seedlings) with a long stem and few or no lateral branches. Most trees, however, are purchased at a larger size, at two or three years old, when they have a framework of lateral branches, which are the basis of the structural framework of the crown of the tree. Formative pruning should start at the time of planting. The growth habit of the tree and its landscape use should determine the method and amount of pruning needed to train the tree, as well as the amount of routine maintenance that will be required.

Broad-leaved evergreen trees

Broad-leaved evergreens require very little routine pruning once the shape has been established. Prune trees in the early autumn or late spring, just as the new season's growth has started. The operation simply involves reducing or removing any dead, dying, diseased, or damaged branches and generally maintaining the correct shape and size.

For formative pruning on broad-leaved evergreen trees, a strong main stem or central leader should be established by training a strong vertical shoot against a cane. This can be removed as the woody stem matures.

Prune out or cut back any shoots competing with the central leader and remove any badly placed laterals during the early years of growth. This process should be repeated until the tree reaches the required height.

If you spot a reverted shoot on your tree (this is a plain green leaf on a variegated plant), this will need to be removed, since these shoots tend to grow at different rates and spoil the effect of the variegated foliage.

Conifers

Conifers can be left to grow naturally unless the shoots are damaged or the leaves become reverted. The basic growth pattern of conifers is for a single main stem to grow with whorls of branches developing at fairly regular intervals along its length. After planting, remove any strong shoots that are competing with the leader. Train a strong vertical shoot against a cane if necessary. Then prune over-vigorous lateral shoot tips to encourage branching and even growth. Repeat this to reach the required height.

Any pruning of mature conifers should be restricted to removing dead branches. Attempts to reduce them in height normally prove unsatisfactory and frequently leave ugly, mutilated plants. Once they have become too tall for the place in which they are growing, it may be necessary to remove the entire tree. Unlike broad-leaved trees, true conifers (not yew) do not normally regrow from mature wood. This is because there are few or no dormant buds present in the older woody branches and stems.

Remove any dead branches to make way for healthy new growth.

Deciduous trees

The most common shapes for deciduous trees are the feathered tree, with a central main stem and branches arranged from ground level to the top of the tree, and the standard tree, with branches starting about 1.8 m (6 ft) above ground level.

Vertical branch spacing is very important, since this influences the overall shape, appearance and structural strength of the tree. Many deciduous trees respond better to pruning either after they have finished flowering or when they are dormant, and this is usually in autumn. However, trees that flower early, in spring or at the beginning of summer, need to be pruned before this, from the middle to the end of summer, to give them as much time as possible to produce the new growth that will bear next year's flowers. Other deciduous trees are prone to bleeding and are better pruned when they are in full leaf, to protect them from excessive loss of sap, which would considerably weaken the tree and may eventually contribute to its death. Once the leaves have fully expanded and matured, they will readily draw back the sap from the pruning wounds.

For a spreading tree, such as red maple (*Acer rubrum*), remove any shoots that compete with the main stem to prevent a branch fork developing. Then remove weak, thin, crossing or overcrowded branches in order to develop a well-balanced framework (see left).

To produce a clear stem on a tree, such as sweet gum (*Liquidambar styraciflua*), after planting remove shoots competing with the main stem and any thin or crossing shoots. Reduce the lateral shoots in spring, then remove them completely in autumn (see below).

Some trees that bleed	
Birch (*Betula*)	*Sophora*
Cherry (*Prunus*)	*Tilia*
Horse chestnut (*Aesculus*)	Walnut (*Juglans*)
Maple (*Acer*)	

Spring- and summer-flowering trees	
Chilean firebush (*Embothrium coccineum*)	Redbud (*Cercis*)
	Robinia
Golden rain (*Laburnum*)	Sweet chestnut (*Castanea*)
Judas tree (*Cercis siliquastrum*)	

Acer palmatum

Betula pendula

Laburnum

renovation pruning

Eventually most trees outgrow their allocated area or become neglected and need some renovation. However, some trees are not suited to this treatment, often because they are unsafe. In this case, replacement is the only solution. Renovation is best carried out in late autumn, especially for those species that bleed if pruned during the growing season (see page 141). It is best to carry out extensive renovation over an extended period of two or three years in order to allow the tree to recover more slowly.

First year
Remove all dead, dying, diseased and damaged wood and any tangled branches.

Second year
Thin out the new shoots and those that cross or rub, so that the crown remains balanced.

crown reduction

This involves an overall reduction of the crown to even out the profile by shortening the branches back to growing points to encourage regrowth. Pruning on the stronger sections of the crown will consist mainly of tipping shoots by pruning back the end third of each shoot – more severe pruning will encourage vigorous growth. On the weaker sections of the crown, pruning can be more severe, with some branches being cut back by about two-thirds of their length.

crown thinning

This involves removing thin, weak, or crossing branches, followed by the complete or partial removal of some healthy branches to achieve an overall reduction in the density of the canopy. Ideally, thinning should be carried out on branch tips, with very few large branches being removed, unless absolutely essential. This has the effect of reducing the density of the foliage, thus allowing more light to reach the centre of the tree, without changing the overall profile of the canopy.

coppicing

This technique of hard pruning is a traditional method of managing specimens such as sweet chestnut (*Castanea sativa*) to give a constant and renewable supply of shoots. Using pruning loppers, the plants are cut back in the spring to about 5 to 7.5 cm (2 to 3 in) above ground level; new shoots will develop from this woody base.

Salix alba 'Britzensis'

Trees suitable for coppicing

Acer cappadocicum 'Aureum'

Common hornbeam (*Carpinus betulus*)

Corylus avellana 'Purpurea'

Mountain gum (*Eucalyptus dalrympleana*)

Salix alba 'Britzensis'

Yew (*Taxus baccata*)

pollarding

This severe pruning technique produces lots of thin, whippy new growths, with young branches that have an attractive bark in the winter. A small canopy of branches is created that does not cast dense shadows on the ground.

1   To develop a pollarded tree, the plant is allowed to grow as a single stem until it reaches a desired height of about 6 feet (1.8 m). In the early spring, all of the side branches are removed to leave stubs of growth about 5 cm (2 in) long.

2   This type of severe pruning will lead to a mass of new shoots developing in the spring and summer, and some of these may need thinning to prevent weak branches forming due to overcrowding. Cut these off, making sure the remaining stems are strong and healthy, as well as being evenly spaced to create a well-balanced display. Any shoots that form on the trunk will need to be cut off as they emerge, since these will spoil the effect of the pollard.

3   Pollarding is essentially an ornamental type of pruning, but it is also a useful technique to use on older trees that have become overgrown or are in need of some form of rejuvenation. It is usually carried out every other year, since this will help to keep the tree in good condition, but it does have the effect of draining away too much of its natural vigour – this is especially important during the first 5 years of establishment in newly planted trees.

Acer pennsylvanicum

Trees suitable for pollarding

Acer cappadocicum 'Aureum'	*Salix daphnoides* 'Aglaia'
Acer pennsylvanicum	*Salix matsudana* 'Tortuosa'
Judas tree (*Cercis siliquastrum*)	*Salix x sepulcralis* 'Erythroflexuosa'
Populus alba 'Richardii'	
Populus x candicans 'Aurora'	*Taxus baccata*
Salix alba 'Britzensis'	White mulberry (*Morus alba*)

hedges and screen plants

Pruning hedges and screen plants basically involves clipping, which is simply a different type of pruning carried out in a certain way to produce a hedge of the desired height and width. The same general principles apply to hedges as for trees and shrubs, and most hedging and screening plants will respond to regular trimming by producing an even covering of dense, compact growth, which makes them useful for creating garden boundaries, divisions, decorative features, or for giving privacy in overlooked gardens. On some sites, hedges can also be very useful as windbreaks, used to protect tender plants by creating pockets of calmer air. Most types of hedge fall into one of two categories – formal and informal. Formal hedges require regular clipping in order to control their growth and to maintain a particular shape. This type makes an effective barrier or shelter or an elegant backdrop for other plants. Informal hedges require less pruning and are an excellent means of displaying plants that produce attractive flowers or fruits.

types of hedge

The aim of clipping is to produce a hedge of the desired size, which is evenly covered with growth over its entire surface. The average hedge, even if composed of the most vigorous species of plants, need not exceed 75 cm (30 in) in width, provided it is pruned and trimmed correctly in the early stages of its development. Formal hedges are often narrower at the top than at the base to make trimming easier to carry out.

Formal hedges
Formal hedges require more work than any other type of hedge and will need regular clipping or trimming to restrict growth and maintain their shape. Conifers, yew (*Taxus*) and beech (*Fagus*) all make excellent formal hedges and create an attractive screen that can provide a perfect backdrop for other ornamental plants in a garden setting.

Informal hedges
Informal hedges, such as *Deutzia*, roses, *Potentillas* and barberry (*Berberis*), need only minimal pruning in order to encourage the plants to flower and prevent them from becoming overgrown. Prune after flowering by removing the flower-bearing stems. Plants that produce hips or berries should not be pruned until after the fruits have finished.

Tapestry hedges
Tapestry hedges are made up of a mixture of plants, such as beech (*Fagus*) alternated with yew (*Taxus*), or holly (*Ilex*), or both. A mixture of deciduous and evergreen species provides a colourful background, since the plants change with the seasons. With no two plants growing at exactly the same rate, however, careful pruning is necessary.

formative pruning

Formative pruning is designed to encourage a dense, bushy growth. Cut the hedge back hard for the first two years, and then all you need do is simply trim it to keep it tidy during the growing season. Upright plants, such as hawthorn (*Crataegus*) and privet (*Ligustrum*), tolerate hard initial pruning, but more shrub-like hedges, including many deciduous flowering varieties, such as hornbeam (*Carpinus*), forsythia and hazel (*Corylus*), suit a less severe pruning regime.

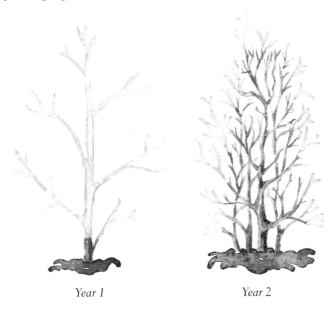

Year 1   *Year 2*

renovation pruning

If a hedge has become diseased or damaged, or has been neglected over a number of seasons for one reason or another, then the first consideration should be whether or not it is worth trying to save. Some hedging and screening plants respond very favourably to severe pruning and are capable of amazing powers of recovery if given sufficient care and attention. Others, however, will never produce new growth to fill any holes that may have developed. If the latter is the case, then the best course of action is to remove the plants and start again. The species of plants involved often determine the best course of action. With a formal hedge, for example, any noticeable damage may spoil its effect, while the more haphazard nature of a tapestry hedge may allow you to replace just some of the

most severely affected plants without ruining the hedge's overall appearance. The most extreme case of renovation pruning involves the plant being cut down to within 10 cm (4 in) of the soil in order to encourage the production of new shoots right from ground level. There are numerous problems associated with taking such drastic action, however, such as lack of privacy and exposing the garden by removing the sheltering benefits of the hedge. Whatever treatment you decide on, in the first year after pruning check that the cut surfaces remain healthy and disease free.

Staged renovation

If pruning plants back to near ground level proves to be too severe a course of action, a less drastic option is to cut one side of the hedge back to the main stems in the first year, and the other side (and top) the following year. Following this type of renovation pruning, feed and water the hedge in order to promote rapid regrowth. Deciduous hedges are best renovated in mid-winter but evergreens should be left until mid-spring. Most conifers do *not* have the capacity to generate new growth from old wood and so are not suited to this type of renovation pruning.

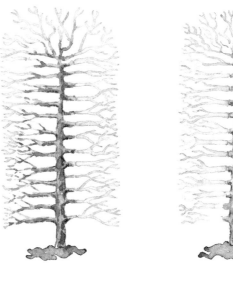

Year 1   *Year 2*

145

when to prune

How and when a particular type of hedge is pruned depends largely on the type of shrub involved and partly on the function of the hedge – as a backdrop for other ornamental plants in the garden, for example, or to provide privacy from neighbouring properties, or to act as a visual full stop and so prevent the eye from taking in all of a small garden at a single glance. As a general rule, the best time to prune is soon after flowering has finished. At this time, you should remove only the flower-bearing shoots. However, some flowering hedges and screens have more than a single season of interest. Plants such as firethorn (*Pyracantha*) or *Rosa rugosa*, which produce attractive berries or hips after the flowers have faded, should not be pruned until after the fruits have finished their display. Plants that require pruning in spring should generally be left until any danger of hard frosts has finished, but if the hedge is used by birds for nesting purposes, then try to complete pruning before nest-building commences.

best tools to use

Broad-leaved evergreens, such as laurel (*Prunus laurocerasus*), should be cut with secateurs for accuracy, to ensure that only whole leaves are removed. Depending on the size and height of your hedge, this can be a time-consuming task, but any leaves that are cut in half develop a brown line where the cells have been damaged and these 'half leaves' slowly turn yellow and die. All other types of hedge can be clipped with a pair of shears. For very large hedges, electric hedge trimmers are a boon.

formal hedges

Evergreen hedges	Ideal maximum height	Best times for clipping
Box (*Buxus sempervirens*)	30–60 cm (12–24 in)	3 x but not in winter
Elaeagnus x *ebbingei*	1.5–3 m (5–10 ft)	1 x mid- to late summer
Escallonia	1.2–2.5 m (4–8 ft)	1 x after flowering
Firethorn (*Pyracantha*)	2–3 m (6½–10 ft)	2 x after flowering and in autumn but avoid berries
Griselinia littoralis	1.2–3 m (4–10 ft)	2 x late spring/summer
Holly (*Ilex aquifolium*)	2–4 m (6½–13 ft)	1 x late summer
Laurel (*Prunus laurocerasus*)	1.2–3 m (4–10 ft)	1 x mid to late summer
Leyland cypress (x *Cupressocyparis leylandii*)	2–6 m (6½–20 ft)	3 x but not in winter
Lonicera nitida	90 cm–1.2m (36 in–4 ft)	3 x but not in winter
Privet (*Ligustrum*)	1.5–3 m (5–10 ft)	3 x but not in winter
Western red cedar (*Thuja plicata*)	1.5–4 m (5–13 ft)	2 x spring/early autumn
Yew (*Taxus baccata*)	1.2–6 m (4–20 ft)	2 x summer/autumn
Deciduous hedges		
Barberry (*Berberis thunbergii*)	60 cm–1.2m (24 in–4 ft)	1 x in summer
Beech (*Fagus*)	1.5–6 m (5–20 ft)	1 x late summer
Hawthorn (*Crataegus monogyna*)	1.5–3 m (5–10 ft)	2 x summer/autumn
Hornbeam (*Carpinus betulus*)	1.5–6 m (5–20 ft)	1 x late summer

informal hedges

Evergreen hedges	Ideal maximum height	Best times for clipping
Barberry (*Berberis darwinii*)	1.5–2.5 m (5–8 ft)	1 x after flowering
Cotoneaster (*Cotoneaster lacteus*)	1.5–2.2 m (5–7 ft)	1 x after fruiting
Firethorn (*Pyracantha*)	2–3 m (6½–10 ft)	2 x after flowering and in autumn but avoid berries
Holly (*Ilex aquifolium*)	2–4 m (6½–13 ft)	1 x late summer
Lavender (*Lavandula*)	50 cm–1 m (20–39 in)	2 x spring/after flowering
Tassel bush (*Garrya elliptica*)	1.5–2.2 m (5–7 ft)	1 x after flowering
Viburnum tinus	1–2.5 m (36 in–8 ft)	1 x after flowering
Deciduous hedges		
Barberry (*Berberis thunbergii*)	60 cm–1.2 m (12 in–4 ft)	1 x after flowering
Forsythia x *intermedia*	1.5–2.5 m (5–8 ft)	1 x after flowering
Hawthorn (*Crataegus monogyna*)	1.5–3 m (5–10 ft)	1 x winter
Rosa rugosa	90 cm–1.5 m (36 in–5 ft)	1 x after flowering

hedge clipping

1   When working with new hedges or hedges that need reshaping, place an upright post at each end of the hedge and stretch a line between them set at the desired height. This will give you a guide to the height without you having to step back all the time, but do beware of cutting through the line.

2   Start at the bottom of a hedge and work upwards so that clippings fall out of the way. If a hedge trimmer is used, cut upwards with a sweeping, arc-like action, keeping the cutting bar parallel to the

hedge. For safety with hedges over 1.8 m (6 ft) high, use two step ladders with a standing board in between.

3   Once the hedge has reached the height you require, cut the top down by about 30 cm (12 in). This encourages the upper shoots to thicken and bush out and any stumps from the pruning cuts will be hidden by new growth. With formal evergreen hedges, remember to maintain the sloping angle so that the bottom is wider than the top.

fruit

While pruning fruit trees is usually seen as a winter task, pruning is often carried out in summer in order to encourage the trees to produce more fruit or, in the case of plums and their relatives, to avoid the risk of infection. Dwarf pyramid trees also need pruning in summer, to maintain their shape. For training new fruit trees, refer to the project on pages 150–53.

trained fruit trees

The standard method of summer pruning is called the 'Modified Lorette System'. It helps to maintain a constant supply of fruit buds, and suppresses vigorous shoot growth. It is carried out in late summer, once the young shoots have become woody at the base.

1   All new lateral branches growing directly from the main stem or a main branch that are longer than 22 cm (9 in) should be cut back to three to five leaves above the basal cluster. Side shoots growing from spurs and existing laterals must be pruned back to just one leaf above the basal cluster of leaves. This job will continue throughout late summer.

2   To prevent secondary side shoots from developing below the earlier pruning cuts, leave a small number of longer shoots unpruned. These shoots will draw in sap and therefore discourage any secondary growth from developing. After the fruit has been harvested, in mid-autumn, prune back these 'sap-drawing shoots' to a single bud.

fruit susceptible to fungal disease

Plums, greengages, damsons and all relatives of the cherry are prone to a fungal disease called 'silver leaf' (*Chondrostereum purpureum*), the spores of which appear in the autumn and winter, entering the plant through pruning cuts. Cut back any affected growth in the summer to reduce the risk of the infection spreading.

maintaining the shape of dwarf fruit trees

The dwarf pyramid tree was developed for commercial growing of apples and pears but it is also ideal for small gardens. The shape saves space, with the upper branches being shorter than the lower ones, and the fruit is accessible, making harvesting easier. The size and shape of the tree must, however, be maintained by regular pruning. Once it has reached the required height of about 2.5 m (8 ft), restrict the tree's growth by cutting back the main stem to one bud in the early summer each year. Throughout the summer, shorten shoots growing from main branches to leave just three leaves, and cut back side shoots growing from existing laterals to one leaf above the basal cluster of leaves.

repairing damaged branches

In fruit trees that produce an unexpectedly large crop, and trees such as plums that often produce heavy crops, the sheer weight of the fruit may cause branches to break or split. These damaged branches must be pruned back or removed in the summer to prevent any invasion of pests and diseases.

pruning soft fruits

Soft fruits that grow on canes, such as blackberries, loganberries and raspberries, are pruned in the summer, after fruiting, to produce plenty of new growth for the following year. The canes also need to be trained on a post-and-wire support.

Blackberries and loganberries

1   As the new canes grow in the late spring and early summer, they are gathered up and loosely bunched together in the centre of the plant. This makes it much easier to pick the fruit, which grows on last year's canes.

2   Immediately after harvest, cut down all the old fruiting canes at the base of their stems, close to ground level.

3   Remove the ties from the bunch of young canes in the centre of the plant, carefully spread the canes out and train them along the wire supports, removing any canes that are surplus to your requirements. Leave a gap in the centre of the plant, into which the new canes can grow.

Raspberries

1   All of the fruited canes should be cut down to ground level immediately after harvest. Also remove any thin, weak or damaged canes, so that the shoots that remain are healthy and strong and are given as much growing room as possible.

2   As the canes grow, loosely but securely attach the new shoots to the wire supports, spacing the canes regularly at 10 cm (4 in) intervals. To make sure that the canes have adequate growing space, cut out

any excess canes and pull up any sucker growths that begin to encroach on to the pathway. When the canes reach the very top of the support, the tips must be pruned back to within 8 cm (3 in) of the wire.

training fruit trees

There are various methods of growing fruit trees, but generally they are either free-standing or trained. Trained trees are those that are grown into a formal shape and in a single plane, usually against a wall, fence or some other means of support. The purpose of wall-training is to produce high-quality fruits in a relatively confined space, and to provide shelter as well as additional warmth for plants, such as peaches and nectarines, that are not fully hardy. Two of the most commonly encountered forms of trained fruit trees are the espalier and the fan.

MATERIALS & EQUIPMENT

spade

secateurs

garden twine

wire

canes

fruit tree (see pages 152–153)

The espalier

This tree form involves training two or three tiers of shoots at right angles to the main stem. Horizontal wires, 60 cm (24 in) apart, form the support framework. Fruits most commonly grown as espaliers are apples and pears.

1 Plant a maiden whip in late autumn or early winter. As soon as buds appear, cut the main stem back to a bud 45 cm (18 in) from the base.

2 In the first summer, train the resulting shoots along canes fixed to the wires, angling the two lower shoots at 45° to the main stem; lower these shoots to 90° later in the summer.

3 In subsequent winters, the central stem is cut back to a cluster of three buds 30 cm (12 in) above the top tier. Prune back lateral shoots by one-third.

4 In subsequent years, starting in mid-summer, repeat the process, treating the three new shoots arising from the main stem in the same way as those in the first year. Continue until four or five tiers are produced.

5 Any new lateral growths or spurs on the horizontal or vertical stems should then be pruned regularly in the summer and the leading shoots removed to promote fruiting.

The fan

With a fan-trained tree the aim is to produce and train a series of lateral or side shoots, and their side shoots (sub-laterals), that radiate out in an arc from a short leg or stem. This method is most commonly used for the cherry family, including acid and sweet cherries, apricots, peaches and plums, as well as for figs.

1   Make a support framework of horizontal wires fixed to the wall at 20 cm (8 in) intervals, the lowest one 40cm (16 in) above soil level.

2   After planting the maiden tree, just before growth starts in spring, cut back the main stem to a pair of lateral branches about 30 cm (12 in) above the ground. Remove all other shoots, cutting them close to the main stem.

3   In the first summer, tie the two lateral shoots to canes set at 45°, raising them if necessary to increase vigour.

4   In the first winter, cut back the two side branches to a bud about 45 cm (18 in) from the main stem.

5   The next summer, tie in four shoots on each lateral to angled canes. Cut out other shoots.

6   In the second winter, cut back each branch to leave 75 cm (30 in) of mature wood.

7   In the third summer, tie in the new shoots that have developed from the second year's growth to form an even-shaped fan. Prune back any sub-laterals to avoid overcrowding.

lawn care

Lawn care is a year-round task. In spring, as the grass starts to grow, mowing becomes a regular task. To sustain this growth, the lawn needs to be fed and any weeds killed. There is also usually some repair work to do, such as redefining edges or filling any hollows that have formed over winter. The summer season is when the lawn should be at its best and you can enjoy it to its full. However, there are still maintenance tasks requiring attention. In autumn, mowing is reduced, but other jobs, such as scarifying and treating moss, become important. Diseases are also prevalent in the autumn; fungi and insect pests thrive when the soil is warm and the air moist, and this is the time to act to ensure a healthy lawn for the following year.

the essentials

There is a selection of basic tools you will need to keep your lawn in optimum condition. The size and type of lawn you have will dictate some of your choices. However, everyone needs a lawn mower, since regular mowing to keep grass at the correct height prevents it from becoming yellow and uneven and also prevents scalping.

cutting equipment

For mowing the lawn, cylinder and rotary types are capable of creating a striped effect if they are fitted with a roller behind the cutting blades, while the hover type is useful for creating an even cut on awkward-shaped and sloping lawns. Other manual tools are used for neatening edges, either by cutting through the turf or clipping the grass.

Cylinder mowers
Cylinder mowers have spirally arranged cutting blades forming a cylinder. These rotating blades cut against a fixed blade in a scissor-like action. They can be manual or powered.

Rotary mowers
These mowers have one or more blades, or a toughened nylon cord that rotates horizontally at very high speed, slicing through the grass. They work particularly well on long or tough grass.

Hover mowers
Hover mowers are similar to rotary types except that they ride on a cushion of air. They are light and easy to use and are particularly good for small, awkward-shaped, or sloping lawns.

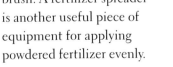

Edging shears
These shears have their handles set at right angles to their cutting blades. They are used from a standing position to trim grass growing over the lawn edge.

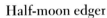

Half-moon edger
This special tool is used for cutting turf and trimming lawn edges. The curved blade is mounted on a spade shaft and handle, making it easy to use standing up.

general equipment

A garden fork is ideal for easing, lifting and spiking the lawn, using the tines to alleviate soil compaction. To rake out moss, collect leaves and remove debris from the lawn, use a fan rake, and for scattering dew, spreading top dressing and breaking up worm casts, use a stiff brush. A fertilizer spreader is another useful piece of equipment for applying powdered fertilizer evenly.

watering equipment

Static sprinkler

A spinning head distributes water in a circular pattern. Coverage depends on the water pressure.

Rotary sprinkler

The rotating arms provide an even distribution of water over a wide area (depending on water pressure). Some sprinklers have adjustable nozzles to regulate the size of the water droplets.

Oscillating sprinkler

A tube with nozzles mounted in a line provides a fan-shaped water pattern. The arm is driven from side to side in an arc, spraying water. The speed of rotation is governed by water pressure.

Pulse-jet sprinkler

A nozzle rotates in a series of pulses, distributing an arc of water to cover all, or parts, of a circular pattern.

Lay-flat seep hose

A flat hosepipe punctured with a series of holes provides a fine spray over the grass at high pressure. At low pressure the water seeps gently from the hose. This system works well in areas of low water pressure, where several hoses can be joined together.

post-winter cutting

1 As soon as the grass shows signs of new growth, use a fan rake to remove all traces of dead grass, debris and worm casts that have accumulated on the lawn during the winter.

2 The grass may be quite long at the beginning of spring so trying to cut the lawn too low may result in clogging the mower, damaging the machine and scalping the grass. Scalping may encourage moss to spread and weeds to grow in the lawn. To avoid this, set the blades to their highest possible setting to encourage growth from the base and root development.

3 Choose a dry day to mow your lawn, since wet grass often produces an untidy effect once it has dried out. Before starting, check there are no stones or branches on the lawn and start mowing by moving forward at a steady pace.

4 Take away the grass clippings. Clean and store the mower, and lower the mower blades ready for the next cut, which will need to be done in about a week.

5 The lawn edge is then re-cut at the beginning of the season with a half-moon edger to redefine the perimeter of the lawn. Place a plank on the edge of the lawn as a guide and to protect the grass. After this, keep the edge trimmed with edging shears.

157

mowing

In order to maintain a healthy lawn, mowing must be carried out regularly throughout the summer. The best approach is to mow little and often, although the frequency of mowing will depend on a number of factors, such as the amount of summer rainfall, the different grasses used to make up the lawn (and how vigorous they are) and the type of lawn required – whether an ornamental backdrop or a hard-wearing play area.

cutting actions

Cylinder mowers

For a good result, the blades of a cylinder mower need to be correctly aligned. This mower type works well on a flat, well-tended lawn but can have problems dealing with long or weedy lawns.

Rotary mowers

The grass is cut by a high-speed, horizontally rotating blade or cord, and cutting height is adjusted by raising or lowering the wheels or rollers. Generally a trouble-free mower design.

Hover mowers

This type of mower has a cutting action identical to that of a rotary. Basic models are inexpensive but do not usually have a grass-collection box, while more expensive and sophisticated models do.

timing

The mowing season usually lasts from mid-spring through to mid-autumn, peaking in the early summer when the grass is growing at its fastest annual rate. After this period, growth will slow down as the grass species and cultivars try to produce flower heads and seed. Drier weather conditions also help to discourage rapid extension growth.

weather

The type of mowing practised depends on the prevailing weather conditions. When the weather has been dry for a long period, or if it is hot and sunny, mow at a slightly higher setting to leave the grass blades longer to provide shade for the roots. This reduces the stress caused by drought and lessens the amount of watering required. After heavy rainfall mow frequently, but at a high setting. Cutting the grass very short, or 'scalping', weakens the shoots and encourages the establishment of moss and weeds. If the lawn is very wet, a hover-type mower can be run over the grass, either at a very high setting or with the blades removed. This will blow the water from the grass and make it sufficiently dry to mow properly within half an hour.

height

Resist the temptation to cut the grass very short in the hope that it will be a long time before it needs cutting again, as this allows moss and weeds to establish themselves while the grass struggles to recuperate. The golden rule is never to reduce the height of the grass by more than one-third at a single cut, and always allow the grass to recover for a couple of days before cutting it again.

Mowing heights and frequencies		
Lawn type	Height	Mowings per week
Very fine ornamental	5 mm (¼ in)	2–3
Average garden	1 cm (½ in)	1–2
Hard-wearing (play area)	2 cm (¾ in)	1

collecting the clippings

Always remove the clippings from the lawn after mowing, since any left behind seldom decompose fully and form a layer of dead grass, or 'thatch', over the soil. This layer can cause yellow patches and prevents water and fertilizer reaching the roots. It also harbours pests and diseases and encourages cast-forming worms. If your mower does not have a box to collect the clippings, remove them with a spring-tine rake. Add them to the compost heap unless the grass has just been treated with chemicals. Bear in mind that taking the clippings away means that more fertilizer has to be used to keep the lawn healthy.

edge trimming

The edges of the lawn need to be trimmed regularly to prevent them becoming ragged and untidy. At the start of the season always cut a clean edge to the lawn with a half-moon edging tool; the best time to do this is after the very first mowing of the season.

1   When cutting a new edge to the lawn, it is easier to achieve a straight line if you use a wooden plank as a guide. Lay the plank on the lawn, close to the edge, and cut against it, clearing the soil and grass away as you work. This should be done only once a year or the lawn will gradually become smaller.

2   After every mowing, the edge can be trimmed with long-handled shears to remove any grass hanging over onto the border or path. For the best effect, cut the grass back as close to the edge as you can. Always remove the grass trimmings and collect them along with the clippings from the mower.

weeds and pests

Weeds not only make a lawn look unsightly, but because of their vigorous growth they can also smother and kill the grass. The more established a weed becomes, the more difficult it is to eradicate. Pests, too, can affect the health of a lawn and need to be dealt with quickly.

mowing to control weeds

Regular mowing will make it difficult for weed seeds blown onto the lawn to establish themselves. Close mowing is effective for controlling many creeping surface weeds, such as clover, daisy, pearlwort, speedwell, trefoil and yarrow, especially if they are spotted before they start to spread. Just before mowing, rake the weeds into an upright position; most of the growth can then be mown off and taken away.

weeding by hand

Tap-rooted weeds, or those that form a flat rosette, such as dandelions, plantain, ribwort and thistles, can be dealt with by hand. Use an old knife with a long blade or a small hand fork to dig or cut out the weed, complete with its tap root. Dig deeply to get the whole root, because if even a tiny piece of the root is left in the soil, the weed may well grow again.

chemical control

The most troublesome lawn weeds are usually too well established to eradicate by mowing or digging out, and you may need to use a selective 'hormone' weed-killer.

1   Measure the area affected to find how much weed-killer you need. Pour the chemical into the sprayer and top up with water as recommended by the manufacturer.

2   Now spray the area to be treated. If only a few weeds are present, you can just spray each one. If the weeds are numerous, systematically work over the whole lawn.

3   Wash out the sprayer thoroughly after use. Within two or three days the weeds will curl up and they can be killed off by mowing. Do not use these contaminated mowings for compost or mulch, since the chemical residue may be harmful to plants.

common weeds

Most lawns suffer from weeds at one time or another – an open expanse of grass is an easy target for wind-borne and bird-borne seeds to land on, where they will quickly develop into weeds. Poor turf and soil preparation is also a common cause for lawn weeds.

Broad-leaved weeds

Symptoms Flat rosettes or spreading weeds that can cause the death of grass, particularly over large areas of the lawn.
Control Eradicate them by applying a selective (hormone) lawn weed-killer in the spring and again in the autumn.

Buttercup   Plantain   Thistle

Weed grasses

Symptoms Dark or pale green vigorous grasses, which colonize the lawn and smother the finer lawn grasses.
Control Paint glyphosate onto the leaves of the coarse grasses and repeat six weeks later if the weeds are still present.

Yorkshire fog   Meadow grass

common diseases

It is a good idea to inspect your lawn regularly for diseases, since the sooner you act the quicker your lawn will return to health. Take good care of your lawn by feeding, aerating and watering it regularly in order to lessen the chances of disease.

Dollar spot

Symptoms This fungal disease only attacks fine-grade ornamental lawns. Small yellow patches of grass gradually merge to form larger, unsightly patches of dead grass.

Control Apply carbendazim- or dichlorophen-based products in the autumn as a preventative measure on lawns containing fescue-type grasses.

Fusarium patch

Symptoms A fungal disease, most prevalent in the autumn, which starts as small yellow patches of grass, gradually merging to form large patches of dead grass.

Control Apply carbendazim- or dichlorophen-based products, spike the lawn and feed with a potash and phosphate-based fertilizer.

Red thread

Symptoms This fungal disease appears in autumn and starts as small irregular patches of bleached-looking grass, which gradually take on a pinkish tinge.

Control Apply carbendazim- or dichlorophen-based products, spike the lawn well and avoid mowing too closely. Feed in late summer rather than autumn.

Fairy ring fungus

Symptoms Two dark circles of lush grass form, with the area between containing dead grass and moss. Toadstools may appear on the outer ring of grass.

Control Apply sulphate of iron to large areas. For smaller areas, dig out the infected area to a depth of 30 cm (12 in) and import new soil.

common pests

Spotting pests quickly is the surest way to prevent them doing lasting damage to your lawn. Once they have become apparent, there are several ways to eradicate them – from chemical methods to removing the offenders by hand.

Earthworms

Symptoms Unsightly coils of sticky brown soil deposits, or 'casts', appear on the lawn.

Control Worm deterrents: lower the pH of the soil with acidic fertilizers. Worm-killers: apply a drench of worm-killer in the autumn as a last resort.

Chafer grubs

Symptoms White flat grubs with a black-brown head, usually curled up into a 'C' shape. Small brown patches of grass appear in spring and summer as the grubs feed on grass roots.

Control Apply a drench of insecticide containing HCH in the autumn.

Leatherjackets

Symptoms These grey-brown legless grubs are found on poorly drained lawns after a wet autumn. In the spring they cause yellow patches from feeding on the roots of the grass.

Control Aerate the lawn, and if necessary apply an insecticide containing HCH.

Moles

Symptoms Large heaps of soil appear on the surface of the lawn, with holes in the lawn occurring as the burrows collapse.

Control An effective method is to reduce the moles' food supply by discouraging worms. Alternatively, call in a mole catcher.

worm management

Most worms prefer a soil temperature of about 10°C (50°F) and will burrow deeper into the soil to maintain this when surface temperatures are colder. Evidence of worm activity tends to be more obvious in the spring and autumn, when they are at their most active. They are rarely seen in summer, since they are resting deeper in the soil.

Beneficial activity of worms

Worms are vital for good soil conditions, since they drag dead plant material, such as grass clippings and thatch, underground and mix it with soil, recycling the nutrients that are present in the decaying matter. They also help the movement of air into the soil as they tunnel and improve drainage.

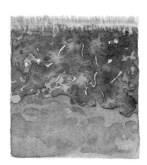

Controlling worms

If you really feel that the only way to have a good ornamental lawn is to reduce the worms in the soil, you can discourage high worm populations by collecting the grass clippings after mowing or by following one of the solutions outlined here.

Worm-killers

Some types of chemical can be applied that will kill the worms that form casts on the soil surface, but will not harm other species of worm. Conveniently, those worms that are killed die in situ and are never seen again. However, it must be stressed that using worm-killers should be considered as a last resort, since worms are more beneficial than not.

Worm deterrents

Worms prefer a soil pH of between 5.5 and 8.5 and dislike acid soils, so lowering the pH of the soil with acidic fertilizers, such as sulphate of ammonia, will encourage the worms to move out of the

lawn and into the surrounding borders. Use a special kit to check pH levels – acid soils are indicated by yellow or orange, neutral is green and alkaline is dark green.

watering

In an average year, a well-kept lawn should be able to survive without watering for at least two-thirds of the year. However, in the height of the summer, or in long dry periods, the lawn may become stressed due to a lack of water and irrigation may be needed. The challenge is to spot the first signs of stress and sort out the problem before it becomes acute.

when to water

A lawn needs to be watered as soon as the first signs of drought start to appear. The symptoms to look for are dull, bluish grass with a hard and fibrous texture and footprints remaining for longer than usual because the grass is limp. If the dry weather persists, the leaves of the grass will gradually shrivel and turn brown and the exposed roots are then in danger of dying off.

how much water to apply

The most common fault is to apply too little water to the lawn, since this encourages the grass to form roots close to the soil surface. These will be the first to dry out in hot weather, making the lawn even more susceptible to drought. Lawns grown on clay soils take much longer to show signs of drought than those grown on light, sandy soils, since clay holds more water than sandy soil. In the height of summer, in hot, dry weather, a lawn can lose about 2.5 cm (1 in) of water over a week. To replace that would take about 27 litres (6 gallons) of water for every square metre (square yard) of lawn.

methods of watering

When watering a lawn, the aim is to replace the water that has been lost in the root zone, rather than on the surface. Wet the soil to a depth of at least 15 cm (6 in); water again when it dries out to a depth of 10 cm (4 in). On very dry soils it is difficult for the water to penetrate and it may form puddles and evaporate, or simply run off on a sloping site. Check the penetration of the water by digging a test hole before and after watering.

To improve drainage on compacted ground, jab the tines of a garden fork into the soil. Work to a depth of 5 cm (2 in) to ensure the hard crust has been thoroughly penetrated.

The most effective method of watering is to use a low-level sprinkler or seep hose, which applies the water slowly and steadily.

feeding

Frequent mowing removes organic matter from the lawn and, when the cuttings are taken away, deprives the grass roots of nutrients. This loss has to be replaced, otherwise the lawn will deteriorate. During the summer, it is quite common to see lawns turning pale green or yellow, which is a sign of nutrient deficiency. This situation can easily be rectified with a fast-acting nitrogen feed to provide the lawn with the boost it needs.

types of fertilizer

To keep the lawn looking green and lush, apply a fast-acting fertilizer, such as sulphate of ammonia, which is high in nitrogen and causes the grass to change colour in 7 to 10 days. This comes in liquid, crystal or dry form. Be careful not to apply too much or you may scorch the grass, which will then turn brown and die.

If the fertilizer is to be applied dry, mix it with soil or sand to avoid scorching the grass. Distribute by hand or fill a special applicator.

applying fertilizer

1   Measure the area of lawn to be fertilized so that you can calculate how much fertilizer is required. Always follow guidelines given by the manufacturer on rates of application.

2   For a liquid fertilizer, measure the correct amount of chemical concentrate or crystals, and pour it into a watering can fitted with a dribble bar. Top up with warm water, as recommended on the container.

3   Work over the lawn systematically to cover the whole area with fertilizer, and walk at a steady pace to ensure even distribution.

4   If there is no significant rainfall within two days after applying the fertilizer, water the lawn thoroughly for at least two hours to prevent the fertilizer scorching the grass.

general maintenance

A lawn is often the largest single feature in a garden, as well as being the most used, but this constant wear and tear can result in even the best-kept lawns beginning to look jaded. Since use of the lawn tends to decline in the autumn, this is the ideal time to carry out a regular and well-planned maintenance programme, ensuring that your lawn is in peak condition throughout the following summer.

soil drainage

Good drainage is essential for maintaining a high-quality lawn. Waterlogging often occurs, however, when the water entering the soil exceeds the amount that drains out, and soils that are compacted or have a high percentage of clay in them are particularly susceptible. The roots of most plants are unable to function properly in waterlogged soil and will eventually die due to a lack of oxygen. As well, wet soils tend to be colder than well-drained ones and this may slow down plant growth in the spring.

Soakaway

There is no point in installing a drainage system if there is nowhere for the water to drain to. So, if you have no natural water outlet, a soakaway must be constructed. This is a rubble-filled pit that holds

the excess water from the surrounding drainage system, and it is constructed in the lowest part of the garden. Usually a pit measures about 1.5 x 1.5 m (5 x 5 ft) and is 1.5 m (5 ft) deep; a layer of coarse rubble sits in the bottom of the pit with a layer of finer gravel just below the soil surface. This is particularly effective on soil that suffers from compaction.

Pipe drains

To make a simple, single-pipe system, lay the pipes in narrow trenches about 15 cm (6 in) wide and 60 cm (24 in) below the surface, on a sloping site. If the site is level, create a fall or slope to encourage the water to drain away quickly. This can be done by laying the pipes 45 cm (18 in) deep at the start of the drain, sloping down to 60 cm (24 in) at the outlet. The pipes are laid on a bed

of gravel and covered over with more gravel, then the trench is filled with a 15 cm (6 in) layer of topsoil.

The 'herringbone' pattern is the most common drainage system used and consists of a main central drain, usually 10 cm (4 in) in diameter with 7.5 cm (3 in) diameter lateral drains running either side of it at an angle of 60°, in the direction of the main drain.

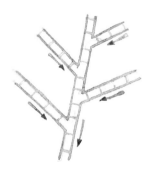

Rubble drains

In small gardens, drainage pipes are not necessary and a simple rubble drain will be sufficient. Narrow trenches, 20 to 30 cm (8 to 12 in) wide and 45 cm (18 in) deep, are used to intercept the water as it passes through the soil, carrying it away from the site. Each trench has a 30 cm (12 in) layer of coarse rubble, followed by 5 cm (2 in) of gravel and 10 cm (4 in) of topsoil.

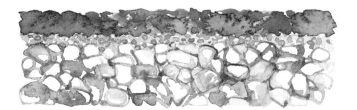

aeration

The basic idea behind aerating the soil is to find some means of allowing oxygen to break through the compacted layer of soil and reach the plant's roots without destroying the existing lawn. In the sequence of lawn-maintenance operations, mowing and scarifying are followed by spiking, and once the holes have been created, a top dressing of bulky material can be spread over the grass and brushed into the prepared holes.

Scarifying

This is the first part of the aeration process and can be tackled at the beginning of autumn, when mowing becomes less frequent and after the dead leaves have been swept away. Scarifying by hand can be done with a wire-tined lawn rake. Remove debris and 'thatch' (the layer of dead grass) by raking the lawn vigorously; then dispose of the rakings. This enables air to penetrate the surface of the lawn and encourages good root growth. If you have a large area of lawn in your garden, you may find it easier to use a mechanical scarifier.

Spiking

Special tine forks with detachable metal spikes can be purchased or hired to aerate your lawn every three years or so. For small areas use a garden fork, especially if the soil is not too severely compacted. Whatever tool you choose, the technique

involves driving channels, either holes or slits, into the zone where the roots grow and down into the soil beneath. This also helps to drain surface water after heavy rain.

1 Start by driving a garden fork into the lawn to a depth of about 10 to 12 cm (4 to 5 in). Gently rock the fork from side to side and ease it out of the ground.

2 This process is then repeated at 20 cm (8 in) intervals across the lawn, working backwards across the lawn to avoid filling in the holes already created.

Top dressing

For free-draining soils, use a top dressing containing two parts peat, four parts loam and one part sand to help improve the water-retaining capacity of the soil.

For slow-draining soils, use a top dressing containing one part peat, two parts loam and four parts sand. This mixture will help to improve the drainage rate of the soil.

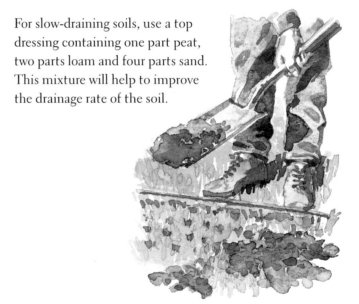

1 After spiking your lawn, apply the top dressing. Use either a special machine or spread the dressing evenly manually with a shovel.

2 Once you have applied the dressing to your lawn, work it into the prepared holes by gently brushing it backwards and forwards.

compaction

During the year, a lawn will be mown, fed, laid on, sat on, walked on and played on. As the air is pressed out of the soil, it becomes compacted. A saying that green keepers and 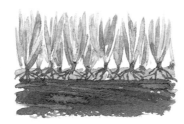 groundsmen will often quote in this situation is: 'Grass grows by the inch, but is killed by the foot.' If the lawn feels hard to walk on and holds water for a long time after it has rained or been watered, there is a strong possibility that the soil beneath is compacted. A compacted lawn looks slightly yellow and the grass appears stunted and thin. Areas of soil also start to become visible. These symptoms are caused when the roots are unable to penetrate through the compacted soil and are left with only a very shallow root system. The lack of air between the particles of soil can cause the death of plant roots, drive away the worm population and impede drainage. The best cure for a compacted lawn is to thoroughly aerate it (see page 166).

moss

The appearance of moss in the lawn is actually a symptom rather than the cause of a poor lawn. Just raking out or applying a moss-killer is not the answer, and the only way to eradicate moss permanently is to remedy the underlying problem. Moss appears when the grass is growing slowly as a result of soil compaction, poor drainage, extremes of pH, or poor light levels, where the lawn is shaded by overhanging trees or piles of fallen leaves.

Mosses with an upright growth habit, green growth at the top and brown stems at the base are symptomatic of dry, acidic soil.

Trailing mosses with a flat growth pattern and pale green foliage and stems are symptoms of a shaded lawn with poor drainage.

Cushion mosses have tiny upright stems and a compact, dense growth habit. They appear in lawns mown too close to soil level.

Moss control

Moss can be eradicated with chemicals spread by a special machine or distributed by hand. Apply when the grass is moist so that the chemical sticks readily to the moss.

1   Do not mow or walk on the lawn for at least two days after treatment. The treated moss will turn black within a few days and after about three weeks the dead moss will turn a golden brown. Any green patches must be immediately treated again.

2   When all of the moss has turned golden brown, you need to rake it out with a fan rake. For larger areas, use a motorized lawn scarifier. Start raking from the edges of the moss patch into its centre to avoid contaminating the areas not infested. Always burn or dispose of the moss, but never compost it – some of the moss may survive and start to spread over the lawn again.

making an
ornamental grass garden

If you do not have the time, or the climate, to grow the fine grasses suitable for a lawn,
it is still relatively easy to create an ornamental grass border by using grasses, sedges and
bamboos. As well as being tough and resilient, grasses vary widely in shape, habit, form
and colour, with architectural qualities making them a striking feature in any garden.

MATERIALS & EQUIPMENT

organic matter

garden fork and spade

granular general-purpose fertilizer

container-grown grasses (see page 170)

hand trowel

watering can

mulch (organic or inorganic)

1   Choosing the site

Ornamental grasses are ideal for the labour-saving border. Most grasses prefer a well-drained sunny site, although some will do well in shade or partial shade and, provided they are hardy, they will tolerate exposed sites quite readily. These plants are suitable for planting in a border, backing onto a wall or fence.

2   Preparing the site

Once you have chosen a suitable site, dig over the soil with a garden fork, removing any weeds, and incorporate plenty of organic matter to improve moisture retention and soil texture. Then mix a base dressing of a granular general-purpose fertilizer into the top 10 cm (4 in) of soil.

3   Positioning the grasses

Use the planting plan below as a guide to positioning the plants in your border. These container-grown grasses will fill a bed measuring about 3 x 1 m (10 x 3¼ ft).

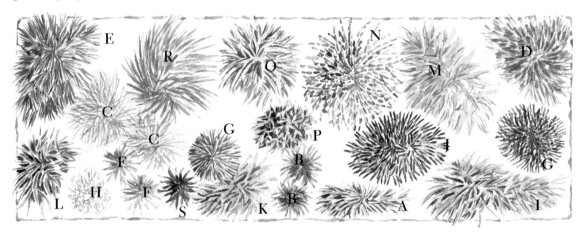

KEY

A *Alopecurus pratensis* 'Aureovariegatus'

B *Carex dipsacea*

C *Carex elata* 'Aurea'

D *Carex kaloides*

E *Carex muskingumensis*

F *Carex testacea*

G *Chionochloa rubra*

H *Deschampsia flexuosa* 'Tatra Gold'

I *Hakonechloa macra* 'Aureola'

J *Imperata cylindrica* 'Rubra'

K *Luzula sylvatica* 'Hohe Tatra'

L *Luzula sylvatica* 'Marginata'

M *Milium effusum* 'Aureum'

N *Miscanthus sinensis* 'Zebrinus'

O *Miscanthus sinensis* var. *purpurascens*

P *Pleioblastus viridistriatus*

Q *Schoenus pauciflorus*

R *Spartina pectinata* 'Aureo Marginata'

S *Uncinia rubra*

4 Planting the grasses

Dig a hole slightly larger than the root ball of the grass to be planted. Gently remove the grass from the container and place it into the planting hole. Position the root ball so that the top is just below soil level and fill in.

5 Firm the plant into place and level the soil around the planting hole before watering thoroughly.

6 Spread a mulch over the soil between the plants, 10 cm (4 in) deep, to suppress weeds. This also prevents the grasses and bamboos from drying out. Protect small plants as you apply the mulch by covering them with a large pot turned upside down, lifting the pots off once you have finished.

Care and maintenance

• In the autumn trim off any old, untidy growth with a scythe or shears and remove it.
• Occasional infestations by aphids can be sprayed with a translocated insecticide.
• Treat the fungal disease 'rust' with a fungicidal spray as soon as orange rusty spots are seen.
• To control invasive plants, a large plastic pot with its base removed can be plunged into the border and the young grass plants planted within the pot.

creating a new lawn

Autumn is a good time to create a new lawn, particularly while the weather is still mild, by preparing the soil and either sowing seed or laying turf. This will establish a sturdy root system slowly over the winter period that will rapidly grow away once spring arrives. Always begin by removing all traces of weed and incorporating plenty of organic matter to improve moisture retention and soil texture.

creating a new lawn from seed

To encourage rapid germination, sow your seed when the soil is warm and dry on the surface but moist underneath. It is a good idea to use a mixture of grass seeds that imparts its specific strengths into the type of lawn required. Do not select too many species, however, since this may lead to uneven germination and patchy growth.

Preparing and sowing the site

1   Start by raking the soil surface with a fine rake, so when the seed is sown it will come into contact with moist soil.

2   Using pegs and string, divide the lawn area into 1 m (39 in) square sections and measure 30 to 45 g (1 to 1½ oz) of seed into a container for each square.

3   Sow the seed evenly over each square. Sow half of the seed across the area, and then the remainder at right angles to the first sowing.

Germination
In good conditions, grass seed will germinate within 10 to 14 days. About three weeks after germination, lightly roll the grass to encourage 'tillering' (new clusters of leaves formed from the base) to thicken up the coverage.

Some suitable lawn seed mixtures

Hard-wearing lawns

10%	Browntop bent
40%	Chewings fescue
20%	Creeping red fescue
30%	Perennial rye grass

Banks and slopes

20%	Browntop bent
30%	Chewings fescue
45%	Creeping red fescue
5%	Timothy

Fine lawns

20%	Browntop bent
40%	Chewings fescue
40%	Creeping red fescue

Quick-growing utility lawns

40%	Chewings fescue
30%	Perennial rye grass
20%	Crested dog's-tail
10%	Rough-stalked meadow grass

Ornamental lawns

20%	Browntop bent
80%	Chewings fescue

Lightly shaded lawns

10%	Browntop bent
30%	Chewings fescue
35%	Creeping red fescue
25%	Smooth-stalked meadow grass

creating a new lawn from turf

For an instant lawn, turf can be used, though this is more expensive than sowing from seed. Turf is best laid in the early autumn when the top growth is slow and the warm, moist soil encourages rapid root growth. Turves are usually cut in sections 1 m x 30 cm (39 x 12 in) and rolled along their length for easy transportation and storage. Do not store the rolls for more than a few days, since the grass will turn yellow due to a lack of light.

1   On a well-prepared site, mark the outside edges of your lawn. Lay out the turves on at least two edges of the area by opening each one out and pressing it firmly into position against the preceding one.

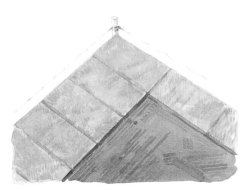

2   Place a plank on the row of turves that has just been laid, to firm the turf into position and to prevent it being damaged. Arrange the turves so that the joins are staggered, like the pattern of bricks in a house wall.

3   When you need to cut a turf to make it fit, lay one piece over the other one, then trim the lower one to size with a knife so that the top piece fits neatly into place.

4   To establish the edges, use a wooden plank or a length of garden line as a guide for straight edges; use a hosepipe or thick rope for curved ones. The best tool to use for cutting the turves is a half-moon turfing iron or, failing that, a sharp spade.

5   Finally, sweep the surface with a stiff brush to lift the flattened grass and remove any loose stones and dirt. If the area is dry, water with a sprinkler.

Mowing
Cut the grass about 10 to 14 days after the turf has been laid, cutting at a height of 4 cm (1½ in). This checks top growth and encourages the roots to penetrate the soil.

planting ground cover

There are plenty of perfectly good alternatives to grass for ground cover that
look equally attractive and also save on mowing. In shady areas, especially beneath trees,
grasses often struggle to survive, but plants such as epimediums, some geraniums, ivies and
Pachysandra will readily cover the soil. Grass on sloping sites and awkward-shaped areas is
notoriously difficult to manage, but plants such as baby's tears (*Soleirolia soleirolii*), shown
here, *Polygonum affine*, *Rubus tricolor* and thymes all spread and surface-root as
they grow, and can be used to cover and stabilize the soil.

MATERIALS & EQUIPMENT

garden fork

weed killer

suitable plants (see page 177)

sheets of black plastic to cover the site

spade

knife

trowel

organic or inorganic mulch

Preparing the site

1 For ground-cover plants to work effectively, the site in which they are going to grow must be well prepared and free from all traces of perennial weeds. Dig over the soil and pull out the weeds, applying chemical weed killers if necessary.

2 Lay out the plants in their containers over the site to determine the position of each one. Avoid spacing them too close together or they will become overcrowded as they establish.

3 After marking the position of each plant with a stick or label, remove the pots and dig the planting holes with a small trowel. Each hole should be large enough to accommodate the plant's entire root system.

4 Before planting begins, place a sheet of heavy-gauge black plastic over the site, cutting it to fit as necessary. Stretch the plastic as tight as you can, then bury the edges, at least 15 cm (6 in) deep, with a spade. It is possible to plant ground-cover plants without using a plastic mulch, but this will involve a great deal of work during the first two years to keep the area free from weeds. Once established, however, the plants cast sufficient shade over the ground to discourage weed seeds from germinating.

5 The air will be colder where the planting holes have been dug, and this will cause condensation to form on the black plastic sheet directly above them. At each point where you see this, cut a cross in the plastic with a sharp knife. Then you can fold back the flaps to reveal the hole beneath.

Planting the ground cover

6 Holding each plant by its stem or leaves, gently remove it from the container.

7 Then take the plant by the root ball and pass it through the plastic into the hole, so that the base sits firmly on the bottom of the hole.

8 Using a trowel, pull the soil back into the hole and firm gently around the plant. Make sure that the surface of the compost is covered by soil, and leave a slight depression around the stem. Water each plant thoroughly.

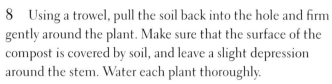

9 Immediately after planting, fold the flaps of plastic back over the soil so that they sit snugly around the base of the plant.

10 The plastic will need to be covered over to protect it from exposure to the sun, to stop it blowing away and to make the area more attractive while the plants are establishing themselves. Use a layer of organic material, such as bark chippings or wood chips, or an inorganic material, such as gravel. Spread it evenly over the plastic and around the base of the new plants.

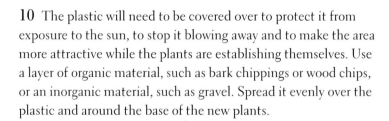

Suitable ground-cover plants

Slow-growing clump-formers	Quick-growing colonizers
Alchemilla mollis	*Ajuga reptans*
Brunnera macrophylla	*Cerastium tomentosum*
Geranium endressii	*Hedera colchica*
Hebe rakaiensis	*Hypericum calycinum*
Marjoram (*Origanum vulgare*)	*Luzula maxima*
Nepeta x *faassenii*	*Pachysandra terminalis*
Persicaria campanulata	*Pleioblastus auricomus*

lawn repairs

If a lawn is used regularly, a certain amount of wear and tear is inevitable; edges become ragged or trodden by walking too close to the lawn edge, and bare patches occur due to mower settings being too low or the removal of a mat-forming weed. Although these blemishes look unsightly, they are quite easy to repair and the lawn can recover its health and appearance remarkably quickly.

repairing a damaged lawn edge

1   Mark out a square around the damaged area with pegs and string and, using the string as a guide, cut out a square of turf from behind the damaged edge using a half-moon edger.

2   Using a spade or turfing iron, cut horizontally under the turf to a depth of about 5 cm (2 in); this will sever the roots, enabling the turf to be lifted up.

3   Lift the section of turf with a spade and turn it 180°, which will place the damaged edge within the lawn and leave a crisp firm outside edge. Gently firm the section of turf back into place until it is level with the surrounding lawn.

4   The original damaged edge is filled with a sandy top dressing or garden soil and firmed until it is the same level as the lawn. Grass seed is then sown onto the top dressing and watered in. If the weather is dry, place a piece of loosely woven hessian sacking over the seeded area to prevent drying out and encourage rapid germination. Within 6 weeks the areas should have fully recovered.

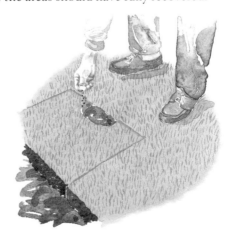

repairing a damaged patch

1 Using a fan rake, rake away all traces of old dead grass and debris to leave the patch of soil on the lawn bare.

2 Then use a hand fork to jab into the surface of the soil to a depth of about 2 cm (¾ in). This breaks up the surface and eases soil compaction.

3 Then, using the fan rake again, rake the surface of the soil to a depth of about 2.5 cm (1 in) to create a fine tilth for a seedbed, ready to take the new grass seed.

4 Sow the grass seed evenly over the prepared area, at a rate equivalent to 30 g/sq m (1oz/sq yd), and immediately after sowing lightly rake the seed into the soil surface. A useful tip is to lay a piece of loosely woven hessian sacking over the seeded area to prevent it drying out, to encourage rapid germination and to deter birds from eating the seed.

repairing humps and hollows

1 Using a half-moon edger, cut two lines into the lawn to form a cross, with the centre of the cross in the centre of the affected area. Make these cuts large enough so that they exceed the area to be levelled.

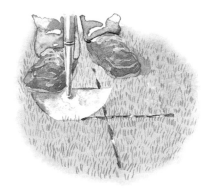

2 Using a spade or turfing iron, cut horizontally under the turf to a depth of about 5 cm (2 in). This will sever the roots, enabling the turf to be lifted up. Cut from the centre of the cross out, into and under the lawn, since this causes less damage to the surface of the lawn.

3 Peel back the four sections of turf to expose the soil beneath; uncovering a large area of soil will allow plenty of room to work within the affected lawn area.

4 For a hollow, fill the space beneath the turf with topsoil and firm gently until it is level with the surrounding soil. For a hump, remove soil until the area is level with the surrounding soil.

5 Finally, carefully replace the folded turf into its original position and firm gently until it is level with the surrounding lawn, or fractionally higher to allow for settling. Cover this area with a 1 cm (½ in) layer of sandy top dressing or sieved garden soil and then brush it into the joints to encourage the grass to re-establish its roots quickly.

introducing plants into your lawn

Though frequently undervalued as merely a flat, green expanse that often requires a great deal of work, the lawn has an important contribution to make to the garden. A lawn is a basic feature of many gardens and can be purely functional. However, the addition of plants within the lawn area can make it a more colourful and highly ornamental feature.

planting bulbs

Groups of bulbs can be planted beneath the turf in your lawn to introduce interest or lead the eye in a particular direction.

1   Use a half-moon edger to cut an 'H' shape in the turf. Cut under the turf with a spade or turfing iron and pull back the edges.

2   Loosen the soil and place the bulbs into the hole in an upright position, and press down into the soil. Then pull the soil back into the hole over the bulbs and firm in.

3   Carefully pace the turf back over the bulbs and firm in place. If the soil is dry, water thoroughly immediately after planting. This will settle the soil around the bulbs and remove any air pockets under the turf.

Allium moly

Galanthus 'S. Arnott'

Ornithogalum arabicum

Suitable bulbs
Allium moly
Snowdrop (*Galanthus*)
Star-of-Bethlehem
　(*Ornithogalum*)

planting trees and shrubs

A single tree or shrub can be used to add a focal point in a garden lawn. Be careful, however, in your choice of plant; trees such as birch (*Betula*) and honey locust (*Robinia*) are a good choice as they have a thin canopy and cast only a little shade over the grass.

1   With canes and string mark out a circle for the hole to at least twice the width of the plant's root system.

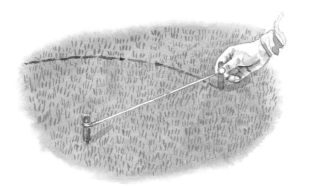

2   Remove the turf with a spade and stack it away from the working area.

3   Dig a hole that is at least twice the width of the plant's root system and deep enough to accommodate all of the roots.

4   Using a garden fork, break up the soil in the bottom of the hole. This will allow the new roots to spread into the surrounding soil and so help the plant to become established more quickly.

5   Taking the plant by its stem, carefully place it into the centre of the prepared hole, and use a bamboo cane to check that the plant is level with the surrounding soil.

6   Start to back-fill the hole with the soil that was removed, spreading it evenly around the roots. Shake the stem of the tree to settle the soil between the roots. This will also remove any air pockets around the roots.

7   Continue filling the hole with layers of soil, periodically shaking the tree stem, and firm each layer with your boot heel until the hole has been filled to its original level.

8   Apply a top dressing of fertilizer to the soil around the plant and mix this into the top 5 cm (2 in). This will gradually be washed down into the root zone.

making a herb walkway

The use of herbs was very popular in medieval England for carpeting green walkways. Chamomile was widely used, as was thyme, which has the added qualities of being covered in a carpet of pinkish-purple flowers in the summer and having a wonderfully aromatic smell. Growing a whole lawn can be expensive and time consuming, since you would need hundreds of plants to create an instant display, so creating walkways around the garden is a much simpler method of introducing small stretches of these attractive plants.

MATERIALS & EQUIPMENT

organic matter

general-purpose fertilizer

trowel, garden fork and rake

suitable herbs (see page 185)

watering can

shears

Soil preparation

1 Herb lawns will usually occupy the same site for many years, which means that the soil must be well cultivated before planting begins. Dig over the soil and remove all weeds to reduce problems when the lawn is establishing. Incorporate plenty of organic matter to improve moisture retention and texture.

2 Add a dressing of general-purpose fertilizer and mix it into the top 10 cm (4 in) of soil. Then rake the site level.

Planting

3 Choose your herb (here we are illustrating lawn chamomile, but see opposite for other suitable plants) and space the offsets about 15 to 30 cm (6 to 12 in) apart – closer spacing simply means that the lawn will establish quicker. Start by digging a planting hole large enough to accommodate the complete root system. Avoid planting when the soil is wet and sticky. This can lead to compaction, which may impede plant establishment.

4 Hold each plant by the stem or leaves and gently remove it from its tray or pot – if the plants come in clumps, you may need to separate them with a knife, but leave as much soil as possible around the roots.

5 Place the plant in the hole with the base of the root ball firmly on the floor of the hole, making sure that the top of the hole is level with the top of the root ball.

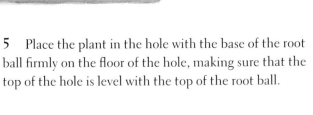

6 Using a trowel, pull the soil back into the hole around the plant and firm it gently into place. Make sure that the surface of the root ball is covered by soil.

7 Immediately after planting, water the new 'lawn' to settle the plants and help them establish quickly.

Maintaining the herb lawn

8 Very little mowing is required for many plants and they need only an occasional trim. Use shears or a rotary mower, with the blades set at a height of 5 cm (2 in), and trim away any long or straggly growth that is spoiling the overall appearance of the lawn.

9 Hand weeding is the only effective method of control in a herb lawn, since there is no acceptable chemical available that will kill the weeds without harming the lawn-making plants – some weeds, such as yarrow, are very close relatives of the lawn plants.

Other plants suitable for a non-grass lawn

Buttonweed (*Leptinella atrata*)

Chamaemelum nobile 'Treneague'

Corsican mint (*Mentha requienii*)

Lawn chamomile (*Chamaemelum nobile*)

Pennyroyal (*Mentha pulegium*)

Wild thyme (*Thymus serpyllum*)

T. serpyllum 'Elfin'

pond care

The secret of successful pond care is doing the right thing at the right time. The pond calendar year really begins in spring, as water temperatures rise, fish become more active and frogs come out of hibernation and begin to breed. Many water plants and marginals are also propagated at this time of year. The summer should be the time to sit back and enjoy the pond, but if left to their own devices, many of the plants will become too large, crowding out their less vigorous neighbours, so plants have to be lifted and divided. It is all too easy to put the pond to the back of your mind once the water lilies have gone over, but autumn preparation will help to determine how well the pond and its contents survive the winter.

pond maintenance

General pond maintenance tends to be fairly minimal if carried out on a regular basis, and you need not empty the pond every year unless it has been neglected. After a number of years, however, silt and debris will accumulate on the floor of the pond, which may lead to pollution levels so bad that both plants and fish begin to suffer. But the water of even a healthy pond is quite literally alive with masses of microscopic plants and other organisms. In the summer, unfortunately, some of them can multiply so rapidly that they have a detrimental effect on the quality of the water. Weeds are also at their most prolific during the summer season. Both can have an adverse effect on the pond plants as well as the fish, so keep a watchful eye and resolve any problems as soon as they become apparent. Leaks may also occur as a result of frost damage, ground subsidence or heave, or even deterioration through age. Any leaks must be dealt with as soon as you notice them.

water colour

Brown, murky water is often the sign of a healthy ecosystem, since it usually means that the fish are actively feeding at the the bottom of the pond or that they are busily breeding. If the water is blue or black, however, or has a thick whitish scum floating on the surface and foul-smelling bubbles, the pond has probably become polluted by rotting vegetation on the pond bottom. This robs the water of oxygen and may kill fish and water snails. The only long-term solution to this is to drain the pond and clean it out (see opposite).

1   First remove the fish and plants from the pond and store in buckets of water. Drain the pond using a pump, or siphon off the water.

2   The debris that has collected in the bottom can then be scooped out and the lining cleaned. Refill the pond, but before returning the plants and the fish, allow the water to settle and warm up slightly.

pond water pH

Ideally the pond water should be slightly acid to alkaline, that is between 6.5 and 8.5 on the pH scale. If your water gives a higher or lower reading than this, the plants and fish may suffer. Check the pH level regularly with a special kit available from pet stores or some garden centres. You can use hydrated lime to raise the pH, but add only a small amount at a time to allow the pond life to adapt to the new conditions.

water levels

In hot, dry weather, the water level in the pond can drop by as much as 5 cm (2 in) over a week due to the effects of evaporation. Topping up the water regularly will help to prevent the liner, especially if it is plastic, cracking in the heat. The addition of fresh water will also help to keep the fish and plants healthy. When topping up, allow the water to cascade into the pond from a height of about 90 cm (36 in). This creates the turbulence that is necessary to introduce more oxygen into the water.

pond cleaning

When a thorough clean is required, choose a mild day in late spring, when the water is clear and it is easy to see the plants and fish in the pond. Temporary storage containers for the plants and fish can include barrels, buckets or even large plastic bags.

1   Store any fish taken from the pond in containers placed in the shade, and keep them in water consisting of half clean water and half pond water. This helps to prevent the fish suffering from shock or stress.

2   Remove as many of the plants as possible before lowering water level, taking out the marginal plants first, the deep-water aquatics when some of the water has been drained away, and the floaters and oxygenators when they are within easy reach.

3   Completely drain the pond of water. To do this, use an electric pump, bail out or siphon off the water.

4   Then remove all silt and debris from the floor of the pond and scrub the walls with a stiff-bristled brush, regularly dipping it in clean water, but take care not to damage the lining of the pond.

5   After the pond has been cleaned, allow the sides to dry for a few hours. This will kill off any pest and disease residue that may have escaped the cleaning process. Refill the pond with slow-running water.

6   Add the plants to be submerged by lowering them gently into the water when it is almost up to the required level. Add the marginals and floating plants last once the water has started to clear. Do not introduce the fish until the water is almost clear, since they may suffocate due to the particles in the cloudy water clogging their gills.

spotting and repairing a leak

If the water level in your pond falls, do not automatically assume that it has a leak, as this may be due to surface evaporation, especially in hot or windy weather. A constant drop in water level during cool, still weather is often the first indicator that your pond is leaking, and one of the commonest causes of damage to the pond liner is frost damage, which usually shows up in the spring. Allow the water level to fall and stabilize – this indicates the level of the damaged area. The first stage is to empty the pond: follow steps 1 to 3 as for 'Pond Cleaning' (see page 189). Then brush away dirt or weed residue and allow to dry.

Repairing flexible liners

1   Cut a patch from a liner repair sheet at least twice as long and twice as wide as the damaged area. Clean the patch and the damaged area with methylated spirits (to ensure good adhesion).

2   Apply a liberal covering of waterproof bonding cement or double-sided waterproof adhesive to both the patch and the damaged area of the liner.

3   When the adhesive feels 'tacky', place the patch over the damaged area and smooth down to ensure good bonding and remove any air bubbles. Check the repair after 24 hours, and if it is firmly bonded to the liner, refill the pond (see steps 5 and 6 in 'Pond Cleaning').

Concrete liner

1   Using a hammer and mason's chisel, chisel out some of the concrete around the crack to make it a little wider than the original damaged section – this will help to strengthen the final repair.

2   Brush out all loose dirt and debris from the crack and carefully fill the crack with a special waterproof mastic cement.

3   Once the mastic cement is dry, paint the whole lining of the pond with two or three coatings of waterproof pond sealant. Leave this to dry for at least 24 hours, and then refill the pond.

making a small pond

In many respects, the basic question about making a pond is a simple one – how to make a hole in the ground that will hold water for long periods of time. The solution is to line the hole with some form of waterproof material, and in this respect there is a wealth of choice, including concrete, flexible and semi-rigid liners and moulded pre-formed liners. Flexible liners are the most satisfactory solution, since they can be moulded into any shape. They are also the most economical method of lining a pond, as well as being the lightest for handling.

MATERIALS & EQUIPMENT

length of hose or rope

spade

plank and spirit level

old carpet or fibreglass insulation material to fit hole

synthetic rubber or plastic lining sheet to fit hole

slabs or bricks for edge

mortar

pond plants (see page 194)

1   Mark out the shape of the pond using a length of garden hose or thick rope. Consider the shape and size in proportion to your garden. Dig out the soil to a spade's depth – this is the correct depth for the first layer of shelves, which is where the marginal plants will be sited.

2   Now excavate the rest of the hole to the required depth. For an average-sized garden pond, this will be about 50 to 60 cm (20 to 24 in). As you dig, take care to form any shelves around the sides that will be needed for positioning submerged plants later on.

3   Using a plank and spirit level, make sure that the rim of the pond is level. It is particularly important to get the pond horizontal if the ground is uneven. Compact the surfaces of the hole, including the base, sides and shelves.

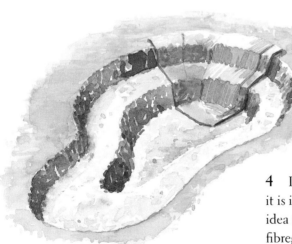

4   If the soil contains sharp stones, these may puncture the liner once it is in place. If they cannot easily be removed from the pond, it is a good idea to line the surface of the hole with two layers of old carpet or fibreglass loft insulation material.

• Bog plants should be placed around the edges in permanently moist soil.

• Marginals are planted in shallow water, either on shelves around the edges or raised on bricks.

• Deep-water aquatics and water lilies have their containers placed on the bottom of the pond with their foliage either submerged, or, as with the flowers of water lilies, floating on the surface.

• Floaters can simply be placed on the surface of the water where they will move freely around the pond in the wind.

5 Now measure the hole to determine the amount of liner needed: it should measure the maximum length plus twice the maximum depth, by the maximum width plus twice the maximum depth. Then add 30 cm (12 in) to the width and length to allow for the flaps around the top edge. Cut out the liner and spread it over the excavated hole that will form the pond, and place weights, such as bricks or rocks, around the edges of the liner to hold it taut and in position.

6 Slowly fill the pond with water to stretch the liner and press it against the contours of the excavated hole. Cut any surplus sections from the liner, leaving a margin of 30 cm (12 in) over the rim of the hole.

7 Edge the rim of the pond with a row of slabs or bricks laid on a bed of mortar. This edging should overlap the rim of the pond by 7 to 8 cm (3 in), to hide the liner. Make sure that no mortar falls into the pond water, since this will harm the fish and plants when they are finally introduced.

8 If you are installing a fountain, stand a submersible pump on the floor of the pond to circulate the water and spray it out of the fountain head. Most ponds do not need a filtration system. If you have large amounts of fish and plants, however, you can fit a filter onto the suction inlet on a submersible pump.

9 Before you introduce any new pond plants, let the water stand for several days so that the temperature reaches that of the outside air. Decide which plants you want and prepare them for the pond. Finally, place them in suitable positions in and around the water.

introducing new plants

Aquatic plants should be moved or transplanted while they are actively growing, since they re-establish better if moved during the growing season. The best time to move them is therefore the late spring or early summer, since this gives them a long time to establish themselves in their new surroundings before the onset of winter.

planting aquatics

Most aquatics are planted and grown in submerged basket-like containers. These give the water gardener a greater degree of control over the growing environment and make the plants more readily accessible for inspection and propagation. The usual material used for containers is heavy-gauge rigid plastic – wood and metal containers should be avoided because they may produce toxins harmful to fish and other water life.

If you are planting water lilies, trim any rotting or dead sections of rootstock and any damaged leaves before planting.

1   Line the mesh container with sacking or heavy-gauge paper, to stop the compost spilling out through the mesh.

2   Half-fill the basket with compost and trim off any surplus liner around the outside of the container.

3   Place the plant firmly into the centre of the basket, add more compost and pack it around the plant so that it is held firmly in position.

4   Fill the basket until the compost is 2 to 3 cm (1 in) from the rim and top up with a 1 cm (½ in) layer of gravel over the compost.

5   Water the container thoroughly to soak the plant and help settle the compost around the roots.

6   To lower the basket into the pond, it is a good idea to attach string handles to the sides of the basket, so you do not have to drop it in position.

summer plantings

Although aquatic plants are best planted in the late spring and early summer, you can delay planting until the late summer in most cases. Those that are planted later will simply have less time to become established before the winter, although some may not fully recover until the following spring. Choose different types of plants – floaters, oxygenators and deep-water aquatics – to create a balanced environment within the pond, and feed them as they develop to maintain their health.

pond and bog plants

For a water feature of any size to be effective and provide the ideal environment for fish and other pond life to live and breed successfully, plants must be present. They provide food, shade and shelter as well as helping to keep the water sweet and clear.

Floaters

Plants in this group have their leaves and stems on the pond surface, with their roots submerged. They reduce the amount of light reaching the water and so help to exclude algae.

Deep-water aquatics

Growing up from a depth of about 60 cm (24 in), these provide shelter for fish and help to keep the water clear.

Bog plants

These are ideal for a marshy area surrounding the pond, since they prefer a rich, peaty, damp soil that will keep their roots cool. Most bog plants are herbaceous perennials and benefit from being lifted and divided every three years or so.

Marginals

This diverse group of plants thrives in shallow water or damp soil, depending on the species. Marginals are largely decorative, although they do attract insects and provide cover for other wildlife.

Oxygenators

These types of plant help to keep the water aerated by releasing oxygen as a by-product of photosynthesis. Keep them fully submerged, with only the flowers on or above the water's surface. Aim to include about three oxygenating plants per square metre (square yard) of pond surface.

Deep-water aquatics
Aponogeton distachyos
Nymphaea
Nymphoides peltata

Bog plants
Lobelia x *gerardii*
Matteuccia struthiopteris

Floaters
Hydrocharis morsus-ranae
Lemna trisulca
Stratiotes aloides

Marginals
Calla palustris
Juncus effusus 'Spiralis'

Oxygenators
Chara aspera
Elodea canadensis
Myriophyllum spicatum

propagation

Many water plants will be flowering and growing rapidly in the summer season, often providing suitable material with which to increase your stocks, whether from seeds or cuttings. Some may even have exceeded their allotted area and will need lifting and dividing into smaller plants to maintain a balanced population and prevent overcrowding. For many of these tasks, the earlier in the summer that they are carried out, the more rapidly the individual plants and the pond as a whole will recover.

seed-raised plants

Many of the bog plants and marginals around the edge of the pond can be increased by raising new plants from their seeds, collected after flowering. In most cases, these seeds can be sown fresh, immediately after collection, but they may need some protection over the winter; seeds of pickerel weed (*Pontederia*), for instance, will not germinate until the following spring.

Seed sowing

1   Select a seed tray (modular trays are best if seedlings are to stay in the tray a long time) and fill with compost. Firm gently to within 1 cm (½ in) of the rim. For very fine seeds, sieve a thin layer of compost over the surface.

2   Sow the seed as evenly as possible over the surface. Place larger seeds individually on the compost and press them in lightly.

3   Sieve a thin layer of fine compost over the seeds and firm the compost gently. Press very fine seeds gently onto the surface, rather than try to cover them with more compost, or they may become too deeply buried.

4   Remember to write the name of the plant and the date the seeds were sown on a label and insert it at the end of the tray.

5   Place the seed tray in a shallow container of water so that the compost takes up water by capillary action. Then allow the surplus water to drain away. This method does not disturb the seeds, making it much safer than overhead watering with a can.

6   Cover the seed tray with a piece of clear glass and a sheet of newspaper to provide the seeds with shade and to prevent the compost from drying out. Place the completed tray in a propagating case or a cold frame to provide a warm, humid environment that will encourage the seeds to germinate.

cuttings

The method of propagation most commonly used for marginal plants and some deep-water aquatics, as well as for bog plants, is by taking cuttings. For fully hardy plants, if you are looking to increase your stock or keep more vigorous plants in check, the best time to take cuttings is in early to mid-summer when plants are growing strongly. Taking cuttings of your less hardy specimens is, however, an essential safeguard. Cuttings should be overwintered somewhere frost-free to ensure that at least some of the stock survives if the parent plants are killed as a result of the cold weather. Oxygenators, deep-water aquatics and marginal plants with thicker roots are best propagated by division (see opposite). Floating plants, which can often be simply propagated from offsets (see opposite), are particularly susceptible to damage caused by cold weather.

Marginal plants

1   To take cuttings from marginals, select non-flowering shoots and then remove the lower leaves and trim back to about 8 cm (3 in) long. Cutting just below a leaf joint helps the development of roots.

2   Insert the cuttings into plastic pots filled with loam-based compost, making holes for the cuttings with a dibber or pencil. Stand the base of the pot in a saucer of water to keep the compost permanently wet.

3   Keep the cuttings in a cool, partially shaded place. For the first week, cover the cuttings with a polythene bag to reduce the risk of the compost drying out.

Deep-water aquatics

1   Take your cuttings in early to mid-summer when the shoots are about 10 to 12.5 cm (4 to 5 in) long. Select non-flowering shoots, remove the lower leaves and trim them to just below a leaf joint (node) to produce a cutting about 7 to 8 cm (about 3 in) long.

2   The cuttings can be planted singly or arranged in bunches of six to eight cuttings, tied together at the base with string.

3   Plant the clump or stem into a mesh basket container suitable for a pond. Fill it with loam-based compost up to the rim and make a planting hole. Insert the plants and firm them in. Then stand the base of the pot in a saucer of water to keep the compost permanently wet and keep the cuttings in a cool, partially shaded place. Position them in the pond in 2 or 3 weeks time.

division

Dividing water lilies

1 Lift the plant to be divided from the pond, then gently remove it from its container. Break the rhizome into two or three sections, each with roots, stems and shoots.

2 Wash each section of rhizome thoroughly to make sure that all of it is clearly visible. Using a sharp knife, carefully cut away any rotting or diseased sections of rhizome and remove any old or weak-looking stems and shoots. Cut off any dead or damaged leaves.

3 Cut the healthy divisions into smaller segments. Keep in a bucket of water until ready to replant to stop them drying out.

4 Replant the new divisions in mesh containers and then reintroduce them into the pond, where they will re-establish.

Bud cutting

1 To produce numerous water lily plants from one rhizome, cut off young shoots arising from a growth bud (called 'eyes').

2 Plant the 'eyes' in small baskets of loam-based compost and submerge in containers of water, so that the compost is only just covered. In the following spring, the 'eyes' will be large enough to be planted in the pond.

Simple division

1 Lift the plant to be divided from the pond, complete with its container, then gently tip it out of its container. For bog plants, simply lift the plant from the soil with a hand fork.

2 Wash the plant thoroughly to make sure all of it is clearly visible. Inspect the plant and remove any rotting or diseased sections and discard any old or weak stems and shoots.

3 Divide the clump of roots carefully into sections, keeping the young, healthy divisions in a bucket of water to prevent them drying out. Replant the divisions into mesh containers suitable for the pond. Trim back any damaged leaves and stems. The older, less vigorous sections of the plant can then be discarded.

Offsets

For floaters, lift the individual plants out of the water, then carefully break off the young healthy pieces of plant you wish to keep, and place them back in the pond. Any old sections of plant or pieces that you do not need can simply be discarded.

making a pebble pond

A pebble pond with a fountain of water jetting through the centre makes an unusual and attractive feature in any garden, and can be adapted in size to suit the space available. A metal or plastic tank, or even a bin, is simply inserted into the ground to act as a reservoir, and to house a submersible pump; the decorative pebbles are then suspended above it on a metal grille. Add shells to the collection of pebbles, if you have any, so that the water splashing over them highlights their shiny surfaces, as well as bringing out any interesting colours or markings.

MATERIALS & EQUIPMENT

peg and string

garden spade

hardcore and sand

60 x 45 x 56 cm (24 x 18 x 22 in) tank or bin made from plastic or galvanized steel

flexible pond liner

submersible pump

waterproof tape

rigid pipe

strong metal grille

pebbles

1 Begin by marking out the shape of the finished pond in your chosen site, which should be clear of all vegetation and large stones. Measure out a circle with a radius of about 60 cm (24 in) by fixing string of this length to a central peg and marking around it (adjust the radius if you wish to make the pond smaller or larger). You may find it easier to use a trowel to mark the circumference in the soil. Then, using a spade, take off the topsoil to a depth of 8 cm (3 in) within the marked circle.

2 To make a hole for the tank, mark a rectangle inside the circle; this needs to be about 60 x 45 cm (24 x 18 in), or slightly larger than the tank. Dig this hole to a depth of 63 cm (25 in), or about 8 cm (3 in) deeper than your tank. Use a marked stick to check the depth of the hole as you work.

3 Place a layer of hardcore about 8 to 10 cm (3 to 4 in) deep in the bottom of the hole and ram it in. Cover this over with a layer of sand to provide a solid base for the tank.

4 Lower the tank into the pit, so that it sits squarely on the bottom. Make sure that the rim is just below soil level. Fill in the spaces around the outside of the tank with soil to steady it in position.

5 Build up the soil on all four sides so that it slopes upwards from the tank to the outer circle. Along the two long sides of the tank flatten the ground to make two strips, 8 cm (3 in) wide; this will form a level base for the grille. Spread a layer of sand over the soil to act as a buffer for the pond liner.

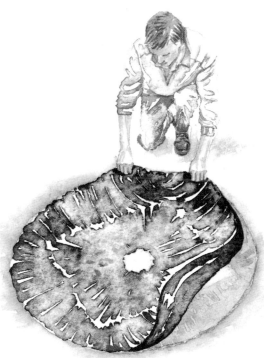

6   Cut a circle of flexible pond liner 8 cm (3 in) larger in diameter than the circle on the ground, then measure and cut a 15 cm (6 in) diameter hole in its centre to accommodate the submersible pump. Lay the piece of pond liner in position, with the hole sitting over the centre of the tank.

7   Lower the submersible pump into the tank so that it rests on the bottom. Run the cable from the pump over the liner, fastening it in place with waterproof tape. Connect a length of rigid pipe to the outlet pipe on the pump so that it sits slightly above the level of the tank; this will act as a fountain head.

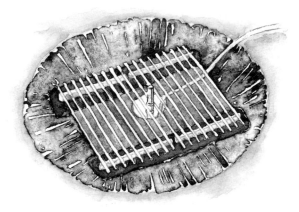

8   To provide the support for the pebbles, lay a strong metal grille, such as a foot-scraper or a piece of stout wire mesh, into position across the top of the tank. Where the edges come into contact with the liner, place extra off-cuts of liner underneath the metal to prevent it from puncturing the material. Adjust the grille so that the fountain head on the pump protrudes between the metal bars.

9   Fill the tank with water, covering over the submersible pump. Switch on the pump to check and adjust the pressure; if your pump will not adjust, raise it on bricks to increase the pressure.

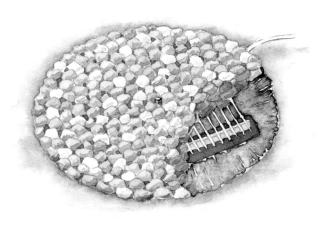

10   Finally, place a layer of pebbles over the grille and the collar of pond liner, filling all gaps. Cut away any excess liner protruding beyond the edge of the circle. Turn the pump on again so that water shoots from the fountain onto the surrounding pebbles, before flowing back into the sunken water tank.

care of established plants

The plants growing in and around the pond will require annual maintenance in the spring. As the season progresses, the water in the pond will gradually rise in temperature, encouraging aquatic plants and marginals to show the first visible signs of growth. However, this is a time for extreme caution, with the weather and air temperature, in particular, being very changeable.

spring tasks

Once established, most pond plants require little attention. Watch out for frost damage at the beginning of the season, however, when the shoot tips and flowers may be scorched by low temperatures or cold winds. Remove any discoloured or withered leaves to encourage the plant to recover – this is important, since any plant debris allowed to accumulate in the water can lead to a shortage of oxygen, which will be harmful to the fish.

Different types of pond plants have different functions in maintaining the natural balance within the pond. Check that your plants are in the right positions and numbers to suit the pond size and environment.

deep-water aquatics

These plants are grown in containers and placed in the bottom of the pond – it is a good idea to cover them with a top dressing of gravel to help weight them down. They will grow up from a depth of 45 to 60 cm (18 to 24 in) and their leaves stretch up and float on the surface. They are useful for providing shelter for the fish as well as a place for them to spawn. Also, the leaves help to keep the water clear, since they deprive algae in the water of food and light. Some of these plants will grow quite happily in moving water and so can be submerged near a fountain or water course; others are particularly well suited to conditions of partial shade or deep water.

Deep-water aquatics	
Aponogeton distachyos	*Nymphoides indica*
Euryale ferox	*Orontium aquaticum*
Nuphar advena	

bog plants

These plants thrive in a rich, peaty, damp soil and they grow best when their roots are in cool, damp conditions close to water. Most of these plants are herbaceous perennials and will need lifting and dividing every three years or so. Grow them close to the pond's edge where they provide shade for the young fish to congregate.

Iris ensata 'Chancellor'

Bog plants	
Anemone rivularis	*Iris ensata*
Cardamine pratensis	*Lobelia cardinalis*
Hosta	*Primula alpicola*

floaters

These plants provide a decorative cover on the surface of the pond, since they float with their leaves and stems above the water with their trailing roots submerged. There are two basic types: the larger-leaved types, such as water chestnut (*Trapa natans*), and the far smaller-leaved floaters, which include ivy-leaved duckweed (*Wolffia*) and fairy moss (*Azolla caroliniana*). The smaller-leaved floaters tend to be very invasive, and in warm conditions these plants can increase rapidly and almost take over the surface of the pond, especially if the spring is mild and moist. Keep them in check by regularly removing any excessive growth.

Floaters
Azolla caroliniana
Eichhornia crassipes
Hydrocharis morsus-ranae
Lemna trisulca
Stratiotes aloides
Trapa natans
Utricularia vulgaris
Wolffia

marginals

Purely decorative, this group of plants does not really contribute to the ecological balance of the pond in the way that other groups of water plants do. Most will grow well in a depth of 15 to 30 cm (6 to 12 in) of water. Marginals growing close to the pond do better if they are lifted and divided every third year, like most other herbaceous perennials.

Marginals
Acorus gramineus
Caltha leptosepala
Decodon verticillatus
Iris laevigata
Mentha aquatica
Ranunculus lingua
Sparganium erectum
Thalia dealbata

Decodon verticillatus

oxygenators

These plants have leaves that absorb carbon dioxide and minerals and, despite their common name, these functions are far more important than their role as oxygen producers. They are also very important for the clarity and quality of the pond water. They should be fully submerged with only the flowers on or above the surface of the water. Plant oxygenators in soil-filled containers, but it is best to keep different species separate to avoid competition. They also provide perfect shelter for fish, as well as food. To create the right balance, there should be about three plants to each square metre (square yard) of water surface.

Oxygenators
Callitriche hermaphroditica
Egeria densa
Fontinalis antipyretica
Mentha cervina
Myriophyllum aquaticum
Potamogeton crispus

water lilies

This group consists of one genus (*Nymphaea*), with a submerged rootstock and roots up to 1.2 m (4 ft) deep, depending on the species. The leaves float on the surface and the flowers, which come in a wide range of colours, are held on or above the water's surface. They prefer full sun and still water and provide perfect shelter for pond fish.

Water lilies
Blue lotus
    (*Nymphaea caerulae*)
Nymphaea 'Aurora'
Nymphaea tetragona
White water lily
    (*Nymphaea alba*)

Nymphaea tetragona

autumn and winter care

Good hygiene is essential to prevent the accumulation of debris and leaves in the bottom of the pool. Such debris uses up supplies of oxygen, harming pond life and fish. Also, the formation of ice can crack rigid pool liners, such as concrete or brick, and can scuff the liner; ponds with sloping sides and flexible liners are better able to withstand frost damage than are ones with vertical sides.

cleaning and hygiene

An oily film on the surface of the water indicates rotting foliage below. Draw a sheet of paper kitchen towel over the surface to soak up the oil.

To remove leaves that have landed on the pond, skim a large sieve through the water, or suspend a net above the pond and empty it regularly.

Dilute the water to prevent the build-up of toxins; suspend a hose above the pond to lower the water pressure, so as not to scare the fish.

frost protection

Pumps can be replaced with a pool heater, which floats on the surface of the water, ensuring that in severe weather at least one area of the pool does not completely freeze over. Check the heater at least once a week to make sure it is not becoming too warm. A low-tech alternative is to float a plastic ball in the pool – it will move about in even the slightest breeze and thus help to stop ice forming. In very cold weather, when the surface freezes over, pour hot water over the ball to melt a little ice and allow oxygen to enter the pond water and toxic gases to be released.

pump care

Lift out pumps and clean them of algae, silt or weed, then wash the inner chamber. Filters can be washed and soaked in a solution of mild detergent to kill off any fungi and bacteria, but make sure that you flush out all detergent before the pump is reused, since the chemical solution may harm the fish. Leave a large pump in place, but run it for half an hour each week to remove any sediment.

plant care

When it comes to caring for your pond plants in the autumn, always assume that the oncoming winter will be a severe one and prepare the pond accordingly. Plants such as water lilies need little or no winter preparation, since they are hardy enough to overwinter outside. However, the pygmy types of water lily, grown in shallower water, do run the risk of frost damage if the winter is severe. To protect them, drain the water away, pack 15 cm (6 in) of straw around the plant and container, and return it to the pond.

Lift tender plants, such as water chestnuts, water hyacinths and water lettuces, and store them in buckets or tubs of water in a frost-free place during the winter.

Remove and divide large, frost-tender specimens before the first hard frost, saving the young, healthier sections of the plant that will survive the storage period.

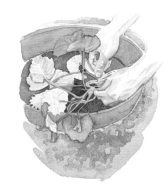

Cut down marginal plants by two-thirds and remove the browned foliage, but never cut them below the water line if they have hollow stems, since they will not survive.

fish care

Careful and thorough conditioning of pond fish can determine not only their survival through an oncoming winter, but also their ability to breed in the following year. The warmest layer of water is at the bottom of the pond, so as the season progresses the fish are seen less and less as they prefer the warmer water lower down. To compensate for the lack of plant cover within the pond, lay a few 10 cm (4 in) diameter clay drain pipes on the bottom or side shelves to make resting and hiding places for the fish, away from predators such as cats or herons. Fish are cold-blooded and tend to stop feeding when the water temperature drops below 5°C (41°F). Feed the fish regularly in early autumn but as they become sluggish, cease feeding.

Temperature tolerance

Each fish species has a temperature range within which it can survive, reproduce and grow. Coldwater fish live a normal and active life at temperatures of 4°C (39°F), which is why they are seen less often in colder weather. These fish can survive at temperatures as low as 0°C (32°F). However, some of the more exotic fish species are unable to survive outdoors over a severe winter and must be housed indoors before the first frosts occur.

Fish species	Lowest water temperature
Goldfish	4–10°C (39–50°F)
Golden orfe	0°C (32°F)
Golden rudd	0°C (32°F)
Golden tench	0°C (32°F)
Green tench	0°C (32°F)
Koi carp	0°C (32°F)
Mirror carp	0°C (32°F)
Shubunkin	4–10°C (39–50°F)

pond weed

As light levels increase in the spring, not only do the ornamental plants begin to grow, but so do the weeds. New ponds, where the natural water balance is not yet fully established, are particularly susceptible, but it is worth waiting for the pond to settle before taking any drastic action to correct the situation. The introduction of healthy plants, including oxygenators, helps to starve weeds of necessary light and nutrients and should help to check their growth. However, you will almost certainly encounter some that appear to be increasing and will need to be eradicated.

Blanket weed

This is an algae that uses light and the nitrogen in the water to grow rapidly in mid-spring. Thick layers of blanket weed can be effectively cleared by dragging it out on a stick or a garden rake. The weed may contain beneficial insects and water snails, so to avoid removing too many of these, leave the piles of blanket weed on the side of the pond overnight to give any creatures the chance to escape and crawl back into the water. For more persistent cases of blanket weed, chemical controls are available.

Duckweed

Duckweed is mainly found growing on still water. This weed is made up of small clusters of leaves with roots attached to them that hang below the surface. It does have some beneficial effect – the fish really seem to enjoy eating it – but it quickly covers the surface of the pond, blocking out the light and killing, or considerably weakening, submerged plants. Drag it out with a fine-gauge net or colander and always make sure that at least a third of the water's surface area is free of duckweed to allow light to enter.

An effective preventive measure is to float a hessian sack of straw or hay in the pond in early spring. Another useful and easy trick is  to stuff the hay into an old pair of tights, secured at the end with a knot, which can then be thrown into the pond. Nitrogen used by bacteria to attack the hay then deprives the blanket weed of the essential nutrients it needs to develop any further.

fish care

If you already have fish established in your pond, you will notice that they become more active in spring as their rate of metabolism increases. As they start to move around they will need to be fed liberally to build up their strength. The food also helps to protect them from the diseases prevalent at this time of year. With new ponds, spring is the time to introduce fish to their new home, but only when the severe weather is over.

looking after your fish

In an established pond, regularly feeding the fish in spring and summer may not always be necessary because of the insect population living in and around the pond. Make sure you do not over-feed pond fish, since this can be harmful, especially in a small pond where uneaten food will decompose and quickly pollute the water.

Watch the movement of the fish to monitor any change in their behaviour. The usual signs of potential problems are either slow and sluggish movement from individual fish, while others remain active, or frenzied swimming, frequent surfacing and body rubbing against the side of the pond. If a problem is suspected, it is essential to have a closer look at them; if possible, lift them with a net and place them in a separate container for examination so that the correct treatment can be administered.

introducing new fish

An average initial stocking rate is ten fish to every 1 square metre (10 square feet) of pond surface. Hardy fish that can live together include goldfish, golden orfe, rudd, tench and shubunkins. Golden orfe and rudd should be introduced

in quantity, since they naturally prefer to swim in shoals. Tench are shy and prefer to live at the bottom of the pond, scavenging on insect larvae.

New fish are usually transported in polythene bags part-filled with water and inflated with oxygen. Ideally, the pond should have been planted at least a month before the fish are introduced to allow the plants to develop new roots and establish sufficiently to start producing new growth. It takes at least this amount of time to establish an ecological balance within the pond.

1   Place the container holding the fish on the surface of the pond to allow the water in the pond and the container to reach the same temperature. This will prevent the fish suffering temperature shock when they are released.

2   After 2 to 3 hours you can open the container and tip the fish into their new environment. Tilt it into the pond water, allowing the fish to adjust and swim slowly into the pond. After an hour, scatter some food over the surface of the pond.

routine care

The growing seasons are exciting times with the introduction of new plants and features, and they are also a period of rapid growth for new and established plants. However, in order to maintain a healthy and attractive garden, there are routine tasks that must be attended to. The beginning of the spring season is ideal for attending to the maintenance of garden buildings and structures and for checking that tools and machinery are in good working order. In summer, do not be seduced into thinking that the garden can look after itself. A summer that brings more or less rain than usual will be one that requires action on your part, but no matter what the weather, pruning, feeding, dead-heading and training are on-going tasks.

forms of winter protection

A combination of frozen soil and cold, drying winds can cause rapid moisture loss that cannot be replaced by a plant's root system. This situation results in the death of leaves and soft shoot tips. Although some plants are tough enough to withstand cold winter temperatures, many need an extra covering to shield them from unfavourable conditions. There are several different materials and methods available for sheltering the plants in your garden. Natural protection comes in the form of hedges, such as yew (*Taxus*), which provide a dense barrier of defence, or from sturdy wattle fences. Alternatively you can construct your own forms of protection using any of the materials below.

hessian

Protecting plants will effectively screen them from extreme weather conditions. A hessian wigwam constructed in mid-autumn will prevent wind damage to branches and stems as well as protecting plants from frost and preventing any further water loss. A wigwam shape is the most effective design, since it shields the top growth and still permits air to circulate, allowing the plants to breathe. If the weather gets warmer, then one side can be opened and tied back, or in even milder conditions the protection can simply be removed. By leaving the support structure in place during the winter the plant may be protected quickly and easily if the weather becomes suddenly cold and windy again.

1   For the example shown here we have chosen to protect a *Viburnum tinus*. Start by selecting four sturdy 1.5 m (5 ft) canes (alter the size to fit your plant) and push them into the soil in an upright position. Each cane should be 30 cm (12 in) away from the plant, forming a square.

2   Draw the tops of each of the four canes in, so that they come together directly over the plant. Tie the canes together with string. This forms the basic framework of the wigwam, which can be left in place throughout winter and used to support the hessian cover whenever it is needed.

3   For the outer protective layer, use hessian, plastic mesh or even thick newspaper. Measure the area to be covered and cut out your material, then wrap it around three sides of the wigwam and attach it to the canes with twist ties. Leave the sheltered side open but seal this off in bad weather.

4   As an extra protective measure, if temperatures drop very low, fill the cavity between the plant and the wrapping with straw, lightly packing it around the leaves and branches. Alternatively, wrap extra layers of covering material around the outside of the wigwam frame, securing it to the canes as before.

cloches

These are best used for small numbers of low-growing plants that need protecting during winter, such as annuals sown in autumn, alpines or over-wintering vegetables. The simplest form of cloche can be made from plastic, stretched over and held in place by wire hoops. The advantage of this type is that you can close off the end by gathering the sheet together and wrapping it around a wooden peg. A sturdier alternative is corrugated plastic or Perspex, which can be bent into an arch and held down with metal pegs. At the top of the range are glass cloches, but these tend to be expensive. Plastic and Perspex offer the most effective frost protection, but they lose heat quickly in late afternoon and evening, with the result that, on occasion, temperatures can be lower under the cloches than outside.

Plastic sheeting over wire hoops　　*A corrugated plastic arch*

polythene

This material is readily available and easy to apply. Tie it in place or anchor down sheets with bricks or stones, making sure it does not touch the actual plants. Leave a gap for air to circulate. Polythene allows the air around the plants to get very hot during the day but this gives way to rapid heat loss during the night, so it is best used only as a short-term defence back-up.

fleece

Loosely woven or spun materials provide better protection than plastic sheeting, with far fewer temperature fluctuations. They are good for wrapping around plants such as conifers and broad-leaved evergreens. Use them in either sheets or strips and secure to your plant with string tied loosely around the outside in three or four places. Fleece can also be spread over the top of low-growing tender plants and vegetables. To hold it in place, make large staples out of thin wire and push them through the fleece and into the soil beneath. This type of insulator does not become very hot during the day but it retains its heat well and keeps plants warm during the night. In areas where windchill is particularly bad, do not worry about keeping this covering in place from autumn right through to early spring, since light and air can still penetrate it.

windbreaks

The best material to use for windbreaks is webbing or netting and polypropylene with 50% permeability. This flexible mesh allows light, air and rain to filter through to the plant but reduces the impact of strong winds and frost. You can buy ready-made windbreaks or construct your own. Using one of the recommended materials, attach lengths between posts or canes at regular intervals, zigzagging it between plants for the most effective protection. Particularly good for plants with weak stems, these screens range in height from 50 cm to 4 m (20 in to 13 ft).

patio and container-grown plants

The majority of popular plants grown outdoors in containers are from temperate and subtropical areas, which grow best in a temperature range of 10 to 18°C (50 to 65°F). These plants are very susceptible to frost damage, particularly around the roots, so if you are unable to bring your containers indoors for winter, protect them with a suitable insulation material.

wrapping a small container-grown plant

1 Lay the container on its side, making sure you do not crack or break it. Wrap it with hessian, bubble plastic, old carpet or cardboard. If you cannot lay your container down, simply wrap the insulation material around the sides.

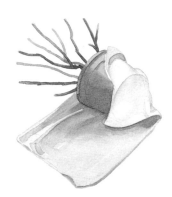

2 In severe cold, straw can be used as an additional insulator. Place wads of straw between the branches of the plant, then gather up the branches and tie them loosely together so that the straw is held in position between the branches.

3 For further protection against wet weather, make your covering waterproof by wrapping a layer of plastic film or sheeting around the insulation material already in place. Remove it when the threat of rain or snow has passed.

Root-killing temperatures for container-grown ornamentals

0 to –5°C (32 to 23°F)
Common box
  (*Buxus sempervirens*)
Magnolia x *soulangeana*
Garland flower
  (*Daphne cneorum*)
Mahonia japonica
St. John's wort (*Hypericum*)

–5 to –10°C (23 to 14°F)
Japanese maple
  (*Acer palmatum*)
Star magnolia
  (*Magnolia stellata*)
Flowering dogwood
  (*Cornus florida*)
Japanese cedar
  (*Cryptomeria japonica*)

–10 to –15°C (14 to 5°F)
Chinese juniper
  (*Juniperus chinensis*)
Oregon grape
  (*Mahonia aquifolium*)
Switch ivy
  (*Leucothoe fontanesiana*)
Viburnum carlesii

Buxus sempervirens

Acer palmatum

Juniperus

packing a large container-grown plant

1 Begin by crushing sheets of wastepaper into balls (single sheets of newspaper are ideal and, provided it is kept dry, has very good insulating properties), roughly equal to the size of a tennis ball.

2 Place the prepared balls of paper in plastic refuse sacks. The sacks should be full but not too tightly packed. Close up the top and tie it up with string.

3 The paper-filled sacks should then be neatly packed around the sides of the container. Tie the bundles in place with string to ensure that they do not blow away.

enclosing large containers

1 A useful method for protecting plants in large, heavy containers is to place 10 cm (4 in) wads of straw between two layers of chicken wire. Cut the chicken wire so that it is slightly taller than the plant and container, and wide enough to fully enclose it.

2 Join the four edges of the wire by twisting it together at the corners. Enclose the container and plant with the straw coat and join the outer edges by twisting the end wires.

3 During the coldest weather it is a good idea to construct a lid to fit over the straw and chicken wire coat. Cut the chicken wire into two circles, place wads of straw between them and then twist the wires together around the perimeter. Place the finished straw lid on top of the side covering. It can easily be removed when the weather conditions improve.

making a raised bed

A raised planter provides a neat, clearly defined growing area where it is possible to work without having to stoop or bend too much. The height and shape add an extra dimension to the garden and a new growing surface. The soil or compost used can be of a different type to that of the surrounding soil, allowing, for example, acid-loving plants, such as rhododendrons, to be grown even when the surrounding soil is alkaline. Plants that like a dry or free-draining site, such as alpines, also do very well in this elevated growing environment.

MATERIALS & EQUIPMENT

pegs and string

hand fork or garden fork

railway sleepers – not treated with wood preservative toxic to plants – or heavy wooden beams or logs of uniform size and thickness

galvanized nails, 15 cm (6 in) long and hammer

coarse rubble and stones

old carpet or turves

compost to suit chosen plants

plants of your choice to suit the soil

Measuring out the bed

1   Using string and wooden pegs, mark out the area
and dimensions of the raised bed.

2   Remove any surface vegetation and weeds from within the
marked area. For small areas, use a hand fork and pull the weeds
by hand. For larger beds, turn the soil with a garden fork.

Making the bed

3   Railway sleepers are ideal for creating a raised bed. However,
an equally attractive effect can be created using heavy beams or
logs. The broad dimensions and weight of sleepers, beams and logs
mean that no concrete or hardcore foundation layer is necessary.
Start off by placing the bottom layer where indicated by the string
and pegs – cut the wood, if necessary, to fit the marked bed. Leave a
2 to 3 cm (1 in) open gap between the end of each sleeper or log to
provide sufficient space to allow surplus water to drain freely away.

4   Repeat this process, working around the wall,
to raise the height of the wall surrounding the
planting bed. If you are using sleepers, it is a good
idea to stagger each level, as you would when laying
bricks, since this will make the structure more
stable. Two courses will make a low wall, or for
a bed about knee high, use four courses.

5 Although the weight of the wood means that the structure will be fairly stable, it is still a good idea to secure it further with nails. Start by driving 15 cm (6 in) nails into the corner joints, at an angle. Then, to fix the top row in position, drive more 15 cm (6 in) nails through the vertical joints, again positioning the nails at an angle.

6 Now that the structure is in place you can prepare the bed for planting. Start by filling the bottom quarter of the bed with coarse rubble and stones to form a drainage layer, and cover this layer over with inverted turves. If you do not have any turves, a section of old carpet will work just as well – this is to prevent any soil or compost being washed into the rubble below, which will restrict the drainage effect.

7 Fill the remaining three-quarters of the bed with soil, compost or a mixture of both. Do not firm this layer, but allow it to settle during planting so that it is approximately 5 to 7 cm (2 to 3 in) below the rim of the bed to allow space for watering.

Planting up the bed

8 Choose suitable plants for your bed and plant up (see the 'New Introductions' chapter for advice on planting techniques). Raised beds are good for plants that prefer dry and sunny conditions. They are also good for acid-loving plants that may be difficult to grow in most garden soils.

Acid-loving plants	
Camellia	*Pieris* 'Forest Flame'
Helleborus purpurascens	*Rhododendron*

feeding

Very few plants can sustain rapid growth without a 'boost' of nutrients during the growing season, since the development of shoots, stems, leaves and flowers can cause a huge drain on the plant's resources. This depletion is made even worse when flowering plants are dead-headed, and the spent flower heads are taken way, since this deprives the plant of a valuable source of organic matter and nutrients. Unless some replacement nourishment is provided, the plant's performance and vigour will decline.

fertilizers

Artificial fertilizers vary greatly in the rate at which they make their nutrients available to plants. Described as slow- or quick-release, the essential difference between them lies in how soluble they are in water. The rate of release is also dependent on the size of the fertilizer particles – the smaller they are, the more rapidly they break down.

Dry feeds

The most common fertilizers come in the form of powder, granules or pellets. They can be used as a base dressing, added to the soil before sowing or planting, or to top dress established plants, including shrubs or hungry feeders such as chrysanthemums, during the growing season. Before applying a top dressing, make sure that the soil is moist. The plant will be able to take up the fertilizer most readily if it has already been incorporated into the topsoil.

Release rates for some common fertilizers	
Fertilizer type	**Plant response**
Slow-release (resin coat)	14–21 days
Quick-acting (top dressing)	7–10 days
Liquid feed (applied to soil or compost)	5–7 days
Foliar feed	3–4 days

Liquid feeds

These come as a liquid concentrate or as granules or powder, which are diluted or dissolved in water. When preparing liquid feeds, it is essential to add the correct amount of water, following the manufacturer's recommendations. It is also important to mix them thoroughly and to keep the solution well agitated. These soluble fertilizers are applied with a watering can or hose, and are ideal for use on most plants.

Foliar feeds

These are specially formulated fertilizers used to correct specific nutrient deficiencies or meet particular needs. Sprays containing  magnesium will assist fruiting, and iron-based preparations are often used on acid-loving plants, such as azaleas and camellias, which are susceptible to iron deficiency when grown on slightly alkaline soils. Spray foliar feeds onto the leaves in dull weather only, since this reduces the chances of leaf scorch.

when to feed

Plants growing in containers, such as hanging baskets and window boxes, are particularly vulnerable because their roots are restricted and they have only a limited supply of food. Even if nutrients are present in the soil, they are effective only if the compost is sufficiently moist. The best approach is to apply a regular liquid feed (every 10–14 days) once the plants have started to flower. For plants growing in the garden soil, if they are repeat flowering, feed after the first flush of flowers; if they bloom only once each year, feed after flowering to promote good-quality flowers in the following year.

The golden rules of feeding
• Always follow the manufacturer's directions.
• Only feed your plants when they are actively growing.
• Never feed plants that are dry, without watering the soil or compost first.
• Do not apply fertilizer in bright sunlight, as this can lead to scorching.
• Wash off any concentrated feed that is spilt directly onto the plant.

composting

Garden compost is another useful source of plant food. Well-rotted plant and animal waste not only provides nutrients (although not the high levels found in fertilizers), it also boosts the activity of earthworms and other beneficial creatures in the soil. Most garden and kitchen waste can be used, but aim for a balance of materials (see pages 254–57).

1 Start by placing a layer of bulky material, such as wood shavings or finely shredded bark, about 10 cm (4 in) deep, in the bottom of the compost bin. A container with a removable front is the easiest to work with.

2 Next, add a layer of green material, such as grass mowings or cabbage leaves, about 20 cm (8 in) deep. Alternating the layers like this will encourage rapid decomposition.

3 To accelerate the start of the composting process, sprinkle a compost primer over the layers. A cheaper alternative is to add a nitrogenous fertilizer, such as sulphate of ammonia, which will also speed up the composting process. Continue building up the compost heap, adding bulky and green material in alternate layers. After two weeks, turn the heap from top to bottom to allow it to compost evenly.

common nutrient deficiencies

	Symptoms	Causes	Susceptible plants	Control
Calcium	Overall reduction in growth, stunted shoot-tip growth, pale margin to the leaves, retarded root development.	Very low or very high soil pH, applying too much potassium and high rainfall.	Most plants, but especially apples and tomatoes (fruit is damaged).	Apply calcium nitrate.
Iron	Pale yellow leaves, stunted shoot-tips and an overall reduction in growth.	High pH and watering with tap water in 'hard water' areas.	Acid loving plants, including *Pieris*, *Camellia*, rhododendrons and heathers.	Apply acid mulches, incorporate sulphur into the soil or apply trace elements or sequestered iron.
Magnesium	Yellow blotches between the veins on the lower (older) leaves.	Soils with low pH, leaching from poor, freely draining soils and loamless composts with high levels of potassium.	Fruiting plants, especially tomatoes.	Apply Epsom salts as a liquid feed or as a foliar feed.
Manganese	Yellowing of the leaves.	Soil pH of 7.0 or more.	Apples, peaches, peas and tomatoes.	Apply fertilizer containing manganese sulphate.
Nitrogen	Dull yellow leaves, thin spindly stems and overall reduction in growth.	Leaching from poor, freely draining soils and loamless composts.	Any plants.	Apply high-nitrogen fertilizer, such as nitrochalk or sulphate of ammonia.
Phosphate	Young foliage is a dull bluish-green, later turning yellow.	Low pH and high rainfall; heavy clay soils locking up the content of phosphates.	Potentially any plant, particularly seedlings.	Apply phosphate or triple super-phosphate.
Potassium	Foliage turns bluish-purple, later changing to yellow with brown, dead margins and tips to the leaves; reduced growth; and poor flowering and fruit.	Growing plants in light or peaty soils, or soils that have a high pH.	Apples, blackcurrants and pears.	Apply sulphate of potash.

Malus 'Golden Hornet'

Pieris japonica 'Geisha'

Rhododendron narcissiforum

watering

Some plants consist of up to 90 per cent water, which is constantly moving around them and being lost from pores in the leaves in a process known as transpiration. Summer, for most plants, is a time of rapid growth. In order to sustain this, the plants need plenty of light and food and copious amounts of water; in particularly hot weather they may need watering twice each day to prevent wilting. Given the huge amount of work this may involve, it makes sense to conserve as much moisture as possible in the soil.

signs of water loss

In prolonged dry conditions, the amount of water that is lost through the process of transpiration can exceed that taken in by the plant's roots. Once the plant has used up its reserves it will rapidly begin to wilt. Wilting manifests itself in the shedding of buds, premature drop of flowers (or poor colour and size in those that do open), early leaf loss, small fruits and increased susceptibility to attack by pests and diseases.

plants most at risk

Some types of plant are more susceptible than others to the effects of prolonged dry conditions. In general, the more sappy the plant and the softer its growth, the more vulnerable it is likely to be to drought. Bedding plants, for instance, will wilt rapidly in dry conditions. Young plants are also especially at risk, since their roots will not have penetrated far into the soil: these include newly planted vegetables, shrubs or trees. Also, plants grown near mature trees, or in the dry soil next to a wall, need to be checked regularly for moisture loss.

preventing dry roots

How much water to apply is difficult to assess because every soil is different. Always add enough to soak the soil to a reasonable depth to encourage plant roots to follow the water downwards. Plants subjected only briefly to drought should quickly recover if given a thorough soaking, ideally by allowing water to run gently onto the soil and soak in.

The effects of long-term drought are difficult to rectify, and the focus should be on measures to prevent it happening in the first place. Preparing the soil deeply with organic matter will help, since it provides a reservoir of moisture for plant roots. Applying a deep mulch, such as bark, to the surface will reduce moisture loss through evaporation.

when to water

Choosing the correct time of day to water your garden can save on the amount of water lost to evaporation from the soil's surface. The soil is cooler and the atmosphere relatively moist in the early morning and late evening, so applying water at these times will allow it the maximum time to soak in and be of most use to the growing plants.

effective watering

1　Water needs to be delivered as close to the roots as possible. Seep- or trickle-irrigation systems work well, with the low pressure and steady flow allowing the water to soak deep into the rooting zone.

2　Another simple but very efficient way of keeping water in the right area to benefit the plant is to create a shallow, saucer-shaped depression around the base of each plant. This way any water that is applied into the depression is held in place until it can soak in.

plant requirements

Plants grown for their edible fruits have two critical watering periods. First, when they flower (to aid pollination and fruit set) and, second, after the fruit begins to show obvious signs of swelling. Other garden plants may have a higher-than-normal requirement for water because of their location – near walls or trees and shrubs, for instance, or because they have been planted in raised beds or other free-draining sites. Plants in pots, window boxes and hanging baskets must be watered at least daily, even when it rains.

water distribution

Hoses and sprinklers (see page 157) are ideal for watering lawns and other large garden areas, but for individual plants an ordinary watering can is best. Use a fine rose attachment for watering seedlings. A water tank, or butt, allows you to fill your can with rainwater.

Water tank
A downpipe from the roof channels rainwater into the tank, which is essential for watering acid-loving plants in hard-water areas.

Watering can
The simplest and most basic method of watering, used for small areas or for young plants and seedlings that may be damaged by high-pressure jets, is a watering can.

controlling weeds

Once plants have become established and started to grow, they will usually sufficiently cover the ground or cast enough shade over the soil to suppress the germination and growth of weed seedlings. Until then, however, nature will need a helping hand, and any weeds that do appear must be removed on a regular basis.

weed problems

As weeds grow, they compete with crops and ornamental plants for light, nutrients and water; they can also act as hosts to pests and diseases that may spread to the garden plants. Groundsel, for instance, may harbour the fungal diseases rust and mildew, as well as sap-sucking thrips and greenfly. Chickweed is a host to damaging red spider mite and whitefly. Some nightshade species host viruses and eelworms that can infect other members of the same family such as peppers, potatoes and ornamental solanums.

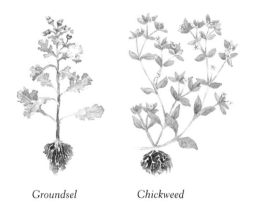

Groundsel   *Chickweed*

annual weeds

The old saying 'one year's seeds make seven years' weeds' has now been the subject of scientific research and, unfortunately, is proving remarkably accurate. Some annual weeds can produce a population of 60,000 viable seeds per square metre (square yard) each year, with the vast majority of these being found in the top 5 cm (2 in) of soil.

Common annual weeds

Annual meadow grass (*Poa annua*)	Groundsel (*Senecio vulgaris*)
Annual nettle (*Urtica urens*)	Hairy bittercress (*Cardamine hirsuta*)
Black nightshade (*Solanum nigrum*)	Ivy-leaved speedwell (*Veronica hederifolia*)
Chickweed (*Stellaria media*)	Knotgrass (*Polygonum aviculare*)
Fat hen (*Chenopodium album*)	
Fumitory (*Fumaria officinalis*)	Pineapple weed (*Matricaria matricarioides*)
Gallant soldier (*Galansago parviflora*)	Shepherd's purse (*Capsella bursa-pastoris*)
Goosegrass (*Galium aparine*)	

---

perennial weeds

These weeds live for many years. Digging them up is an effective way of dealing with them, as long as every bit of the root system is removed. If only a few weeds are present, dig them out with a trowel or tined implement such as a daisy grubber. Do not throw perennial weeds on the compost heap – they will simply regrow. Always burn them.

Common perennial weeds

Bindweed (*Convolvulus arvensis*)	Dandelion (*Taraxacum officinale*)
Broad-leaved dock (*Rumex obtusifolius*)	Elderberry (*Sambucus nigra*)
Clover (*Trifolium repens*)	Ground elder (*Aegopodium podagraria*)
Coltsfoot (*Tussilago farfara*)	Horsetail (*Equisetum arvense*)
Couch grass (*Elymus repens*)	Japanese knotweed (*Fallopia japonica*)
Creeping buttercup (*Ranunculus repens*)	Perennial nettle (*Urtica dioica*)
Creeping thistle (*Cirsium arvense*)	Plantain (*Plantago major*)

---

methods of weed control

There are four methods of weed control commonly available to the gardener: chemical, where a synthetic chemical is applied over the weeds to kill them; mulching, which involves covering the soil to deprive weeds of light; manual, where weeds are physically removed using some form of hand tool (see opposite); and mechanical, which is a method of chopping down or burying weeds using a rotary cultivator. Perennial weeds, which can persist for many years, are best dealt with chemically or by physically removing them.

chemicals

All chemicals used to kill weeds are known as herbicides. They are preferred by non-organic gardeners as their main method of weed control, and they are certainly one of the most effective ways of controlling persistent perennial weeds. The chemicals are either bought in concentrated form, to be diluted with water and then applied to plants through a sprayer or watering can with a dribble bar attachment, or they can be bought as ready-to-use formulations.

Herbicides available in sprays are normally intended for spraying onto individual, scattered weeds – as the weeds start to die, simply pull them out. In large areas, however, it is easier to dig over the soil to bury the weeds, but only if they are dead. Some herbicides are selective in that they will kill weeds in a lawn while leaving the grass unaffected, but you must ensure the spray does not come into contact with any cultivated plants.

mulching

As beneficial as organic mulches are on many levels in the garden, inorganic mulches are more effective for weed control because they form an impervious physical barrier. A typical inorganic mulch is heavy-duty black plastic. New plants can be introduced through slits cut into the plastic. Water the soil well before laying the plastic. However, inorganic mulches look rather unsightly, and in order to get the best of both worlds, this type of mulch is often covered with a thin layer of organic material to make it aesthetically pleasing.

As well as helping to conserve moisture in the soil by minimizing evaporation and providing a decorative surface for garden beds, mulching is also a very effective technique for suppressing weed growth if properly applied. In order to work well against weeds, organic mulches, such as bark chippings or spent mushroom compost, must be at least 10 cm (4 in) thick so that enough sunlight is blocked out to prevent the weed seeds in the soil germinating. Mulches tend to be less effective against established perennial weeds, unless the affected area can be completely covered until the weeds have died out. New planting must then be carried out with the mulch still in place to prevent regrowth. Any weed seeds that germinate in the surface of the mulch can be easily removed simply by pulling them out, as long as they are not left to develop root systems deep enough to reach the soil beneath.

manual methods of weed control

Most weeds are found in the uppermost 6 cm (2½ in) of soil and so the simplest way to deal with them is to remove them physically. The principal disadvantage of this method of control is that it disturbs the soil, potentially exposing weed seeds to light and so

encouraging them to germinate, thus starting the problem all over again. If you do not want to use some form of chemical control, then vigilance is the key: removing weeds as soon as you see them, when they are very young and have only shallow roots, will cause the least possible disturbance to the soil and any nearby established plants.

Combined control
The best way to control weeds is usually a combination of manual and chemical methods. This involves spraying with an appropriate herbicide when the weeds are in full growth; as the weeds start to die, the area is dug over so the weeds are buried in the soil. When the next flush of weeds start to germinate in response to the ground being disturbed, and the young seedlings emerge, they can be sprayed with a chemical (see opposite) while they are at their most vulnerable and thus be quickly dispatched.

hand tools for weed control

If you do not wish to use chemicals to control weeds in your garden, then you will need to remove them by pulling or digging them out, or, if they are small enough, by hoeing them off at soil level. There are many tools available designed to cope with different types of weed. See below from top to bottom: a patio weeder is useful for removing weeds in cracks between paving and other narrow spaces; a daisy grubber removes large weeds from the lawn; a Dutch hoe works best for shallow-rooted weeds; and a draw hoe is effective for chopping up deeper-rooted weeds.

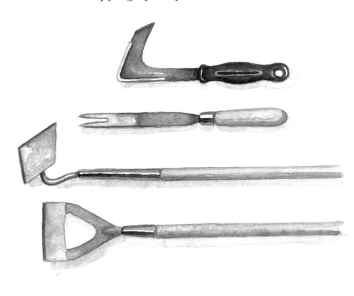

spring protection

As the days lengthen in spring, many plants will still need protection from frost damage, or damage from birds and other pests, to help advance growth and to encourage earlier cropping or flowering. As they grow, many of your taller plants will also need supporting to stop their stems from bending over, and spring is the ideal time to set up a support structure, ready for the plants as they emerge from the soil.

protective structures

Cloches
Glass, rigid plastic and Perspex covers offer the most effective form of frost protection. They can be purchased ready-made and placed over the plants that need protection (see below). However, bear in mind that they tend to lose temperature rapidly in the late afternoon and evening.

Fleece
Loosely woven or spun materials are now readily available. They do not provide a great deal of warmth but they do maintain a steady temperature, thus making them ideal for short-term protection in the early spring.

Plastic film
This material is inexpensive and easy to use. However, the air around the plants gets very hot during the day and loses heat rapidly during the night. Use only for short-term protection and to give plants an early boost.

Screening
The very changeable weather conditions in the spring mean that young plants can be very easily damaged by sun scorch, particularly through glass. Some method of screening from very bright sunlight may well be necessary and should be applied earlier rather than later, after the damage has occurred. For small greenhouses, shade netting or blinds made from split canes can be draped over the roof to filter the sun's rays, but they may interfere with the roof ventilators. If this is a problem, the glass can be painted or sprayed with a proprietary glasshouse shading paint, or with diluted white emulsion paint.

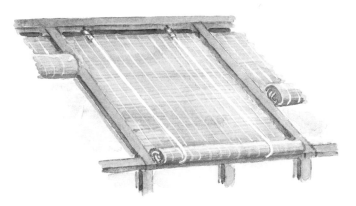

making a protective structure

A simple netting, hessian or plastic casing, held in place with canes, will prevent wind and frost damage while still permitting air circulation and allowing the plants to 'breathe'. When the weather improves, it can easily be removed.

1 Insert bamboo canes (four is usually enough) into the soil around the plants to be protected, making sure that the canes are taller than the actual plants.

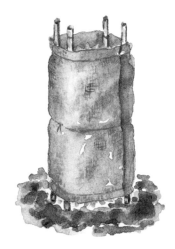

2 Wrap netting, plastic mesh or hessian around the sides of the bamboo frame and secure with string, tied around the top, bottom and middle of the casing.

Creating the framework

1   Mark out the route for your path with brightly coloured string stretched between pegs. The pegs are set at least 7 to 8 cm (3 in) wider than the intended edge of the path to allow for the retaining pegs inserted in step 3.

2   Dig out the soil within the coloured string lines to form a shallow trench about 20 cm (8 in) deep. Then rake the base of the trench level and compact it thoroughly using either a garden roller or a motorized compactor plate.

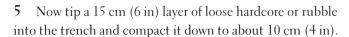

3   Knock in retaining pegs along the string line marking the edge of the path, placing them about 1 m (39 in) apart all along the length – the purpose of these is to form an outside support to hold the retaining boards in place along the sides.

4   Lay out the retaining boards along both sides of the path and nail them to the insides of the retaining pegs. Use a spirit level to check that they are level, both down the sides and across, from one side of the path to the other side.

5   Now tip a 15 cm (6 in) layer of loose hardcore or rubble into the trench and compact it down to about 10 cm (4 in).

6   Add a base layer of sand over the hardcore so that it is about 5 cm (2 in) deep and rake it over until it is roughly level. Lightly compact it.

7   Next, prepare the strips of wood that cross the path. Lay them in position over the sand and mark the angles where they need to be cut. Carefully cut them with a saw.

Wooden strips embedded in concrete can shrink and lift out. To prevent this happening, knock 7.5 cm (3 in) galvanized nails into the underside of each board, every 30 cm (12 in), leaving about 4 cm (1½ in) protruding from the board. The heads of the nails will then set into the concrete as it dries and this will prevent the boards from lifting out of the path.

Making the path

8 Make the concrete that will form the surface of the path. In a wheelbarrow, mix 1 part cement to 3½ parts sand and gravel (aggregate) and add water until it is porridge-like in texture. Add the concrete to the layer of sand, working in 1 m (39 in) sections, and rake and lightly compact it until it is roughly level.

9 For each section, while the concrete is still wet, push the wooden boards that will create the chequerboard effect into position by gently tapping them with a lump hammer until the upper surface is level with the concrete.

10 To finish off the decorative effect, push pebbles into the concrete, between the wooden strips, by gently wiggling them from side to side, up to about halfway, which should bed them securely into the concrete.

11 Repeat this whole process for each section, until the full length of the path is complete.

12 After about 4 hours, brush over the pebbles and wooden boards with a stiff-bristled brush, which should be regularly dipped in water – this will clean all traces of concrete off the pebbles and boards, considerably improving their appearance.

13 Cover the path with polythene sheets for about 3 days to allow the concrete to set.

14 After about a week or so the pegs and retaining boards can be removed.

summer protection

It is not unreasonable to expect the best weather of the year during the summer months, but conditions may still pose a hazard to plants. In addition, pests are often attracted to the colourful and tasty flowers and fruits of this season and deterrents will need to be put in place. Since summer is the main holiday season, measures may also need to be taken to ensure that your plants survive any short periods of neglect.

protecting blooms

The blooms of some plants are very delicate and are easily damaged by rain, dew and mist, which may mark the petals. For many years, chrysanthemum enthusiasts have 'bagged' their prize blooms. This involves covering the young flower with a greaseproof paper bag as a protection from moisture and dirt. Cover the flower as soon as the bud shows colour – but not before, or the developing flower may become distorted.

holiday protection

If you do not want to return to an overgrown, neglected-looking garden after a holiday, make sure you carry out such tasks as lawn mowing, tidying borders, feeding and watering before you leave. Container, house and bedding plants are the most vulnerable, since they have a limited root run and only small reserves of food and water.

Providing shade

For indoor plants, move the containers away from the windows so that they are not in direct sunlight. Outdoor container plants can be pushed closer together so that they provide shade for one another; grouped like this they will also trap humidity to create their own microclimate. Larger container plants growing outdoors on a deck, patio or balcony can either be moved into a more shaded area or, if they are too heavy to move, a light screen of netting or fleece can be draped over them to filter the sun's rays. Elevate the netting on canes to avoid it touching the plants and damaging them.

Providing water

Small pot plants can be kept moist and humid by placing them on upturned saucers in a bath or sink with 2.5 cm (1 in) of water in the bottom. The pots should not sit in the water or the roots will rot. For larger plants, place a bowl of water beside each one and run a 'wick' of capillary matting or other absorbent material from the water into the compost. Another method of keeping plants moist is to water the plant well and then place the pot in a polythene bag. Tie the bag around the stem to recycle the water inside and prevent evaporation. You can put the bag over the whole plant, but only use this method for short periods or the plant may start to rot.

protecting fruit

For many fruits the need for protection is not just from the elements; more frequently, marauding birds will enjoy the best of the season's crop if the ripening fruit is left unprotected. You can grow the fruit inside a permanent cage made with fine mesh wire, or drape a soft string or nylon mesh over the plants and peg it in place to provide cover until picking has been completed.

Fruits that may need covering

Blackberry	Grape	Redcurrant
Blackcurrant	Loganberry	Strawberry
Blueberry	Nectarine	Whitecurrant
Cherry	Peach	
Gooseberry	Raspberry	

Cherry

Peach

supporting fruit trees

Fruit trees often need another form of protection, since in some years the burden of fruit may be so great that the stem and branches are unable to bear the weight and they may be physically damaged. The easiest way to prevent this is to select a stout stake that is at least 60 cm (24 in) taller than the tree, and tie it in an upright position to the trunk or main stem. Use a proprietary tree tie or wrap the stem well with sacking to prevent rubbing or slipping. Run lengths of string from the top of the stake out to the branches, and tie them in place about two-thirds of the way along to provide support until the fruit is harvested.

protecting low-growing fruit

Low-growing plants often need protection from the soil to keep them clean and prevent damage from soil-borne pests and diseases. Strawberries produce their fruit very close to the ground; as the berries develop they rest on the soil and are easily attacked by slugs and insects. Straw or plastic laid around the plants, before the berries swell, can overcome most of these problems.

pests and diseases

There is a vast range of pesticides and other chemicals that can be applied to control and eradicate most of the pests and diseases affecting plants. Reaching for the chemical carton, however, should be a last resort. The first course of action should be to practise crop rotation and good general garden hygiene, such as clearing away any rubbish and disinfecting tools and equipment, and always to buy healthy plants. Also, regular inspection of plants allows you to spot problems early on, which means that chemicals may be needed only in small quantities.

diseases

Botrytis
A fungus that attacks fruits and flowers.
Symptoms: a covering of grey felt-like mould; the infected parts of the plant rot and rapidly decay.
Control: remove and burn badly affected plant parts, or spray with fungicide.

Clubroot
A soil-borne fungus that attacks the roots of plants.
Symptoms: swollen distorted roots and yellow wilting leaves, causing the plant to collapse and die.
Control: grow resistant cultivars in well-drained soil; use fungicide on new plants.

Mildew
A fungus that attacks flowers, fruits, leaves and stems.
Symptoms: discoloured, yellow leaves, with white patches on the underside of the leaf, causing slow death.
Control: spray with fungicide, grow resistant cultivars and burn any infected plants.

Rust
A fungal disease that invades the leaves, eventually killing the whole plant.
Symptoms: orange-brown spots and yellowing of the leaves and stems; general reduction in growth.
Control: grow resistant cultivars, improve air circulation, remove infected plants; apply fungicide.

Silver leaf
A fungus that enters the woody tissue of members of the plum and cherry family.
Symptoms: the leaves take on a silvery sheen, branches die back, and the plant itself gradually dies.
Control: prune out infected branches during summer, and remove and burn badly infected trees.

Virus
This very simple organism lives and feeds on the inside of the plant.
Symptoms: yellow distorted leaves and stems, poor weak growth, stunted shoots and striped, misshapen flowers and fruits.
Control: purchase virus-free plants, control aphids, and burn any infected plants.

pests

Aphids

Large colonies of small sap-sucking insects, which also carry viruses. They range in colour from pale green to greenish black.

Symptoms: distorted shoot tips and leaves and a sticky residue on the lower leaves.

Control: spray at regular intervals with insecticide but remove and burn badly infected plants.

Caterpillars

The larvae of butterflies and moths, varying greatly in both colour and size.

Symptoms: holes in the leaves and young stems, reducing vigour and crop potential.

Control: spray at regular intervals with insecticide or remove by hand.

Eelworms

Microscopic worm-like pests that live in the roots, leaves and stems of plants.

Symptoms: yellowing of the leaves, stunted growth, wilting and small knobbly swellings on the roots.

Control: grow resistant cultivars in well-drained soil; burn affected plants.

Maggots

The larval stage of flies.

Symptoms: brown marks and lesions in roots, flowers, fruits, bulbs and stems, often leaving a residue of brown waste on crops.

Control: sow crops later, in mid-summer, cover with fleece and apply insecticide at regular intervals.

Red spider mites

Tiny mites that feed on the sap of plants.

Symptoms: yellow stunted growth, curled and mottled leaves covered with a fine webbing; reduced vigour.

Control: grow resistant cultivars, maintain good air circulation; use insecticide. Burn badly infected plants.

Slugs and snails

Slugs are tubular, soft-bodied pests, usually black or brown and of varying size; snails are similar but carry a hard shell in the centre of the back.

Symptoms: circular holes in the plant tissue, often causing extensive cavities; slime trails may be visible. Seedlings and young shoots are particularly vulnerable.

Control: keep soil well drained and free from weeds and remove all plant debris. Apply a sharp mulch, such as gravel or soot, around the plants as a physical barrier. Pick off by hand at night when feeding. Or use chemical baits or slug pellets. For biological control, use a slug nematode.

Vine weevils

A shiny black weevil, about 2.5 cm (1 in) long, usually only seen on plants in the late evening.

Symptoms: semicircular holes in the leaf margins; the larvae devour plant roots.

Control: incorporate insecticide in the soil; for biological control, use a nematode to kill the grubs.

repairs

Just as you take care of the plants in your garden, so must you regularly check and maintain all the equipment and the structures that play such an important part in the health and appearance of your garden. The beginning of spring is the ideal time to carry out repairs of garden tools in preparation for the coming growing season.

greenhouse repairs

If any sheets of glass are broken, they should be replaced immediately, because without attention, in addition to the loss of heat, the wind will enter through the hole and cause more damage to the glass and the plants inside.

Aluminium alloy greenhouses

Remove the sprung metal clips that hold the glass in place, and take out the cracked or broken pane. Replace it with greenhouse or horticultural glass and return the metal clips.

Wooden greenhouses

With most wooden structures, the glass is held in place by a combination of a layer of putty, onto which the glass is pressed, and small glazing nails called 'sprigs', which hold the glass to the wooden glazing bars.

1   Start by removing the old glazing sprigs with a pair of pliers, and carefully take out any broken sections of glass that remain. Then chop out any old dry putty with a hammer and glazing knife or chisel.

2   Spread an even layer of soft putty over the area where the old putty was removed from the glazing bars. Slide the new sheet of glass into place and carefully press it onto the bed of putty. Care must be taken to apply pressure to the glass evenly or the sheet of glass will crack. Using a damp knife, remove any surplus putty from the glass and glazing bar.

3   Fix the sheet of glass into position by knocking the new sprigs into the glazing bars. When the glass is secured, it can be cleaned with a damp cloth.

timber maintenance

Preserving wood

Wooden gates, fence posts and other wooden garden structures will require regular applications of a suitable wood preservative to prolong the life of the wood and to guard against extreme weather conditions, such as rain and sun scorch.

1   Remove any surface mould or lichen with a wire-bristled brush and make sure that the wood is dry before painting begins – this is to ensure that the material will soak deeply into the wood for maximum protection.

2   Apply the preservative with an old paint brush or garden sprayer. Take great care to protect any nearby plants by pulling them well away from the structure and covering them with polythene sheeting before any painting begins. It may be necessary to consider applying a second coat for sections close to ground level or where the end grain of the wood is exposed.

Repairing a rotten fence post

1 Prise out the fixing nails holding the side panels into the post and ease the fence panels away from the post.

2 Dig around the base of the post until it is loose and lever it out of the ground. Then saw through as much of the post as necessary to remove all traces of rotten wood.

3 Refill the hole and compact the soil to make it as firm as possible, leaving the surface level. Then hammer the new fence spike into the soil.

4 Set the repaired wooden post into the 'cup' in the top of the spike and fix the post into position so that it is steady and secure in the ground. Replace the side panels of the fence by pushing them back into line with the post. Use a spirit level to check that the top of each of the panels is still horizontal. Finally, fix them to the wooden post by nailing them into their original positions.

garden tools

Early spring is a good time to thoroughly check over all gardening tools and equipment, since poorly maintained equipment tends to be ineffective and can damage plants by making ragged cuts. They may also be a danger to the gardener.

Cutting tools

Clean knives, loppers and secateurs with vinegar to remove any dried sap and dirt from the blades. Then wash them with water to remove all traces of vinegar and dry them. Finally, wipe the metal parts of the tools with an oily cloth to prevent rusting.

The blades should be run through a sharpener; this will need to be done throughout the growing season if they are to maintain their effectiveness.

Cultivating tools

These can be cleaned with an oily rag (see below), and any splits or splinters in the handles should be smoothed over by rubbing them down with sandpaper.

making a sink garden

Tubs, sinks and troughs of various kinds can be recycled to make excellent containers for plants, and by adding a special coating they can be made to look like natural stone. Alpines are one of the most diverse groups of plants we grow, and when planted out in containers, such as old earthenware sinks, provide an excellent display. Low-growing or mat-forming shrubs and conifers are also good subjects, with some covering the surface and others trailing over the rim. Place the sink in position before you start work – it may be too heavy to move once planting is complete.

MATERIALS & EQUIPMENT

old sink

wire brush and mild detergent

sponge, sand and water

cement, sand and peat

stiff-bristled paintbrush

pot shards

capillary matting

free-draining loam-based compost

spade

hand trowel

suitable plants (see page 247)

gravel mulch

1 Clean the sink thoroughly using a mild detergent and a wire brush, scrubbing the outside and rim as well as the inside.

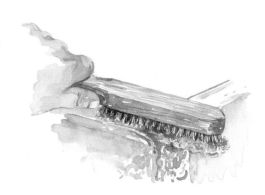

2 Clean the sink again, including the top and the upper inside edge, using a sponge dipped into a paste made up of equal parts of fine sand and water. This will scour the surface of the container and help the coating to bind to it.

3 To create a weathered stone look, make up a coating using equal parts of cement, sand and peat. Mix the ingredients thoroughly together and then gradually add enough water to form a stiff paste.

4 Using an old stiff-bristled paintbrush, spread a 6 mm (¼ in) layer of the coating over the surface of the sink, not forgetting the rim and the top 8 cm (3 in) of the inside. Leave the coating to dry.

5 After two or three days, apply a second layer 1 cm (½ in) thick and leave this to dry.

6 Place a layer of pot shards, 8 cm (3 in) deep, in the bottom of the sink, and cover this with a sheet of capillary matting. This will prevent the compost being washed down into the shards and impeding drainage.

7   Fill the sink with a free-draining compost. Firm the surface gently with the spade. Top up with more compost as necessary to fill the sink to within 5 cm (2 in) of the rim.

8   Using a trowel, dig planting holes and place the new plants in them, leaving the top of each root ball slightly high. Firm them in gently.

9   Position the trailing species near the edges of the sink, so that they can spill over the sides as they grow. During planting, check that each plant has enough room to develop comfortably. Avoid overcrowding or the plants will have to struggle to survive.

10   When planting is finished, spread a 2.5 cm (1 in) layer of fine gravel over the surface of the compost in between the plants. To protect the plants while you do this, cover them temporarily with inverted pots. The gravel mulch will help to retain moisture in the compost, improve surface drainage in winter, inhibit the germination of weed seeds and prevent slugs from attacking the plants.

Alpines suitable for growing in sinks and troughs

Arenaria nevadensis	*Helichrysum coralloides*	*Raoulia australis*
Carduncellus rhaponticoides	*Juniperus communis* 'Compressa'	*Salix reticulata*
Cyclamen coum	*Lewisia* hybrids	*Saxifraga* 'Tumbling Waters'
Daphne petraea 'Grandiflora'	*Petrophytum caespitosum*	*Sedum spathulifolium* 'Cape Blanco'
Erinus alpinus	*Potentilla tommasiniana*	
Gentiana septemfida	*Ramonda myconi*	

soil management

Soil, although we often take it for granted, is the most important resource in the garden and is a very complex material. It can be very delicate and must always be well managed and cared for if it is to provide an adequate environment for plant growth. A basic understanding of your soil type is the first step towards creating the best possible conditions for all the plants in your garden. Good soil management includes the use of fertilizers and manures to improve quality and texture, planned crop rotation to prevent the invasion of pests and diseases and help return nutrients to the soil, and the addition of organic matter to improve moisture retention. All these measures will help to improve the soil's ability to support plant life.

improving your soil

In order to get the most from your soil you must first have a thorough understanding of its structure. The gardener need only be concerned with the first two levels of soil. The top level, referred to as 'topsoil', is the biologically active area, occupied by millions of bacteria, fungi, insects, worms and other life forms. It is usually a dark colour and can vary in depth from 5 cm (2 in) in more chalky soils, to 1 m (3¼ ft). The layer lying immediately below this is called 'subsoil', and can be distinguished by its paler colour, caused by a lack of organic matter; it can sometimes also be identified by orange and yellow flecks of iron oxide.

determining your soil type

It is important to identify the nature of the soil in your garden since this can have a significant effect on the growth of your plants. Once you have categorized your soil type, unless it is perfect, there are various methods you can employ to improve the situation and create a more healthy environment for your plants to grow in.

Texture
The first thing to do is to test the texture of your soil as any variations can significantly affect its drainage capabilities. Simply pick up a handful from the garden and rub it between your fingers and thumb to determine its characteristics.

Clay: This is a heavy, sticky soil that can be rolled into shape. Clay suffers from poor drainage but is rich in plant food. To improve its quality you need to open it up by digging in manure, compost, gravel or lime.

Sandy: Characterized by a light, dry texture, this soil is free draining but tends to lack essential nutrients and needs frequent watering. Improve this soil by removing large stones and adding manure and fertilizer.

Soil pH
Measured on a scale from 0 to 14, anything above 7 is alkaline and below 7 is acidic; 7 indicates neutral soil. Use a special kit to test your soil pH, matching the prepared sample with the colour scale provided. Dark green indicates alkalinity, gradually changing to orange for acidic soils. A reading of 6.5 is ideal since most plants prefer a slightly acidic soil. If your soil is too acidic, it probably lacks phosphorus and an application of lime will raise alkalinity. To raise the acidic content, however, add peat or flowers of sulphur.

fertilizers and manures

Applying fertilizers and manures is all part of the process of soil preparation and must be done before any planting. Most garden soils will need a certain amount of improvement in order to sustain the plants. The main nutrients needed to improve plant growth are nitrogen, phosphorus and potassium and these are available as both fertilizers and manures. You can either apply these nutrients separately or use a general fertilizer that contains all three. Different plants use up different amounts of nutrients and you should choose your fertilizer accordingly. Nitrogen, phosphate and potassium should be applied in early autumn as you prepare your soil for new plants.

Bulky organic manures

Incorporating quantities of bulky organic matter provides nutrients and fibre for a garden soil as well as improving its water content. Green vegetation and manures with animal content will provide some nutrients almost immediately, but very little fibre. The more woody and fibrous materials are better for opening heavy soils, and on lighter soils they improve moisture retention. Long-term improvements occur as they decompose, contributing to the formation of humus, which then absorbs other applied nutrients.

Percentage of nutrients (approximately)			
Material	Nitrogen N	Phosphate P	Potash K
Bark	0.3	0.2	0.2
Garden compost	1.5	2.0	0.7
Leaf-mould	0.4	0.2	0.3
Manure – chicken	2.0	2.0	1.0
Manure – cow	0.6	0.3	0.7
Manure – horse	0.7	0.5	0.6
Manure – pig	0.6	0.6	0.4
Manure – sheep	0.6	0.3	0.7
Manure – turkey	2.0	1.5	1.0
Mushroom compost	0.6	0.5	0.9
Peat	0.7	0.2	0.2
Sawdust	0.3	0.2	0.2
Seaweed	0.6	0.3	1.0
Sewage sludge	1.0	0.6	0.2
Spent hops	1.1	0.3	0.1
Straw	0.5	0.2	0.7

Fertilizers

These can be applied as base dressings, when an application of fertilizer or bulky organic matter is added to the soil surface and incorporated before planting or seed sowing begins. They can also be introduced into the soil as a top dressing: fertilizer or bulky organic matter is applied to the soil surface and incorporated around the base of the plant once it is in position. Fast-action fertilizers are good for giving your plant a quick boost and are easier to control. However, the application of slow-release types is far less time consuming.

	% Nutrient	Type	Action
Nitrogen N			
Ammonium nitrate	34	inorganic	fast
Ammonium sulphate	21	inorganic	fast
Bone meal	5	organic	slow
Dried blood	12	organic	fairly fast
Hoof and horn	12	organic	fairly fast
Nitrate of potash	13	inorganic	fast
Nitrate of soda	16	inorganic	fast
Nitro-chalk	25	inorganic	fast
Phosphate P			
Basic slag	14	inorganic	slow
Bone meal	24	organic	slow
Superphosphate	19	inorganic	fast
Potash K			
Muriate of potash	60	inorganic	fast
Nitrate of potash	44	inorganic	fast
Sulphate of potash	50	inorganic	fast

Green manure

Instead of using composts and manures, you can grow plants to incorporate into the soil as an improver. Plant them in the autumn and dig into the soil once they have grown to about 20 cm (8 in). Green manure returns more to the ground than it has taken out and will eventually form humus within the soil. Choose plants with a rapid growth rate that mature quickly, such as legumes.

Green manure	% Nitrogen
Borage	1.8
Comfrey	1.7
Mustard	2.0
Red clover	3.0
Ryegrass	1.2

soil cultivation

The ideal time to dig is in the autumn or early winter, when the soil is often quite dry and not as wet as when the winter rain starts. Lighter soils, such as sandy loams, should not be cultivated over winter as the wind, rain and frost can damage the soil structure. Digging opens up the soil to allow air penetration and helps to bury annual weeds and plant debris, which return nutrients back into the soil, improving drainage and the formation of a deeper root system.

simple digging

Simple digging is where a spadeful of soil is lifted, turned over and dropped back into its original position. This technique of shallow cultivation is very useful for clearing the surface of the soil and for digging around existing plants, since it does not disturb their roots.

single digging

1   Dig a trench about 25 to 30 cm (10 to 12 in) wide and the depth of the spade or fork, and move the soil.

2   Facing the trench, dig a second trench and use the soil from this one to fill in the one made in the previous step.

3   Twist the spade a little when putting the soil into the first trench so that the upper layers of soil and any weeds go to the bottom.

4   Repeat this process down the length of your plot, filling in the final trench with the soil taken out of the first trench.

double digging

Use a digging spade and a fork. Turn so that you are digging across the trench and roughly divide the trench into three times the width of the spade's blade; it is helpful to mark out the area with garden line and pegs. Make sure each trench is about the same size so that a similar amount of soil is moved from trench to trench and the plot remains level. Try to avoid mixing the topsoil with the subsoil, since it is better to concentrate your efforts on increasing the fertility of the topsoil (though some gardeners believe that mixing the two layers will eventually help to increase the depth of fertile soil).

1   Start by digging out a trench about 60 cm (24 in) wide and the depth of the spade's blade. As you remove the soil, place it in a pile to one side of the trench.

2   Stand in the trench and use a fork to break up the bottom to the full depth of its tines. The soil has now been cultivated to an overall depth of about 50 cm (20 in).

3   Mark out another 60 cm (24 in) wide trench, parallel to the first one. Soil taken from the second trench can now be used to fill in the first one.

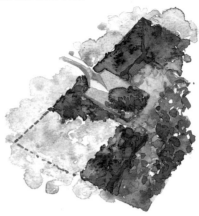

4   Fork over the second trench and fill in as before. Continue this technique up to the last trench, filling this one in with the soil from the first trench.

zero cultivation system

A growing practice that is increasing in popularity is a system of zero cultivation. The aim is to incorporate large quantities of organic matter into the soil by double digging, and then the soil is left relatively undisturbed. The reasoning behind this system is that cultivating the soil creates an ideal environment for the germination of weed seeds, as well as destroying the soil's natural structure and causing a loss of plant nutrients. This system minimizes problems with weed control since, by not digging, the seeds cannot be brought up from the lower depths of the soil. The usual method of weed control is to use a surface covering of organic mulch to suppress weed seed germination by causing a lack of daylight. The mulch is incorporated into the soil by the activity of earthworms, which, in turn, increases humus content and fertility, as well as naturally improving the soil structure. These mulches also create a more even soil temperature, which encourages plant growth by reducing the overall stress on the plant.

making a compost bin

A compost bin, made to look like a traditional beehive, is both practical and decorative. Making a feature of your bin is particularly useful in a small garden where it would be difficult to hide an unsightly one. This construction is relatively straightforward and can be painted to fit in with your garden scheme. Almost any form of vegetable material is suitable for making compost, provided it is not diseased or contaminated with chemicals. Grass clippings, soft prunings and hedge clippings, leaves, annual weeds, straw, vegetable and household waste are all suitable.

MATERIALS & EQUIPMENT

sawn timber (see steps, over page)

shuttering ply or other exterior-grade plywood (see steps, over page)

galvanized nails, 5 cm (2 in) long

glue (waterproof PVA)

2 roof bolts, 7.5 cm (3 in) long

2 wooden pegs, 15 cm (6 in) long

1 litre (1 quart) rubberized paint

1 litre (1 quart) microporous paint

1   Choosing a site

Compost heaps should always be built on soil, rather than an impermeable surface such as concrete, since this allows the liquids formed during the process of decomposition to drain away and also allows worms to work their way into the compost.

2   For the sides cut the following pieces in sawn timber:
4 uprights, 1 m x 6.5 x 6.5 cm (39½ x 2½ x 2½ in)
2 top boards, 68 x 20 x 1 cm (27 x 8 x ½ in)
2 rims, 68 x 4 x 4 cm (27 x 1½ x 1½ in)
10 feather boards, 68 x 15 x 1 cm (27 x 6 x ½ in)
For both sides, nail a top board between two uprights, leaving 5 cm (2 in) of each upright protruding from the top. Then nail the rim directly underneath the board.

3   Nail 5 feather boards below the rims with the thin edge uppermost, overlapping them by 1 cm (½ in) so that they fit exactly between the rim and the base of the uprights; position the nails nearer the thick edge.

4   For the back, cut the following pieces in sawn timber:
1 top board, 70 x 20 x 1 cm (28 x 8 x ½ in)
1 rim, 75 x 4 x 4 cm (30 x 1½ x 1½ in)
5 feather boards, 70 x 15 x 1 cm (28 x 6 x ½ in)

5   Fix the back pieces to the sides, positioning them to cover the sawn outer edges on the side sections.

6   For the front cut the following pieces in sawn timber:
2 posts, 1 m x 4 x 4 cm (39½ x 1½ x 1½ in)
1 top board, 70 x 20 x 1 cm (28 x 8 x ½ in)
1 rim, 75 x 4 x 4 cm (30 x 1½ x 1½ in)
5 feather boards, 70 x 15 x 1 cm (28 x 6 x ½ in)

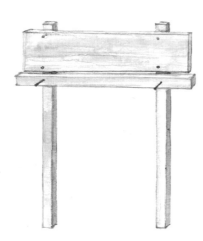

7   The front door is a separate piece. Attach the front sections to the posts, positioning the posts 7.5 cm (3 in) in from the side edges. Nail to secure.

8   Slot the front door between the sides. Drill a hole through the front posts and into the uprights on the sides, near the top, to take a roof bolt – this closes the front. For further security, fix two 15 cm (6 in) wooden pegs into the ground at the base of the door.

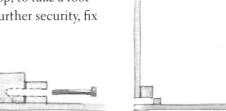

9 Making the lid

For the base, cut the following pieces in sawn timber:
2 sections, 79 x 5 x 5 cm (31 x 2 x 2 in) for the front and back
2 side sections, 81 x 5 x 5 cm (32 x 2 x 2 in)
Cut halving joints at each end and fix them with glue and
nails to make a frame.

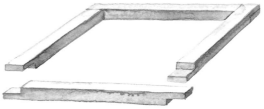

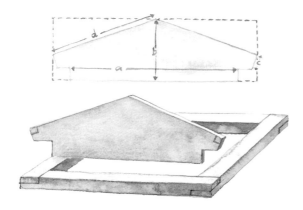

10 For the roof ends, cut two shapes, each from a 90 x 25 x 1 cm
(36 x 10 x ½ in) sheet of plywood, using the following measurements.
a: 69 cm (27 in), b: 25 cm (10 in), c: 5 cm (2 in), d: 45 cm (18 in).
Make the end cuts at right angles to the sloping roof. Slot the ends
inside the lid base, front and back, and nail in place from the inside.

11 For the roof pediments, cut the following in sawn timber:
4 pieces, 45 x 5 x 5 cm (18 x 2 x 2 in)
Bevel both ends on each piece so that they join neatly in the middle
and fit the shape of the roof at the sides. Glue and nail two to each
roof end, lining up the top edges.

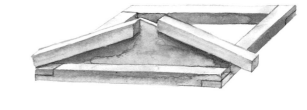

12 For the roof cut the following in plywood:
2 pieces, 46 x 82 x 1 cm (18 x 33 x ½ in)
Bevel one long edge on each piece so that they fit
together at the top. Line the back edge up with the
back pediment and let the front edge overlap slightly.
Glue and nail to secure.

13 Paint the interior with rubberized paint and the exterior
with microporous paint. Allow to dry before using.

14 Build up the heap in thin layers starting with a fibrous
material, such as straw or green hedge clippings, then use
alternate layers of a carbon-rich material, such as wood
shavings, with nitrogen-rich layers of green material, such as
grass mowings. Keep the heap moist in dry weather, covering
the top with plastic to retain moisture. Turn the heap after
two weeks to allow the material to compost evenly.

glossary

A

Aerate

To loosen soil, either by physical or mechanical means, to allow the penetration of air.

Algae

Primitive green plants which form a scum-like layer in ponds.

Alpine

A plant originating in mountainous regions; the term is often applied to rock-garden plants.

Alternate

Buds or leaves that occur at different levels on opposite sides of the stem.

Annual

A plant that completes its reproduction cycle in one year.

Aquatic

Any plant that grows in water (may be anchored or free floating).

Axil

The angle between a leaf and stem.

Axillary bud

A bud that occurs in a leaf axil.

B

Bare-root

Plants with no soil around their roots. Bare-rooted plants are usually grown in a field before being dug up for sale.

Basal

A shoot or bud arising from the base of a stem or plant.

Base dressing

An application of fertilizer or organic matter incorporated into the soil around the base of a plant.

Bedding plants

Plants arranged in mass displays (beds) in order to form a colourful but temporary display.

Bed system

A highly productive system of growing vegetables in closely spaced rows to form blocks of plants.

Biennial

A plant that completes its life cycle in two growing seasons. It produces roots and leaves in the first year and these are followed by flowers and fruit in the next.

Bleeding

The excessive flow of sap, usually from plants pruned in spring. Bleeding can often be minimized by pruning when plants are in full leaf.

Bog plant

A plant that prefers to grow in damp soil conditions.

Bolt

The premature flowering and seed production of a cropping plant.

Branch

A shoot growing directly from the main stem of a woody plant.

Brassica

Belonging to the cabbage family.

Broadcasting

The technique of spreading fertilizer or seeds randomly.

Broad-leaved

Deciduous or evergreen plants that have flat, broad leaves.

Bud

A condensed shoot containing an embryonic shoot or flower.

Bud union
The point where a cultivar is budded onto a rootstock. Most often employed to control the ultimate height of a plant.

Bulb
A storage organ consisting of thick, fleshy leaves arranged on a compressed stem.

C

Callus
The plant tissue that forms as a protective cover over a cut or wounded surface.

Chamfer
A 45° bevel, made along the edge of a piece of wood.

Chilling
A period of low temperature, about 2°C (36°F), required by some plants during dormancy in order to stimulate flower development later in the growing season.

Cloche
A clear structure used for warming the soil or for protecting plants.

Cold frame
A low, clear, portable or permanent structure used for protecting plants and acclimatizing them to normal garden conditions.

Collar
The point on a plant where the roots begin at the base of the main stem, or the swollen area where a branch joins the main stem.

Compost
A potting medium made to a standard formula; loam- or peat-based. The term also applies to well-rotted organic matter, such as garden or kitchen waste.

Conifer
A classification of plants that have naked ovules, often borne in cones, and narrow, needle-like foliage.

Coppicing
The severe pruning of plants to ground level on an annual basis.

Cordon
A plant, often a tree, that is trained to produce fruiting spurs from a main stem.

Crop rotation
A system of moving crops in a planned cycle to improve growth and help control pests and diseases.

Crown
The growing point of a herbaceous perennial originating at soil level.

Cultivar
A plant form that originated in cultivation rather than from the wild.

Cutting
A portion of a plant used for propagation.

D

Dead-heading
The deliberate removal of dead flower heads. Often prolongs the flowering period of a plant.

Deciduous
Plants that produce new leaves in the spring and shed them in the autumn.

Disbudding
Removal of unwanted buds to produce fewer, but much larger, flowers.

Division
A technique used to increase the number of plants by splitting up a single parent plant into smaller units for replanting.

Dormancy
A period of reduced growth, usually extending from late autumn through the winter months and finishing as the weather warms in spring.

Drill
A narrow straight line made in the soil for sowing seeds into.

E

Earthing up
A process of mounding up the soil around the base of a plant.

Espalier
A tree trained to produce several horizontal tiers of branches all growing from a vertical main stem.

Evergreen
Plants that retain their actively growing leaves through the winter.

F

Fan
A tree or shrub that is trained to create a network of branches spreading out from the main stem.

Feathered
A young tree with small lateral branches.

Fertile
A soil rich in nutrients and biological life.

Fertilizer
An organic or inorganic compound used to help plants to grow.

Fibrous roots
The fine, multi-branched roots of a plant.

Floating mulch
A sheet of plastic or woven material used for protecting plants from frost.

Force
Induce plants to grow earlier than usual.

Formative pruning
The pruning of young plants designed to establish a desired plant shape and branch structure.

Framework
The main permanent branch structure of a woody plant.

Fruit
The seed-bearing vessel on a plant.

Fungicide
A chemical used to control fungal disease in plants.

G

Germination

The development of a seed into a plant.

Grafting

A propagation method that involves the joining of two or more separate plants.

Graft union

The point where a cultivar is grafted onto a rootstock.

Ground cover

A term to describe low-growing plants.

H

Half hardy

A plant that can tolerate low temperatures but is killed by frost.

Hardy

A plant that can tolerate temperatures below freezing without protection.

Herbaceous

A non-woody plant with an annual top and a perennial root system or storage organ.

Herbicide

A chemical used to kill weeds.

Humus

The organic residue of decayed organic material.

I

Inorganic

A man-made chemical compound (one that does not contain carbon).

Insecticide

A chemical used to kill insects.

Irrigation

A general term used for the application of water to soil and plants.

L

Lateral

A side shoot arising from an axillary bud.

Layering

A propagation technique where roots are formed on a stem before it is detached from the parent plant.

Leaching

The loss of nutrients by washing them through the soil.

Leader

The main dominant shoot or stem of the plant (usually the terminal shoot).

Legume

A member of the pea family that bears seeds in pods.

Lime

An alkaline substance formed from calcium.

Loam

A soil with equal proportions of clay, sand and silt.

M

Maiden

A young (one-year-old) budded or grafted tree or bush.

Marginal plant

A plant that prefers to grow in damp soil conditions or partially submerged in water.

Mulch

A layer of material applied to cover the soil.

Mutation

A plant change or variation occurring by chance, often referred to as a 'sport'.

N

Nematode

A microscopically small worm-like organism that can be introduced into the garden in order to attack specific pests and so reduce the need to use chemical pesticides.

Nutrients

The minerals (naturally occurring or introduced in the form of fertilizers) used to feed plants.

O

Opposite

Plants in which leaves, buds or stems are arranged in pairs directly opposite one another.

Organic

Materials derived from decomposed animal or plant remains.

Ovule

The body in a seed-bearing plant that contains the egg cell. It is the egg cell that will develop into the seed once fertilization takes place.

Oxygenator

An aquatic plant that releases oxygen into the water. Lack of oxygen in garden pond water can lead to the poor growth of aquatic plants and ill-health in fish.

P

Peat

Decayed mosses, rushes or sedges.

Perennial

A plant which has a life cycle of three years or more.

Pesticide

A chemical used to control pests.

pH

The level of acidity or alkalinity in a soil, measured on a scale of 1 to 14; 7 is neutral, below 7 is acid, and above 7 is alkaline.

Pinching out

The removal (with finger and thumb) of the growing point of a plant to encourage the development of lateral shoots.

Pollarding

The severe pruning of the main branches of a tree or shrub to the main trunk or stem.

Propagation

Different techniques used to multiply a number of plants.

Propagator

A structure in which plants are propagated.

Pruning

Cutting plants to improve their growth, to train them to grow in a particular way or to restrict their growth to prevent them becoming too large for their allocated space.

R

Renewal pruning

A method of pruning based on the systematic replacement of lateral fruiting branches.

Rhizome

A specialized underground stem that lies horizontally in the soil.

Root ball

The combined root system and the surrounding soil or compost of a plant. Plants are often sold in this form, wrapped in hessian.

Root pruning

The cutting of the roots of live plants to control their vigour or ultimate height.

Rootstock

The root system onto which a cultivar is budded or grafted.

Runner

A stem that grows horizontally close to the ground, such as in strawberry plants.

S

Sap

The solution of mineral salts, sugars and other nutrients that circulates in and nourishes a plant.

Scale

A modified leaf of a bulb that is used in propagation.

Scion

The propagation material taken from a cultivar or variety that is to be used for budding or grafting.

Shoot

A stem or branch of a plant.

Shrub

A woody-stemmed plant.

Side shoot

A shoot arising from a stem or branch.

Sport

See Mutation.

Spur

A short flower- or fruit-bearing branch.

Standard

A tree or bush with a clear stem of at least 1.8 m (6 ft).

Stooling

The severe pruning of plants to within 10–15 cm (4–6 in) of ground level on an annual basis.

Stratification

The storage of seed in cold or warm conditions in order to overcome dormancy.

Sucker

A shoot arising from below ground level.

T

Tap root

The main large, anchoring root of a plant.

Tender

A plant that is killed or damaged by low temperatures, usually –10°C (14°F).

Tendril

A thin, twisting, stem-like structure used by some climbing plants to support themselves.

Thatch

A layer of dead organic matter on the soil surface of a lawn.

Tilth

A fine crumbly layer of surface soil.

Tip pruning

Cutting back the growing point of a shoot in order to encourage the development of lateral shoots.

Top dressing

An application of fertilizer or bulky organic matter added to the soil surface.

Transplanting

Moving plants from one site to another in order to give them more growing room or to move them to a more suitable site.

U

Union (graft union)

Where a cultivar is grafted onto a rootstock.

V

Vegetative growth

Non-flowering stem growth.

W

Whip

A young (one-year-old) tree with no lateral branches.

Whorl

The arrangement of three or more leaves, buds, or shoots arising from the same level of a plant.

Wilt

The partial collapse of a plant due to water loss or root damage.

useful addresses

Garden Centres

**Alexandra Palace
Garden Centre**
Alexandra Palace
London N22 4BB
020 8444 2555
www.capitalgardens.co.uk

Blooms of Bressingham
Bressingham
Diss
Norfolk IP22 2AB
01379 688585
www.bloomsof
 bressingham.co.uk

Bridgemere Nurseries
Bridgemere
Near Nantwich
Cheshire CW5 7QB
01270 521100
www.bridgemere.co.uk

Burncoose Nurseries
Gwennap
Redruth
Cornwall TR16 6BJ
01209 860316
www.burncoose.co.uk

The Chelsea Gardener
125 Sydney Street
London SW3 6NR
020 7352 5656
www.chelseagardener.com

Clifton Nurseries
5A Clifton Villas
London W9 2PH
020 7289 6851
www.clifton.co.uk

Deacons Nursery
Moor View
Godshill
Isle of Wight PO38 3HW
01983 840750
www.deaconsnursery
 fruits.co.uk

Kinder Garden Plants
Sunnyfield Nurseries
Wragg Marsh
Spalding
Lincolnshire PE12 6HH
www.kindergarden.co.uk

Highfield Nurseries
School Lane
Whitminster
Gloucester GL2 7PL
01452 740266
www.highfield-nurseries.co.uk

Hillier Nurseries
The Stables
Ampfield House
Ampfield
Romsey
Hampshire SO51 9BQ
01794 368733
www.hillier.co.uk

Notcutt's Garden Centre
Woodbridge
Suffolk IP12 4AF
01394 445400
www.notcutts.co.uk

Rolawn (turf growers)
Main Street
Elvington
York YO41 4XR
01904 608661
www.rolawn.co.uk

Scotts Nurseries
4 Higher Street
Merriott
Somerset TA16 5PL
01460 72306
www.scottsnurseries.co.uk

**The Van Hage Garden
Company**
Great Amwell
Near Ware
Hertfordshire SG12 9RP
01920 870811
www.vanhage.co.uk

Wyevale Garden Centre
Kings Acre Road
Hereford HR4 0SE
01432 266261
www.wyevale.co.uk
Branches nationwide.

For Hedges, Trees and Shrubs:
Beechcroft Nurseries
Appleby-in-Westmorland
Cumbria CA16 6UE
01768 351201

Crowders Garden Centre
Lincoln Road
Horncastle
Lincolnshire LN9 5LZ
01507 525252
www.crowdersgarden
    centre.co.uk

R. V. Roger Ltd
The Nurseries
Pickering
North Yorkshire YO18 7JW
01751 472226
www.rvroger.co.uk

Weasdale Nurseries
Newbiggin on Lune
Kirkby Stephen
Cumbria CA17 4LX
01539 623246
www.weasdale.com

For Aquatics:
**Anglo Aquarium
Plant Company**
Strayfield Road
Enfield
Middlesex EN2 9JE
020 8363 8548
www.anglo-aquarium.co.uk

Stapeley Water Gardens
London Road
Stapeley
Nantwich
Cheshire CW5 7LH
01270 623868
www.stapeleywg.com

For Roses:
David Austin Roses
Bowling Green Lane
Albrighton
Wolverhampton
West Midlands WV7 3HB
01902 376300
www.davidaustinroses.com

Mattock's Roses
A division of the Notcutts
Group; see Garden Centres
for details.
www.mattocks.co.uk

For Bulbs:
Avon Bulbs
Burnt House Farm
Mid Lambrook
South Petherton
Somerset TA13 5HE
01460 242177
www.avonbulbs.com

Jacques Amand
The Nurseries
Clamp Hill
Stanmore
Middlesex HA7 3JS
020 8420 7110
www.jacquesamand.com

For Seeds:
Johnsons Seeds
Gazeley Road
Kentford, Newmarket
Suffolk CB8 7QB
01638 554123
www.johnsons-seeds.com

Marshalls
01480 443390
www.marshalls-seeds.co.uk

Mr Fothergill's Seeds
Gazeley Road
Kentford, Newmarket
Suffolk CB8 7QB
01638 751161
www.fothergills.co.uk

Suttons Seeds Ltd
Woodview Road
Paignton
Devon TQ4 7NG
0870 2202899
www.suttons-seeds.co.uk

Unwins Seeds Ltd
01480 443395 for catalogue
www.unwins-seeds.co.uk

For Trellis:
Stuart Garden Architecture
Burrow Hill Farm
Wiveliscombe
Somerset TA4 2RN
01984 667458
www.stuartgarden.com

For Polytunnels:
Ferryman Polytunnels
Bridge Road
Lapford
Crediton
Devon EX17 6AH
01363 83444
www.ferryman.uk.com

For Fleece:
Agralan Limited
The Old Brickyard
Ashton Keynes
Swindon
Wiltshire SN6 6QR
01285 860015
www.agralan.co.uk

Agriframes Ltd
Tildenet Ltd
Hartcliffe Way
Bristol BS3 5RJ
0845 2604450
www.agriframes.co.uk

Timber and Building Supplies

B & Q
0845 6096688
www.diy.com

Homebase
0845 0778888
www.homebase.co.uk

Jewson
0800 539766
www.jewson.co.uk

Leisuredeck Ltd
311 Marsh Road
Leagrave
Luton LU3 2RZ
01582 563080
www.leisuredeck.co.uk

Fertilizers and Mulches

William Sinclair Holdings
Firth Road
Lincoln LN6 7AH
01522 537561
www.william-sinclair.co.uk

Tools and Equipment

Atco
0844 7360108
www.atco.co.uk

Black & Decker
Stockists nationwide.
www.blackanddecker.co.uk

Butyl Products (pond liners)
11 Radford Crescent
Billericay
Essex CM12 0DW
01277 653281
www.butylproducts.co.uk

Gardena (UK) Ltd
Stockists nationwide.
www.gardena.co.uk

HSS Hire
0161 7494400 for
customer service
www.hss.com

credits

l. = left, c. = centre, a. = above, b. = below, r. = right

The photographer, Anne Hyde, wishes to make the following acknowledgements: English Hurdle, Stoke St Gregory, Somerset, for the loan of wattle fencing; Mr and Mrs Coote, 40 Osler Road, Headington, Oxford; Judy Brown, Masham Manor, East Molesey; Meg Blumson, 20 St Peter's Road, Cirencester; Jean and Ian Housley; The *Gardening Which* Garden, Capel Manor, Enfield; Fran Donovan; Robin Allen; Michael Goulding, Hipkins, Herts; Ruth Thornton, Balfour Road, Northampton; Jon Tye, Lea Gardens, Derby; Malley Terry, Hillgrove Crescent, Kidderminster; Mr and Mrs Nicholas Calvert, Walton Poor, Surrey; Benington Lordship, Herts; Sandy Lodge, Beds; Mrs Rogers, Riverhill House, Kent; The Beale Arboretum, Herts; Milton Lodge, Somerset; Westonbirt Arboretum, Gloucs; H. Groffman, St Quintin Avenue, London; Peter Aldington, Garden Designer of Turn End, Haddenham, Bucks; Vivien and John Savage, Stockgrove Park, Bucks; Mr and Mrs D. Ingall, Irthlingborough, Northants; Mr and Mrs Douglas Fuller, The Crossing House, Shepreth, Cambridge; Merle and Peter Williams, Ickleford, Herts; Glen and Beverley Williams, Ickleford, Herts; Mrs Easter, Harpenden, Herts; Mr and Mrs Siggers, Wichert, Ford, Bucks; Lucy Sommers, 13 Queen Elizabeth Walk, London; Ivan Meers and David Boyer; Heather Montgomery, Wisteria Cottage, Maidwell, Northants; Mr and Mrs Try, Favershams Meadow, Bucks; Vanessa and Vinda Saax; Mrs Huntingdon, The Old Rectory, Sudborough, Northants; Charles Paddick; Capel Manor, Enfield, Herts; Clifton Nurseries, Clifton Villas, Little Venice, London.

All photographs taken by Anne Hyde except for the following: **Endpapers** Melanie Eclaire/Sticky Wicket wildlife garden near Dorchester, designed and created by Peter and Pam Lewis (www.sticky wicketgarden.co.uk); **7** Melanie Eclare/Jim Reynolds' garden 'Butterstream', Co. Meath, Ireland; **10** Melanie Eclare/Daphne Shackleton's garden in Co. Cavan, Ireland; **14 al & bcl** Jerry Harpur; **14 bl** Jerry Harpur/Beth Chatto; **14 br** Melanie Eclare; **24 & 25** Jerry Harpur; **38, 53 & 54** Marianne Majerus; **57 a** Jerry Harpur; **58 & 59** © Andrew Lawson; **62 b** Jerry Harpur; **65** © Andrew Lawson/Chilcombe House, Dorset; **82** Pia Tryde; **83** © Andrew Lawson; **95 bl, bc & br** Jerry Harpur; **109 l** Pia Tryde; **109 r** Jerry Harpur; **116 br** Melanie Eclare; **125 a & c** Jerry Harpur; **128** Jonathan Buckley; **129** Marcus Harpur; **135 l & cl** Jerry Harpur; **135 cr, 137 r & 141 r** Marcus Harpur; **144 l & ar** Stephen Robson; **144 br** © Andrew Lawson; **168 & 169** Andrea Jones; **180 all & 206–207 all** Jerry Harpur; **216 al** Marianne Majerus; **216 bl** Caroline Arber; **216 r** © Andrew Lawson; **224 all, 233 all & 239 l** Jerry Harpur.

All projects designed by Steven Bradley except the Compost Bin Project – designed by George Carter and photographed at the *Gardening Which* garden at Capel Manor.

Also thanks to the Principal at Capel Manor Horticulture Centre, Bullsmoor Lane, Enfield, and the Editor of *Gardening Which*, PO Box 44, Hertford X, SG14 1SH.

index

acknowledgements

In putting this book together, I would like to thank a whole host

of people. In particular, I am most grateful to Toria Leitch

and Caroline Davison for working my fingers to the bone, and my

wife Val Bradley for keeping a straight face while checking my

grammar. I would also like to thank Anne Hyde for her excellent

photographs and Ashley Western and Prue Bucknall

for their design input.